CULT AND RITUAL ABUSE

Its History, Anthropology, and Recent Discovery in Contemporary America

REVISED EDITION

James Randall Noblitt
and Pamela Sue Perskin

Westport, Connecticut
London

Library of Congress Cataloging-in-Publication Data

Noblitt, James Randall.
    Cult and ritual abuse : its history, anthropology, and recent
discovery in contemporary America / James Randall Noblitt and Pamela
Sue Perskin.—Rev. ed.
        p.   cm.
    Includes bibliographical references and index.
    ISBN 0–275–96664–X (alk. paper).—ISBN 0–275–96665–8 (pbk. :
alk. paper)
        1. Ritual abuse—United States.   2. Occult crime—United States.
3. Ritual abuse victims—United States.   4. Multiple personality—
United States.   I. Perskin, Pamela Sue.   II. Title.
HV6626.52.N63   2000
616.85′82—dc21   99–22108

British Library Cataloguing in Publication Data is available.

Library of Congress Catalog Card Number: 99–22108
ISBN: 0–275–96664–X
          0–275–96665–8 (pbk.)

First published in 2000

Praeger Publishers, 88 Post Road West, Westport, CT 06881
An imprint of Greenwood Publishing Group, Inc.
www.praeger.com

Printed in the United States of America

The paper used in this book complies with the
Permanent Paper Standard issued by the National
Information Standards Organization (Z39.48–1984).

10 9 8 7 6 5 4 3 2 1

We rededicate this revision to those
who are helping to break the silence:
to those who are speaking out,
and to those who are listening.

Contents

Preface

We ask the reader's indulgence. As you will no doubt notice, this book has two authors yet is frequently narrated in the first person singular. As the primary author, Dr. Noblitt is conveying information based on his clinical experiences with patients. As secondary author, Ms. Perskin is not a clinician, but she has worked extensively with survivors, clinicians, law enforcement representatives, investigative journalists, and others, particularly in her role as executive director of the International Council on Cultism and Ritual Trauma. We have spent several years reviewing the clinical, historical and anthropological literature related to this topic. This book is the result of our combined efforts to bring to the reader the outcomes of our comprehensive research as well as our different perspectives on the problem.

Acknowledgements

This book would have been impossible without considerable assistance and support from many people. First and foremost, we would like to thank our parents and their parents before them, for their loving support and nurturance. We would also like to express our gratitude to our siblings, both those by birth and by marriage, for their support, encouragement and optimism. And we especially thank our children and future grandchildren for giving us life's greatest privilege and pleasure. We dedicate this book to all of you with love and appreciation.

We would also like to thank the many people who shared their stories of horror and hope. We have learned much from them. To the many patients and survivors who entrusted us with their secrets, we hope this work does you credit. Please note that out of respect for your privacy and our obligation to protect your confidentiality, we have taken pains to provide appropriate pseudonyms and to alter other identifying data.

To Doctors Gary Lefkof, Troy Caldwell, Bennett Braun, Judith Peterson, Charles Whitfield, Catherine Gould: few will comprehend the depth of your commitment and sacrifice on behalf of your patients. We do. Thank you. You are pioneers and a source of inspiration to the rest of us. To Michael Moore, Ken Olson, Diane Humananski, David Calof, and others who have both given and lost much, we appreciate your dedication and courage. To Pamela J. Monday and Jan MacLean, our cofounders of the International Council on Cultism and Ritual Trauma (formerly the Society for the Investigation, Treatment and Prevention of Ritual and Cult Abuse), who responded to this crisis with compassion and unparalleled commitment, thank you for your fellowship and collegiality. To our friends on the board of directors of the International Council on Cultism and Ritual Trauma: Ann Earle, Carl Raschke, Helen

McGonigle, and Michael Newton, thanks for your continued efforts, your friendship and support. To Shari Julian, thank you for your friendship and help during the rough spots. We are grateful for the skill, support, and dedication of the staff of The Center for Counseling and Psychological Services, Licensed Professional Counselors Tory Gustafson, Sheri Miller and Glenda Faulkner, and our administrative support staff, Penny Alecknavage. To Dr. Robert Schwartz, psychiatrist, thank you for the care, commitment and professionalism that you have provided these patients.

Thanks to our colleagues on the Cult and Ritual Trauma online list that provides us with opportunities for continuing professional education and personal support. Special thanks to list moderator Thorsten Becker for your concern and energy.

We extend our appreciation for all of those individuals who advocate on behalf of the victims who have no voice, the children. Thank you to Eileen King, Sherry Quirk, Beth Vargo, Claire Reeves, Sylvia Gillotte, Elizabeth Morgan, Susie Alverson, Katherine Andrews, Maralee McLean, Jackie McGauley, Marymae Cioffi, David Westgate, Dean and Nancy Treadwell, and the many others who devote themselves to the protection of children.

Thanks to Dale Griffis, John Hunt, Steve Baggs, Tony Bovis, Brooks Fleig, and to the many helpful peace officers who participated in the Texas Council of Occult Crimes Investigators for sharing your insights and perspective.

Thank you to Alan Scheflin, Walter Bowart, Karen Jones, and the many others who generously shared with us their knowledge of abusive mind control practices.

Thank you to Chrystine Oksana, Margaret Smith, and Daniel Ryder, for your encouragement and advice.

Thanks to Sara Camilli, our agent, who helps us immeasurably. Thanks to Jan Brumfield and Calvin Glenn of Graphics Group of Dallas for your invaluable assistance in adapting our manuscript to a printable format. Thanks to the University of Texas Southwestern Medical School Library and its helpful staff. You have been our home away from home. And thank you to Greenwood Publishing Group, for demonstrating your confidence in our work by commissioning this new revision.

And finally, our thanks to our readers. This book is not about pleasant or entertaining material. Thank you for your open-mindedness and willingness to consider this disturbing and controversial subject. Social ills and abuses cannot be resolved until they are examined and understood by the public. It all begins with education. Hopefully, this book will be a beginning for many of us.

Introduction

This book is about ritual abuse, a phenomenon reported with increasing frequency throughout the world. For many, the notion that innocent people are deliberately, ritually traumatized is unthinkable, the stuff of science fiction novels or fantasy films. For others, it is an unspeakable but distinct reality, an experience that some say they have actually endured and continue to relive indirectly through nightmares and flashbacks. These claims are made by people who allege to be victims, perpetrators, and witnesses. The public's reaction to these assertions, not surprisingly, has been mixed. In many cases there has been an emotional and polarized response. *Cult and Ritual Abuse: Its History, Anthropology, and Recent Discovery in Contemporary America*, revised edition, reviews both the published and unpublished accounts of ritual abuse and the theoretical commentaries on this subject.

This book also describes one therapist's personal experience evaluating and treating individuals making these allegations, most of whom were seen as psychotherapy patients seeking consultation at a private psychological and counseling practice. Established in the early 1980s, this practice, The Center for Counseling and Psychological Services, P.C., has been devoted primarily to the treatment of highly self-destructive patients. Over time, some of these clients began to reveal that they had been abused in cults that had subjected them to bizarre mind control techniques, unlike anything taught in the course of a traditional university curriculum for clinical psychology. These patients described experiences of ritual torture that caused them to undergo amnesia, mental fragmentation, altered states of consciousness, and a particular psychiatric disturbance, dissociative identity disorder.[1]

My initial response to these allegations was incredulity. I saw no reason to take such claims seriously. After all, psychiatric patients, like the rest of us, can spin a good yarn now and then. However, in spite of my skepticism, I was hearing comparable reports from other patients. In addition to their similar allegations, these patients were demonstrating the same cluster of psychiatric symptoms (e.g., powerful trance reactions, multiple inner identities, and psychogenic amnesia, etc.). Consultations with fellow mental health professionals revealed that they too were encountering patients with comparable stories. It soon became clear that this was a subject in need of further investigation. This research has led to some surprising conclusions.

We began a study of the historical and anthropological background of such practices, including accounts of religions, cults, and fraternal organizations where traumatic rituals were reportedly used for the purpose of creating altered states of consciousness. We found a body of literature where such mental states were sometimes viewed as sacred — as the magical catalyst for profound visions or possession by gods.[2] At the same time, my patients were describing traumatic techniques that were allegedly used to establish a powerful kind of psychological control that, until recently, existed "underground" in secrecy, essentially unknown within the mental health professions.

But the events described by patients and others are neither about the distant past nor exotic, foreign cultures. These traumatic acts of mind control reportedly occur in modern, civilized societies, including contemporary America. The stories are often incredible and include descriptions of abuse in sadistic ceremonies, some of which are allegedly associated with Satanic, Luciferian, and other occult themes. The psychiatric symptom pattern displayed by these individuals appears similar to those described as "possessed" in various other cultures. In probing these patients' allegations, we have been introduced to a world of occultism and other dark traditions and practices. Being persons with neither strong superstitions nor any beliefs in the supernatural, we have tried to make sense of these accounts in purely scientific terms. Consequently we offer some hypotheses about the so-called possession phenomena described over the centuries by theologians, religious leaders, historians, and anthropologists.

Our conclusion is that the diagnosis *dissociative identity disorder (DID)*, is a Western version of what has been known historically and anthropologically as possession.[3] Is it possible that some variants of possession in other cultures in other times have also resulted from such abusive practices? As the reader will see, there is historical and anthropological evidence that this may be the case.

Some readers may view these reports as unbelievable just as we did when we first encountered them. Such skepticism is natural and to be expected. These accounts go well beyond the pale of normal human experience. However, the prevalence and similarity of these reports throughout the United States and in other countries[4] makes one pause. Before dismissing these claims, the community must take some responsibility to investigate them. These outcries cannot simply be ignored without a fair hearing.

Subsequently, a significant controversy has arisen, resulting in bitter disputes among professionals and virtual battlegrounds within families where allegations have been made. As this book is being revised, the situation is grave for many survivors of alleged ritual abuse, as well as for those therapists who are willing to treat them. Patients reporting histories of ritual abuse find it increasingly difficult to obtain psychotherapy for their numerous and often disabling psychological problems. This dilemma is exacerbated by a trend among managed health care and health insurance companies to curtail coverage for the necessary lengthy psychiatric care for the chronically and pervasively mentally ill. Therapists who treat this patient population are the targets of civil suits and complaints to their licensing boards (Comstock & Vickery, 1992). Many of these actions are frivolous, but because these therapists choose to work in a newly identified field, and one that has attracted controversy, they are more vulnerable than the average mental health professional.

How did this happen? Three factors have lead to this predicament: the politics of psychotherapy, a generally unsympathetic and sometimes hostile media bias, and a growing contingent of reactionary individuals who are intent on proving that current allegations of child abuse are overstated.

But is there any hard evidence that these practices are ongoing in modern America? In spite of the numerous reports of ritual abuse, some authors and journalists have chosen to interpret these allegations as the products of either mass hysteria or the vulnerability of fragile psychiatric patients preyed upon by unethical psychotherapists. Although these hypotheses are worth consideration, we have found occasions where the media has tended to distort or suppress facts that should be made available to the public. We will discuss some instances later in this book in which journalists refused outright to publish facts (e.g., legal case findings) about this phenomenon. However, there have been isolated cases in which an effort was made to present facts in a balanced and evenhanded manner consistent with the best arguments regarding both sides of the controversy.

In September of 1993, we attended the National Conference on Crimes against Children in Washington, D.C. One of the major concerns discussed at this conference was ritual abuse. Among the prominent speakers was Senator Newton Russell from California, whose presentation, *Ritualized Crimes Against Children*, clearly showed that some legislators are beginning to address this phenomenon seriously. Several states have enacted laws against ritual abuse. Former Nebraska State Senator John DeCamp discusses ritual abuse uncovered during the investigation of a failed savings and loan institution in his book *The Franklin Cover Up*. A review of the research by Dr. Kathleen Faller (1994) at the University of Michigan concludes that there are cases of alleged ritual abuse with corroborating evidence. Those who argue that there is no evidence supporting the existence of ritual abuse are simply not accurately representing the facts.

On December 8, 1993, a program produced by the American Justice series entitled *Satan, Rituals and Abuse* was aired on cable television's Arts and Entertainment network. Two cases were profiled in which convictions were obtained in response to children's allegations of ritual abuse at two day care centers, one in Florida and the other in Texas. Significantly, in each case, one of the defendants confessed to some of the specific allegations. I am intimately familiar with the case in Texas, having acted as an expert witness for the prosecution.

Many professed cult and ritual abuse survivors have reported that their perpetrators told them that no one would believe their stories. It is our hope that this book will help shed light on their confusing and deeply disturbing allegations. In so doing, it may be possible to separate the reality of this phenomenon[5] from the illusions, superstitions, and misinformation that have further obscured what is already a complex question. A more realistic and scientifically based understanding of ritual abuse may best prepare us to respond to this problem in an effective and responsible manner.

NOTES

[1] The American Psychiatric Association (APA) publishes a diagnostic manual that categorizes all of the various psychiatric disorders recognized by the APA. Every few years the APA revises this listing of diagnoses. The latest revision of the *Diagnostic and Statistical Manual of Psychiatric Disorders, IV (DSM-IV)* was published in 1994. The *DSM-IV* has renamed what they formerly labeled multiple personality disorder, as dissociative identity disorder. The World Health Organization publishes a diagnostic manual, the *International Classification of Diseases (ICD)*. The most recent edition, *ICD-10*, uses the term, multiple personality disorder for this diagnosis. In this book both terms will be used.

[2] Many Westerners may view such altered states of consciousness as exotic and perhaps mythical phenomena that probably rarely occur in actuality. However, in an anthropological study reported by Bourguinon, the investigators found that 90% of a

sample of 488 societies worldwide demonstrated "one or more institutionalized, culturally patterned forms of altered states of consciousness" (Bourguinion, 1973, p. 11). Furthermore, in 51% of these societies there was evidence of spirit possession phenomena.

[3] Richard Noll (1992) also makes the point that the so-called possession disorders or, as he terms it, possession syndrome, may in fact be multiple personally disorder. However, as Craig Lockwood has pointed out, Noll is skeptical and critical of the idea that ritual abuse actually occurs (Lockwood, 1993, p. 17).

[4] See Core (1991), John (1989), Jonker, & Jonker-Bakker (1991, 1997).

[5] A study by Perry (1992) shows that a large percentage of the members of the International Society for the Study of Multiple Personality and Dissociation who responded to her questionnaire, 88% indicated "belief in ritual abuse involving mind control and programming" (p. 3). In a survey by Bottoms, Shaver, & Goodman (1991) the authors found that 30% of their national sample of members of the American Psychological Association had seen at least one case involving alleged ritualistic or religion-related abuse. Of these, 93% believed that their patients had actually been harmed.

Chapter 1

The Church in Thetford Forest

It is hard to believe that the precipitating incident resulting in a lifelong challenge would seem so innocuous at the time. But in many aspects of life, we do not readily recognize these moments as they occur. Rather, it is only in retrospect that they take on significance and can be seen as important milestones, teaching valuable lessons. This was such an event.

In 1979, I had never heard of ritual abuse and was unaware of its possible existence. The subject of such abuse was never broached during the staff and supervision meetings where I was assigned to the second largest Air Force mental health installation in Europe. Furthermore, like most of the clinic personnel, I had been trained to be skeptical of any allegations of sexual abuse made by the patients. The prevailing attitudes among the staff were influenced by Sigmund Freud's theory that people commonly fantasize about such abuse, particularly during early childhood. As a newly trained psychologist, I was completely unprepared to address the phenomenon of ritual abuse.

A special benefit of this European posting was that outside the day-to-day duties required by the base, hospital, and clinic, it provided numerous recreational opportunities as agreeable diversions. The congenial environment contributed a kind of insulation from the unpleasant stories that the psychiatric patients sometimes told.

It was easy to become immersed in the history and culture of England, unknowingly exposed to the evidence and artifacts of cults that had originated in Britain (and other European sites). At the time, their significance was not apparent to me. However, England was the birthplace of Aleister Crowley, perhaps the most infamous of modern occultists. Similarly, Wicca, or white witchcraft, originated in the United Kingdom, along with several secret, occult fraternal organizations.

I had no interest in occultism but was fascinated by the history and picturesque beauty of the countryside. Our family enjoyed driving and hiking from one ancient ruin to the next. Looking back on that period, I recognize that there were many things there to discover and experience that would be directly relevant to my later work with ritual abuse survivors. For example, we frequently visited a beautiful park on the grounds of the abbey at Bury St. Edmunds, a town not far from the air base. While the children frolicked, chasing after the resident ducks and geese, we explored the ruins and wondered what could have driven the townspeople to rise up against the monks on more than one occasion and destroy the magnificent abbey, one of the most sacred shrines in all of England. According to one of the British locals, the monks were known to escape from the abbey and molest the women of the town. Another curiosity was the twin Stars of David that embellished the massive and beautifully crafted abbey gate. Why, in what had been such an anti-Semitic culture, would a symbol of Judaism[6] decorate the gate of the abbey, which was the sacred burial ground of King Edmund and the site where the English barons gathered to confirm their resolve to force Henry II to sign the Magna Carta? Bury St. Edmunds had also been an infamous site of witch trials in England that became a precedent for the witch persecutions of Salem, Massachusetts. Not far away was a very old country church whose interior displayed a medieval wall painting entitled *The Wheel of Fate*. This pagan subject matter seemed oddly out of place in a Christian house of worship. While curious about these mysteries of history, I did not pursue any tedious research. Instead, my days were pleasantly filled with family, friends, and work.

The assignment to the Mental Health Clinic at RAF Lakenheath, England, was a pleasant job for a young captain and psychologist having just completed an Air Force internship in clinical psychology. With my career at its beginning, the patients' stories were new and fresh. It was at Lakenheath that I met "Bill" my first patient reporting ritual abuse, although at the time I didn't recognize the significance of his story.

His intake form identified him as Sergeant "William Hoffer", but he invited me to call him "Bill." Dressed in his blue Air Force summer uniform, he appeared haggard and distressed. He mumbled that it was embarrassing for him to come to the mental health clinic because as a "private person," he was not accustomed to discussing his personal problems with anyone. Yet, something had happened that was so disturbing that he felt compelled to talk about it. While he spoke, Bill frequently paused and hesitated, wrung his hands, and demonstrated obvious discomfort with the subject that had brought him to my office. He rarely looked me in the eye. Instead, he allowed his gaze to travel around my meagerly furnished office in the Mental Health Clinic. Finally, Bill began to speak.

He said that he came to see me because he had been to "a party." Again he hesitated, and I encouraged him to continue. Suddenly Bill's eyes filled with tears, and he described what appeared to have been a bizarre sex party during which he was sodomized. Bill claimed that the man who assaulted him wore a black robe and a goat's head mask. According to Bill, the room was partially lit with candles, and some of the other people present were also dressed in robes.

The party, he said, started out simply as an ordinary gathering of people, some British nationals and some United States military personnel and dependents. Pockets of individuals and couples conversed and drank. When I asked Bill if drugs were used at the party, he looked away evading my question. Bill said he had been invited to this party by a casual acquaintance with the promise that it was a "really wild group" and that Bill was "sure to get laid." Indeed, as the evening progressed, several of the partygoers appeared to become intoxicated. Eventually, some of those present began to openly engage in sex, and the party degenerated into an orgy. Bill said some of those present shed their clothes while others clothed themselves in dark, hooded robes and chanted to Satan. It was at that point, Bill alleged, that he was raped. The issue that motivated Bill to seek counseling was not so much his brush with the occult as his fear that because he had not actively resisted his rape, he might be homosexual.

I asked Bill where this party had occurred. He told me that this group met in an abandoned church located in the Thetford Forest not far from the air base. With some hesitation, he gave me the directions to the church. Already skeptical of the details of his story, it was at that point I became even more incredulous. I was familiar with the road he described and had never seen a church there. Although he seemed sincere in what he was telling me and showed no signs of being psychotic, Bill's narrative was simply too bizarre to be taken at face value.

Several days later, I happened to drive by the location described by Bill. Thetford Forest is a thickly wooded area, difficult to navigate in many places because of the lush undergrowth of ferns and other vegetation and the abundance of trees. Along the perimeter, the dense green panorama is interrupted by occasional stone and flint cottages and farmhouses. I drove slowly along the road looking off into the forest and saw what appeared to be a small, flint-studded church, partially obscured by trees. There was neither footpath nor road by which to approach the church from my car. For a moment, I considered parking my car at the side of the narrow English road and attempting to walk to the building. I decided against it and drove back to the base.

Bill's sessions with me focused primarily on his fear that he was a latent homosexual. Eventually, he satisfied himself that he was not. I concluded that he had become involved with a group of people who were drawn toward kinky sexual practices and that they used the occult and demonic trappings in order to maximize the "forbidden fruit" fantasy of their sex games. I assumed that Bill's story probably represented a relatively rare kind of experience, as I was unfamiliar with any similar cases in the professional literature of psychology.

I was, however, aware of one precedent to Bill's story, the notorious Hell Fire Club.[7] This organization, led by Sir Francis Dashwood in 18th-century England, allegedly existed for the purpose of providing male aristocrats with opportunities for sexual debauchery. According to one of my undergraduate history professors, these sexual escapades were conducted in a manner that included acts of blasphemy along with the simulation of demon worship. The professor pointed out, however, that these "rituals" were not authentically Satanic, but merely a decoy for the real purpose of the organization, which he claimed was sexual license.

This group had historic significance because it provided a connection between Benjamin Franklin (who is said to have visited the club in 1758) and certain important English aristocracy and representatives of the British government who were also members of this club[8] during the time when America was seeking its independence. With so little material published on the subject of occult-inspired sexual practices, I decided that they must not occur very often, and so I thought that I would probably never again see a patient like Bill.

NOTES

[6] As I was later to learn, the Star of David, or *Magen David*, was not in use as a symbol of Judaism until a later time - long after the building of the Abbeygate. At that time in history, the hexagram was an occult symbol (see Walker, 1983, pp. 401-403).

[7] At that time, I was not aware of the controversy associated with the Hell Fire Clubs, notably the one made infamous by Sir Francis Dashwood more accurately known as the "Friars of Medmenham." Some authors viewed Dashwood's enterprise merely as a group that provided an opportunity for sexual license (e.g., King, 1991). Others considered it to be a truly diabolical organization (e.g., Raschke, 1990). Howard (1989) argued that the Friars of Medmenham were associated with Freemasonry and other occult but not strictly Satanic groups. Certainly, some combination of these various interpretations could also be true. See also Ashe (1974), Chancellor (1925), Colquhoun (1975), Mannix (1959), McCormick (1958), and Towers (1986).

---

[8] Dashwood himself was a Member of Parliament and Chancellor of the Exchequer. Some of the other members were also highly placed in the British Government, reputedly with connections to the royal family.

Chapter 2

On the Borderline

Clinically, I had particularly wanted to work with patients suffering with phobias and anxiety disorders, but such patients were relatively rare in the Air Force. As one of the most junior ranking of the officers at the Mental Health Clinic, I paradoxically tended to be assigned many of the seriously disturbed and more challenging patients. Such patients, with their relatively chronic and severe problems, are often frustrating to those who try to help them. Typically, their progress in therapy is slow and only marginal. On the other hand, it can be dangerous to limit or deny treatment to such individuals because of their risk of suicide, self-mutilation, or harm toward some other person.[9] Many of the senior mental health providers avoided working with these demanding and frequently dangerous patients by referring them to me. Consequently, I began to gather a sizable caseload of these patients, many of whom met the diagnostic criteria for borderline personality disorder.

One such patient was "Annie." The wife of a young enlisted man, Annie had a complicated psychiatric history consisting of episodes of depression, suicide attempts, and self-mutilation. Most of the time, she was charming, friendly, and talkative. On other occasions, Annie flew into rages, often for no discernible reason. Annie was overly dependent on her husband, typically refusing to drive alone or go places without him. Yet, when they were together, she was usually quite emotionally aloof. She was extremely critical of herself and felt unloved and unworthy of love. She said she felt "dead" inside in spite of her usually intense and often lively outward expression of emotion. Her speech, sometimes poetic, often reflected a sense of poignancy about life and the others around her. Annie did not understand why she was in such constant and uncontrollable turmoil. Annie said that another doctor once told her she had a "chemical imbalance" in her brain and that her emotional problems were a result of faulty neurochemistry. When I asked her what she thought, she responded only with an empty and melancholy silence.

Annie was a person with many contrasting moods, ideas, and feelings. Sometimes when I saw her, she appeared to be gregarious, dramatic, and animated. At other times, her face was devoid of expression or stained with partially dried tears. Periodically, Annie deliberately cut herself, and afterward, ironically, described feelings of relief. Sometimes before these incidents, she was observed staring into space chanting, "I've got to see blood; I've got to see blood." Those involved with her care tried to prevent her acts of self-mutilation through hospitalization. But even in a protected hospital environment, Annie found ways to inflict self-harm. Once when she was hospitalized, she successfully concealed a sharp object that she used to scratch and superficially cut herself. In the morning, she was discovered with blood smeared on her body and on the walls of her room. I didn't have an opportunity to continue Annie's therapy because her husband was reassigned to another station. But there were many others in my caseload who lived in a similar state of chronic mental torment.

Borderline personality disorder is a psychiatric diagnosis about which little is known. Important and basic questions, such as its cause, are still not clearly understood. But beyond its status as a scientific curiosity, borderline personality disorder represents significant suffering, lingering unhappiness, and, sometimes, the reality of suicide. Borderline personality disorder is characterized by deeply conflicted emotions, running the gamut from rage to terror, from depressed apathy to turbulent agitation. Patients with borderline personality disorder often experience self-loathing that alternates and coexists with self-absorption or narcissism. Their frequent acts of self-destructiveness, including self-mutilation and suicide attempts, bewilder and frighten their families, friends, and caregivers. These individuals typically have deeply unsatisfying interpersonal relationships and appear to alienate those who care for them, while at the same time expressing fears that they will be abandoned. Patients with this disorder often appear uncooperative in therapy and are frequently accused of sabotaging their own treatment. The condition of such patients is considered chronic with intermittent self-destructive episodes. Curiously, these patients often respond in unusual or unpredictable ways to psychiatric medications.

Many of these patients perceive their lives to be unsatisfying and empty. However, in spite of their numerous psychological frailties, there is often a richness of character present. With lives that often parallel those of the anti-heroes of the modern cinema, they frequently appear to be rebels or eccentrics. Like Don Quixote with his compulsion to do combat with windmills, their aggressive energies frequently seem diverted toward pointless or unwinnable conflicts, but at the same time their impractical battles often reveal their sentimentality.

Some of these patients are reminiscent of well known creative personalities who periodically appear in the course of history. Like Vincent van Gogh, Peter Tchaikovsky, and Edgar Allen Poe, these patients typically live chaotic, turbulent, eccentric lives. Although they often lack the simplest understanding of many of their own more mundane and routine experiences, they will periodically have profound and creative insights.[10]

Upon discharge from the Air Force, I went into private practice in a suburb of Dallas, Texas. Although I wished to develop a practice specializing in the treatment of phobias and anxiety disorders, my experience and willingness to work with patients with borderline personality disorder soon became known and resulted in a sizable caseload of these individuals. However, the professional community was — and is — divided about the proper regimen of treatment for such patients. My review of the numerous books and professional journal articles on the subject of borderline personality revealed no clear consensus regarding the appropriate treatment of this disorder. A book by Waldinger and Gunderson (1987) lists six different psychodynamic[11] approaches to conceptualizing and treating borderline personality disorder. However, even this roster is not comprehensive. Other theories and therapy methods have been used in treating these patients.[12]

Doctor Wilhelm Abse wrote about the origins of the term *borderline*:

> In 1891, George M. Beard wrote a series of essays in the *New York Medical Record* in which he introduced the term *border-liners* and applied it to 'that large class of nervous persons, sometimes hypochondriacal, sometimes neurasthenic, sometimes hysterical, sometimes epileptic, sometimes inebriate, sometimes several of these united who,' he wrote further, 'are almost insane at times and yet may never become insane, though sometimes they may cross the borderline.' (1983, p. 340)

Abse explained that the current psychiatric diagnostic manual at the time, the *DSM-III*, stated very conservatively, "Child abuse and other forms of severe emotional trauma may be predisposing factors." In citing the *Diagnostic and Statistical Manual of Mental Disorders, Third Edition*

(American Psychiatric Association, 1980, p. 258), Abse added, "I have never found severe psychic trauma to be absent in such cases" (1983, p. 340). Also writing about borderline patients, Nagel (1989) observed, "Therapists frequently say they do not see many patients who have experienced incest, molestation, or physical brutality. This is not necessarily because their patients have not had these experiences but, rather, because therapists overlook, deny, or ignore the existence of these problems" (p. 402).

Reluctantly, I have to admit that I was such a therapist. I had gotten out of the habit of specifically asking about sexual abuse in the histories of my patients, often because early in the history taking, patients frequently deny abuse even though later in therapy some report that child abuse had actually occurred. Think about it for a moment. Imagine yourself as a patient having your first session with a mental health professional. Although he or she is a stranger to you, you are asked to disclose intimate details of your personal life. You feel nervous, embarrassed, and emotionally overexposed. You are unsure about confidentiality. You wonder whether anything that you say about yourself will later be used against you (e.g., if your mental health records are subpoenaed in a divorce or child custody hearing). The question of sexual abuse in your childhood comes up.[13] What would you say?

I cannot blame the patients for their reluctance to identify accurate histories of sexual abuse. I myself have never liked hearing about childhood sexual abuse. I often simply hoped that my patients would not bring the subject up. Hearing adults sobbing while recounting a childhood rape by a drunken parent is a not a pleasant experience for the therapist. I hoped that the numerous incidents of this horror reported by some of my colleagues were an exaggeration.[14] As I later read in *The Challenge of the Borderline Patient*:

> Borderlines frequently and increasingly report sexual abuse (as well as physical and emotional abuse) having occurred during their childhood and adolescence. Attempts to explain away this phenomenon by invoking the borderline's hysterical suggestibility stimulated by greater public awareness and publicity of childhood sexual abuse appear inadequate and even malicious. (Kroll, 1988, p. 41)

The author continues:

> It is more likely that professionals have become more aware of the need to ask the relevant questions and patients have become less reluctant to acknowledge and discuss these

usually recurrent childhood and adolescent sexual assaults. Certainly there is much better evidence for the occurrence and centrality of sexual abuse as an important etiological factor in the development of borderline symptoms and style than there is for the mythical "not good enough mothering" of the separation-individuation phase. (Kroll, 1988, p. 42)

Other researchers and have found childhood trauma and sexual abuse to be frequent in the histories of individuals with borderline personality disorder (Herman, Perry, & van der Kolk, 1989; Zanarini 1997). One of the diagnostic criteria for borderline personality disorder is self-mutilation. Self-mutilation has been found to be associated with histories of child abuse (Walsh & Rosen, 1988) and incest (Turell & Armsworth, 2000).

Some clinicians have attempted to describe the phenomenology of individuals with borderline personality. One of these conceptualizations, known as *object relations theory*, originated with the British psychoanalyst Melanie Klein. This theory is sometimes used to explain the "inner world" of these patients that is described as consisting of internal representations of other people and the self with the notion that these internal representations are often themselves fragmented. Thus, according to this theory, many of these patients have internalized "people" and fragments of people in their "inner world."[15]

Today, this concept parallels what therapists who work with dissociative identity disorder (multiple personality disorder) call *alter personalities* or *alter fragments* which, in the language of object relations theory, are labeled *internal objects* and *internal part objects*. During my research on and active treatment of borderline personality disorder patients, I did not notice a connection between the two diagnoses because I had never seen a patient whom I recognized as having multiple personality disorder.

In fact, at that time, I viewed the diagnosis multiple personality disorder with great suspicion and questioned whether it was a legitimate diagnosis or simply an artifact of sloppy or poorly conducted psychotherapy. I wondered if overzealous and naive psychotherapists inadvertently created the disorder in their patients through suggestion. Never having seen the disorder among my patients, I believed it to be very rare. When I was a graduate student, the only reference I heard with regard to MPD occurred when an instructor declared it to be so scarce that we would probably never see a case in the course of our professional careers. It was not until much later that I read reports by other authors who expressed the view that the diagnosis borderline personality disorder had much in common with multiple personality disorder[16] and that MPD was not actually rare. MPD was, according to some authors, more often unrecognized and, thus, underdiagnosed.

The idea that MPD is underdiagnosed is related to the notion that few mental health professionals know how to make the diagnosis. Furthermore, patients with MPD frequently cope with it through denial. This argument is similar to observation of many alcohol treatment specialists, that alcoholism is frequently underdiagnosed because professionals do not typically know how to correctly make the diagnosis and because most alcoholics are in denial. According to Confer and Ables (1983), "A disorder that is rarely considered and only partially understood is unlikely to be frequently diagnosed, especially when specific skills are required to make the proper diagnosis. Such is the status of multiple personality" (p. 13).

A study by Hayes and Mitchell (1994) may further illustrate the reasons that professionals underdiagnose MPD. In a national sample of 207 psychologists, psychiatrists, and social workers, Hayes and Mitchell found 24% of them to be moderately to extremely skeptical about the MPD diagnosis. Additionally, their data showed that professionals' skepticism was inversely related to their knowledge about multiple personality disorder. Finally, Hayes and Mitchell found that MPD was less accurately diagnosed than schizophrenia and that misdiagnosis of MPD was associated with skepticism about MPD. Why would mental health professionals allow bias and lack of knowledge to affect their diagnostic thinking? This question is important and will receive further attention in subsequent chapters of this book.

Some argued that MPD is a questionable diagnosis without a scientific basis or that the diagnosis was accepted by few mental health professionals. Over time research began to accumulate addressing these questions. In a study by Dunn, Paolo, Ryan, & Van Fleet (1994), the authors surveyed 1,120 psychologists and psychiatrists employed by the Veterans Administration. Eighty percent of their respondents endorsed belief in the legitimacy of the DID diagnosis. Another study by Mai (1995) surveyed 180 Canadian psychiatrists and found that 66.1% believed the diagnosis was legitimate, 27.8% did not, and 3.3% were unsure. Pope, Oliva, Hudson, Bodkin and Gruber (1999) also studied 301 board certified psychiatrists. The authors found that 15% of the psychiatrists thought that DID should not be included in a future revision of the diagnostic manual, 43% thought it should be included with reservations and 35% though it should be included without reservations. In response to a question, "In your opinion, what is the status of the scientific evidence regarding the validity of Dissociative Identity Disorder," 20% endorsed "little or no evidence of validity," 51%

endorsed partial evidence of validity," and 21% endorsed "strong evidence of validity" (p. 322).

Surveys of professionals' beliefs about a diagnosis do not necessarily reflect the actual scientific characteristics of a particular diagnosis. Professionals do at times have biases and may be misinformed. Because psychiatric diagnoses are abstract and based on subjective reports of patients, it is often difficult to directly measure specific scientific characteristic of the diagnosis. However, interrater reliability is one scientific index of psychiatric diagnoses has been relatively well researched. Studies of the interrater reliability of the DID diagnosis made with structured interview methods show that DID has perhaps the highest interrater reliability of any psychiatric diagnosis (Ross,1997).

The courts have also upheld the finding that DID is a scientifically accepted diagnosis. In 1999 the Washington state supreme court determined that the diagnosis of dissociative identity disorder met the criteria for the Frye rule.[17] This ruling meant that expert testimony about dissociative identity disorder was admissible in court because the court had determined that the diagnosis was generally accepted in the mental health field.

NOTES

[9] Unfortunately, as previously mentioned, current trends in health care insurance are increasingly limiting sufficient coverage to adequately treat chronic psychiatric disorders.

[10] Weissman's (1993) book, *Of Two Minds: Poets Who Hear Voices,* provides an interesting discussion of Homer, Virgil, Shakespeare, Milton, Smart, Blake, Wordsworth, Coleridge, Tennyson, Arnold, Bronte, Browning, Rosetti, Dickinson, and Yeats, with regard to the notion of poetic inspiration via hearing voices.

[11] The term *psychodynamic* is often used to refer to psychological approaches that assume that the mind has inner processes that interact among themselves in predictable ways, just as in engineering and physics the term *thermodynamics* refers to the interactive properties of heat, temperature, work, and energy. Not all psychological treatment methods are psychodynamic in nature. Some are more behavioral and focus on external observable features of psychological functioning.

[12] For example, Marsha Linehan (1993) has developed a primarily behavioral treatment approach for individuals with borderline personality disorder.

[13] See J. Patterson & P. Kim (1992) who report that in their national survey which inquired about sexual abuse, "almost half" (p. 125) of their respondents who admitted to being sexually abused in childhood also indicated that they had never told anyone before about the abuse.

[14] Unfortunately, the recent studies on child abuse seem to indicate that it is more prevalent than most of us have previously recognized. See Chapter 18.

[15] I sometimes use the expression *inner world* to refer to a state or states of subjective experience. A person's inner world consists of thoughts, sensations, emotions, etc. For some people, their inner world also consists of internalized images and conceptualizations of other people. In some cases, these internalized entities give the

appearance of exerting influence or control over the person. Nevertheless, this kind of language is meant to be metaphorical.

[16] See Benner & Joscelyne (1984), Bliss (1980), Buck (1983), Clary et al. (1984), Horevitz & Braun (1984).

[17] *U.S. v. Greene*, 1999

Chapter 3

Entering Uncharted Territory

I continued working with patients with borderline personality disorder and other related diagnoses.[18] Although many of my patients appeared to make progress in therapy, the work was still often frustrating and exhausting. I hoped that it would be possible to identify a specific collection of therapy techniques and strategies that would help these patients toward recovery in a briefer, and thus more humane, period of time. In the pursuit of this goal, I began to study a variety of different therapy methods with the hope of distinguishing those that would be most productive and efficient. As time went by, I came to believe that books and journal articles were not as instructive as the experience of actually working with these patients, who proved to be excellent teachers. What would happen if mental health professionals gave up their preconceived ideas about this disorder and simply listened to their patients?

Of the many hours spent providing therapy for these clients, I especially valued and learned from working with them in group therapy. There are many different ways to approach group therapy. Some groups are highly structured by the facilitator, occasionally focusing on a particular theme or group exercise. Other groups are less defined in their particular format and topic, and the group participants are encouraged to talk about anything meaningful or emotionally significant to them. Many groups alternate from a structured to unstructured style in order to implement a variety of different goals.

Group therapy is often an effective treatment modality for people who feel that they are alone in life, misunderstood and unworthy of love. Many groups are emotionally supportive, and in this nurturing environment people often learn that others share similar fears, secrets, and painful experiences. People also learn to experience social acceptance in terms of their individuality and diversity, developing a sense that each person has a right to respect and that they need not be the same as one another in order to have worth. Thus, patients are often able to improve their social skills and frequently feel great relief through their participation with others in social interactions in which honesty and caring are usually appreciated and respected. In the group setting, people are able to explore their relationships and gain insights about the way their behaviors are perceived by others through methods such as role playing and role reversal as well as through other group therapy techniques.[19]

For a time, I regularly conducted inpatient group therapy with borderline patients on the psychiatric unit of a local community hospital. On one occasion, I brought a toy doll to the group and proposed a group exercise involving the doll. I asked the group members if they would be willing to hug the doll, one at a time, imagining they were holding themselves as children. I requested the group participants to hold the doll individually and describe the feelings that resulted from the experience. The purpose of the exercise was for the group members to explore their capacity for self-nurturing, their attitudes about themselves, their self-perceptions, and their feelings about their childhood experiences.

The outcome of this exercise was dramatic, although not immediately. Early in the exercise, many of the participants felt, not surprisingly, self-conscious and even ridiculous engaging in behaviors so inconsistent with normal adult roles. However, some of their reluctance had nothing to do with the apparent absurdity of the therapy task. Many of the patients refused to hold the doll because their self-hatred was so great they could not stand the idea of holding themselves, even symbolically.

As we explored these feelings over several days in group therapy, some of the patients began to report improvement in their attitudes toward themselves. Eventually, many of the patients were able to embrace the doll and some would tearfully talk about experiencing small amounts of self-acceptance for the first time. Many of these group members previously had little insight about the nature of the conflict between their strong feelings of self-revulsion and their emotional neediness. As a result of the exercise, some said that they understood their feelings better. Others simply seemed able to integrate these opposing emotional states. It was such a moving experience that the head nurse of the unit later purchased a similar doll for me as a personal gift, but also to be used in future groups.

Some time later, I was asked by a neurologist colleague at the same medical facility to consult on one of his patients, a married woman in her late 30s. "Susie" was hospitalized for intractable headaches and the neurologist suspected that her pain was at least partly related to psychological factors. When I visited Susie in her hospital room, she showed no outward appearance of distress but described intense, excruciating headaches. While she spoke her facial expression was so pleasant and congenial that I wondered if she really was experiencing any discomfort. Because her hospital room was dimly lit, I turned on the overhead light in order to write my case notes as we talked, but simultaneously with the light coming on, Susie grimaced painfully.

When I switched the light off, she showed considerable relief. This reaction provided some objective evidence that Susie was experiencing actual physical pain because it is common for headache patients, particularly those with vascular headaches, to experience more pain in bright light. However, her pleasant mood was conspicuously out of place. Her behavior showed what some clinicians call *la belle indifference,* or an attitude of incongruous unconcern about her identified problem. This style of behavior is often associated with the old and now rarely used diagnostic category *hysteria* although it is also seen in individuals with other psychiatric disorders.

Hysteria is a label that once represented an official diagnostic category within the nomenclature of the American Psychiatric Association but in modern usage, has generally been replaced with the diagnostic terms *conversion disorder* and the *dissociative disorders.*[20] Patients with conversion disorder often develop physical ailments that are not attributable to a physical disorder and for which a psychological cause accounts for the symptoms. An example would be the case of a woman who develops a psychological (rather than neurological) paralysis that prevents her from attending the funeral of her mother.

Dissociative disorders are a category of diagnoses that, in the *DSM-IV,* include dissociative amnesia, dissociative fugue, dissociative identity disorder, and depersonalization disorder along with a miscellaneous category for dissociative disorders not listed elsewhere as dissociative disorder not otherwise specified. According to the *DSM-IV,* "The essential feature of these disorders is a disruption in the normally integrated functions of consciousness, memory, identity, or perception of the environment" (American Psychiatric Association, 1994, p. 477). Dissociative amnesia is the inability to remember important and extensive personal information because of a psychological cause other than dissociative identity disorder. Dissociative fugue refers to a condition wherein the patient may experience amnesia upon finding that he or she has traveled to some unfamiliar or distant place. The diagnosis dissociative identity disorder represents the experience of two or more different personalities that, at different times, exert "executive control" over the person's behavior and when there is amnesia for important personal information. The experience of depersonalization and the disorder by the same name refer to the experience of feeling detachment from one's self or physical body (e.g., an "out-of-body" experience).[21]

Susie and I talked for awhile, and I administered a psychological test, the Minnesota Multiphasic Personality Inventory (MMPI). After she completed the test, I reviewed her test data and returned to see her the next day. Susie's psychological testing appeared more consistent with the diagnosis borderline personality disorder than one of the hysterical diagnoses. In any case, it was common for people with the diagnosis borderline personality disorder also to have some of the characteristics of hysteria (i.e., either conversion or dissociative symptoms).

As I became acquainted with Susie, I came to know her as a person who wanted to portray herself as being well-functioning but who was, in reality, moody, periodically explosive, and at times, desperately needy. When I asked her about her experiences growing up, she told me that her family was wonderful. In later sessions, however, Susie related that her father was an alcoholic who physically and sexually abused her. She described strong feelings of revulsion and self-hatred. Susie reminded me of the patients with whom I worked in the group therapy milieu who were initially unwilling to express affection, even symbolically, to themselves when imagining themselves as children.

I asked Susie to imagine that she could see herself as she was when she was a child. Then I asked her to picture herself in the present, as an adult comforting and nurturing the child she once was. Susie closed her eyes and was quiet for awhile. I waited, then after a few moments asked her what she was feeling. Susie's eyes opened and, with a gleeful expression she responded in a soft, high-pitched, and childlike voice, saying, "Hello, Doctor Randy."

In our previous sessions, Susie addressed me as Dr. Noblitt. I was bewildered by her different speech and behavior, "Susie," I asked, "are you okay?"

"Silly, I'm not Susie. Susie went away."
"You're not Susie?"
"No-o-o," she playfully drawled.

"Then who are you?" I asked.
"I'm Little Susie."

Looking at her in her hospital bed, I saw a fully-grown woman, of normal weight and slightly taller than average. Yet, despite the evidence of my eyes, the patient's voice had the intonation, rhythm, and articulation of a little girl. "Little Susie" told me that she was four years old and that she came out to talk to me because she had watched me talk to "Big Susie," and decided that she liked me. She complained that no one would listen to Big Susie and that Big Susie felt alone and scared. Little Susie thanked me for listening to Big Susie and gave me some additional historical information that the patient had not previously revealed.

After this conversation between Little Susie and myself, the patient became quiet again. A few moments later, Susie's expression and voice returned to their previous adult-like quality. She showed no signs of having any recollection for the conversation between Little Susie and myself and, when I asked her if she knew anyone by the name of Little Susie, she said she didn't know what I was talking about. She did say that something about the session had made her feel better, but she did not know what it was.

I left her hospital room puzzled and confused. What I had just witnessed appeared to be a textbook case of multiple personality disorder. But how could this be — given that I did not consider MPD to be a legitimate diagnosis?

In proceeding with the evaluation of this patient, I looked for any alternative explanation other than the MPD diagnosis, but could find none. In fact, the patient began to present with more of these alternate identities as the assessment continued and some of her alter personalities began to narrate stories of cruel and sadistic abuse in Susie's childhood. The personalities were different from one another. Some were expressed as children, some were in the role of teenagers, and some were portrayed as adults. The memories of these alternate identities were also occasionally different, and at times arguments would ensue among the personalities regarding the veracity of their various reports. I was unable to find an alternate explanation for Susie's behavior other than the diagnosis, multiple personality disorder.

Some of Susie's emerging alternate identities reported that the allegations of abuse were just "made up." I tried to explore both sides of this inner controversy in order to arrive at the truth. For example, a particular alternate identity would present and speak: "I'm Billy. The stories your hear are just made up. In fact we don't even have MPD." I asked "Billy" why he used a different name from Susie. "Billy" had no answer and simply disappeared for the moment. Other alternate identities expressed great relief that I was willing to listen to "them." Some expressed fear that there would be retaliation, usually by other internalized identities, because some of the other alters were "telling the secrets."

Although this idea of secrecy seemed to be a paramount theme in Susie's narratives, she also verbalized an urgency to express her powerful pent-up feelings. When describing the repeated incidents of abuse, alters would sometimes weep pitifully, and at other times they would recount these stories wearing the blank and glassy expression characteristic of individuals in a state of shock. Occasionally, child alter identities would playfully emerge just to make friendly conversation.

One of the male alters seemed particularly angry and hostile, often making threats toward me and denying the accounts of childhood abuse and that the patient had MPD. Initially, this alternate identity would not identify "himself," but once when provoked, "he" stood up in front of me and defiantly announced, "I am the 'Evil One.' " When the alter identified "himself" in this way, I incorrectly assumed that "he" was presenting "himself" merely as an evil alternate identity. Much later, I came to realize that the "Evil One" was an internal representation of the devil.

This clarification did not become apparent until after approximately two years of therapy with Susie, when stories of ritual abuse in a Satanic cult began to emerge. As time went by, her stories became more bizarre and unimaginable. However, the alternative explanations were even more incredible. Suffice it to say that at this time, I believed that this patient was demonstrating symptoms consistent with a diagnosis of multiple personality disorder. The notion of ritual abuse had not even occurred to me. The idea of MPD alone was sufficiently bizarre to stretch my capacity for new concepts to its limits.

NOTES

[18] Many patients are said to show some signs or symptoms of borderline personality disorder, but not enough to accurately make that diagnosis. Many of these borderline-like patients are considered to be within what some clinicians have designated the "borderline spectrum."

[19] In role playing, the patient plays the role of someone else in a group exercise organized and presented somewhat like a skit. For example, a shy person might play the role of a more extroverted individual in order to examine internal processes (e.g., thoughts and feelings) related to introversion-extroversion. In role reversal the participants are paired together and asked to reverse their roles. One person plays the role of another person and vice versa. This exercise helps people to empathize with others and see different points

of view (which naturally result when playing the role of another person and while experiencing that other person acting out one's own style of behavior).

[20] Although the *DSM-III-R* published in 1987 listed the term, *hysterical neurosis*, in parentheses along with the diagnostic labels conversion disorder and dissociative disorder, the *DSM-IV* published in 1994 no longer uses references to hysteria in context with these diagnoses.

[21] Psychiatric diagnoses do not represent universal or unchanging categories of mental illness. They are revised every few years. The criteria whereby the various diagnoses are included and defined in the diagnostic manual are based on the opinions of the American Psychiatric Association's task force assigned to revise the manual. Obviously, these opinions will vary.

Chapter 4

Multiple Personalities

It was difficult for me to acknowledge multiple personality as a scientifically valid concept. Until the time I consulted with Susie, the very idea of this diagnosis ran counter to all my training and clinical experience. Furthermore, a study by Nicholas Spanos and his associates (1986) indicated that alternate identities could be created by hypnosis. I had heard from some other professionals that all of the cases of MPD that had been reported thus far were found in individuals who had undergone hypnosis. It seemed reasonable to assume that MPD was created in patients who were highly suggestible[22] by practitioners who were using hypnosis. Some authors even observed that individuals with MPD appeared to go into spontaneous trances (e.g., Bliss, 1984a).

Although I had not used hypnosis with Susie, she did appear to go into trance states during our sessions. Was she experiencing spontaneous trances? Other authors reported that spontaneous trance states were common among persons with multiple personality disorder. Was it possible that Susie did not have MPD before she met me? What if Susie was merely an extremely hypnotizable person who sometimes entered a trance state without a formal hypnotic induction? When I asked her to imagine herself as an adult nurturing herself as a child, was it possible that I inadvertently put the idea in her mind that she might be two different people? Might she have responded to this as if it were a suggestion *and then* developed MPD? What if I were the one who caused her MPD?

An article in the professional literature addressed this question (Spiegel, 1974). According to Spiegel, there are certain highly hypnotizable individuals whom he calls "grade 5s," corresponding to a test of hypnotizability that he developed and calls the Hypnotic Induction Profile (HIP). According to Spiegel, these highly hypnotizable individuals are very prone to take on the attitudes and beliefs of their therapists and are so suggestible that he warns against the use of introspective psychotherapy with them. Spiegel and Spiegel (1978) further elaborate this theory in the book *Trance and Treatment*. In these publications, the authors recommend a differing approach to treatment based on the patient's measured hypnotizability, but no data are cited that demonstrate that highly hypnotizable patients improve more with the treatment approach they recommend as opposed to other alternatives. Furthermore, according to a report by Cohen (1984), tests of hypnotizability, including Spiegel's, have not been readily accepted by clinicians: "The data lead to the conclusion that none of the tests of hypnotizability have yet proved their efficacy to even significant minority of clinicians" (p. 79).[23]

In working with Susie, I also wanted to explore the extent to which therapy may have contributed to her mental fragmentation, her memory lapses and the appearance of her various alter identities. As each alternate identity appeared, I attempted to get an individual history of that particular identity by asking questions such as "When did you first come into existence?" and "When did you first come out?" Although the various alternate identities were different, some being helpful and cooperative while others were hostile and adversarial, most were willing to give an individualized history and claimed they had been created by Susie's mind when some overwhelming or traumatic event occurred. For example, "Little Susie" told me that she had first come into existence when Susie's father forced her to stand on the hot metal grating over a gas floor furnace that burned the soles of her feet. The notion that trauma was related to the creation of these alter identities was not suggested to the patient by me. At that time I was unaware of the relationship between trauma and dissociation. Furthermore, in all cases, when I obtained a history of a particular alternate identity's experiences and memories, the alternate present told me that "he" or "she" had come into being at some time long before I worked with the patient.

As I worked with Susie I became aware that there were professional publications that described what I was observing in this patient. The first book that I found on this subject was Frank Putnam's (1989) *Diagnosis and Treatment of Multiple Personality Disorder*. It was surprising that an entire book had been written on what was assumed to be an obscure and rarely used diagnosis. Nevertheless, Putnam was clearly describing the same phenomena that I was observing. The book also addressed the question of whether MPD could be created by therapeutic methods such as hypnosis. His book indicated that many of the alternate identities had histories that occurred long before therapy commenced. Putnam noted that the pseudo-personalities supposedly created by hypnosis had markedly different characteristics than genuine alternate identities seen in patients with MPD.[24]

This has also been my experience. In attempting to help patients stabilize, I have sometimes suggested to them that they would be able to create more "helper" alternates, but this strategy has never been successful. Although it is possible to change an already-existing alter's name, habits, sense of identity, and job, I have never been able to use hypnotic suggestion to create alter identities who have any enduring reality or significance to the patient. Additionally, the task of modifying the characteristics of alters already in existence is not easily accomplished (e.g., in a few sessions of hypnosis), but normally engages the patient and therapist in lengthy, difficult, and often grueling work. The suggestibility of individual patients has not proven to be an effective conduit for any meaningful or lasting change. Otherwise, multiples could simply be encouraged to say to themselves, "Every day, in every way, I am getting better and better." Experience has taught that such an approach does not work with these patients.

Frequently Susie, the host persona, would deny any awareness of the other identities, and they sometimes expressed resentment that she did not acknowledge them. Occasionally, the alternates would do things to prove to Susie that they were real. They sometimes took control and she would later discover that she had engaged in behaviors that Susie neither appreciated nor approved. In some cases, Susie remembered engaging in the harmful or undesirable behaviors but, in other cases, she was amnestic for the events that occurred. Sometimes the alter identities wrote notes to Susie and, occasionally, to me. Susie also frequently had no memory of having written them. On other occasions, the alters described traumatic events for which Susie had no recollection. When confronted with such reports of abuse made by her inner "personalities," Susie sometimes recognized the veracity of what the alters reported to her, but on other occasions she was unsure. Because these alter identities described an existence and a history that antedated my interactions with the patient, and because I was unable to enact any significant changes in them simply by suggestion, I concluded that it was extremely unlikely that they were produced by therapy. Nevertheless, this is a most curious phenomenon. Why would some individuals dissociate as separate selves in the presence of trauma?

This question was not readily solvable. My days were consumed by patient appointments and consultations, leaving little time to speculate about the possible causes of dissociative phenomena. There seemed to be an endless stream of people with incomprehensible mental anguish that were finding their way to my office. Many of these patients initially had no conscious awareness of the cause of their suffering. Instead, they came to my office with a long list of psychiatric symptoms.

One such patient was "Pat." She was in her 40s, small and emaciated, and she looked much older than her stated age. Her hair was styled in a short pixie cut, and her eyes appeared sunken, empty, and sad. She told me that she had panic attacks and agoraphobia for which she had been unsuccessfully treated by a nationally known phobia specialist. She was fearful of leaving her house, driving a car, or being in crowded places such as shopping malls. She was anorexic and had a severe hand-washing compulsion. Her hands had bleeding scabs from the self-inflicted dryness and excessive wear from her compulsive scrubbing. She claimed to experience chronic fatigue because she had an exhaustive and time-consuming house-cleaning ritual that occupied so much of her time and energy. However, her very low caloric food intake was also presumably a factor. Furthermore, Pat's cleaning compulsion left her without any free time to enjoy recreational activities or any of the other pleasures of life. She was very depressed and felt hopeless that her life would be any more than a tortuous drudgery at its best.

This patient's long history of treatment, including a lengthy psychiatric hospitalization, left her feeling frustrated and without hope. Together, we engineered a treatment plan designed to gradually reduce her compulsions and phobic behavior and increase her intake of food. Although she made slow but steady progress toward her treatment goals, she also appeared to be experiencing a kind of passive resistance. It was like the cliché, "pulling teeth." We discussed this observation and she agreed, indicating that she also felt that there was some resistance[25] within her, but she didn't understand it or why it was there. I proposed that we could explore this question further using the therapy technique of role-playing.

I asked Pat to consider the idea that part of her mind wanted to get well, and it was for that reason that she sought therapy in the first place. I also addressed the possibility that part of her mind might not want to get well and so, as a result, she might experience some resistance to her therapy. I asked her to imagine that she was no longer speaking only for herself, but that she could act out and verbalize the thoughts and feelings of the part of her mind that might not want to get well. I told her that together we could discuss the possible reasons she might have for not getting well in this role-playing exercise. She was familiar with role playing, and so we were able to proceed without any difficulty.

I addressed her as "Part," which was short for "part of your mind that might not want to get well." I said, "Part, why don't you want to make more progress in therapy?" She paused for a moment and then began to detail her own feelings of self-hatred and her belief that she was unworthy of enjoying a normal life. As she continued to elaborate on this theme, her speech subtly changed to a slower tempo and, after a while, she was silent and stared down at the floor with a blank expression on her face. Her silence prompted me to ask, "Part, could you tell me more about. . . . " She interrupted me with a hostile glare, and, in a harsh voice, snarled, "Don't call me that." I asked her, "What do you want me to call you?" In slow, angry, strident tone of voice, she responded, "The Evil One."

At that moment, I was at a loss for words, but I regained my composure and simply tried to keep her talking. I remembered Susie's alter identity, the "Evil One," and saw similarities in Pat's persona by the same name. Both presented with strikingly similar characteristics. Both glared at me menacingly and spoke in a low-pitched, raspy voice. Both referred to the self[26] in extremely critical, pejorative terms and in the third person (i.e., "she"). I encouraged her to continue talking, and she did so.

Eventually she paused, again with her eyes lowered toward the floor, and an empty expression on her face. I asked her to tell me more about what she was feeling. The patient began to speak, but her voice was different. It was soft, higher-pitched, and childlike. I was reluctant to ask her to tell me her name in the event that such a question might put the idea in her mind that a different "person" was expected to be present. Yet, she *seemed* like a different person. In order to get around this dilemma, I simply asked her to spell her name for me.

"B-A-B-Y," she responded with an impish grin.[27]

"Baby" initially began talking to me in a friendly, cheerful manner, but her mood became increasingly somber as she began to describe sexual abuse by her brother, with whom she was forced to sleep in childhood. Again I was at a loss for words. After awhile, she looked at me with a curious and somewhat disoriented expression. It appeared as if she did not know what we had been talking about.

"How do you feel?" I asked her.
"Fine," she responded.
"Tell me what you remember about our session today," I inquired.

Pat was able to describe what had transpired during our appointment until she came to the part of our session where she had talked to me using the names of Evil One and Baby. I pressed her for more detailed information, but she was simply unable to recall that segment of our therapy hour.

As I continued seeing more patients with these symptoms, I had to consider the possibility that MPD and dissociation of identity, as clinical phenomena, were not as rare as the professional literature reported. I obviously needed more information about this diagnosis, and I extensively researched all available resources. I also joined a local MPD study group organized and facilitated by Gary Lefkof, M.D.,[28] a local psychiatrist skilled and knowledgeable in this field. In my discussions with other therapists, I learned that some of them were developing experience with MPD and were becoming acquainted with a related topic that some of my patients had just begun to speak of — ritual abuse.

I continued to pursue additional education in the area of dissociation and MPD. I joined the International Society for the Study of Multiple Personality Disorder and Dissociation (ISSMP&D).[29] The ISSMP&D's monthly newsletters and its quarterly journal, *Dissociation*,[30] became a major source of information. In one of its articles, Bennett Braun, M.D., described what he called a "BASK" model of dissociation (1988a, 1988b). According to Braun, these patients were capable of dissociating along several psychological dimensions, specifically, behavior, affect, sensation, and knowledge.

But what exactly is dissociation? Why would the human mind sometimes separate knowledge from behavior, for example, in cases where individuals were unable to remember things that they had actually done? Why would the mind separate any of its functions that normally worked in concert? Different authors offered different hypotheses and explanations.

The modern concept of dissociation is often traced historically to the French neurologist and psychologist, Pierre Janet. He was the first to incorporate ideas about dissociation and trauma into a theory of psychopathology. However Janet's theory was soon eclipsed by Freud's psychoanalysis. Sigmund Freud viewed dissociation as an unconscious method of coping, a defense mechanism. In a paper written in 1894 entitled "The Neuro-Psychoses of Defence"(1962) Freud presented his idea of defense mechanisms. These ideas were later elaborated by his daughter, Anna Freud (1946), and other psychoanalysts (e.g., Laughlin, 1970). Essentially, the theory of defense mechanisms postulates that people are able to protect themselves from emotional discomfort, pain, or even trauma through a variety of unconscious mental maneuvers. The individual is said to be usually unaware of the ongoing defensive mental processes. In modern psychology and psychiatry dissociation is sometimes viewed as such a defense mechanism.[31] Although this theory seems widely and popularly accepted among mental health professionals, it is difficult to test scientifically because it postulates hypothetical entities and functions not directly measurable by an outside observer. But then, this is one of the central problems in psychology. Internal mental and emotional processes are not normally observable in a purely objective manner. Psychology is, at its best, the objective study of subjectively reported phenomena.[32]

As my caseload of patients with dissociative disorders continued to increase, I began to notice the high incidence of poverty among these individuals. Prior to working with this patient population, my practice largely consisted of affluent residents of prosperous areas of North Dallas. However, it soon became evident that a large proportion of the MPD patient population were only marginally functioning in the workplace, and many were often unemployed or underemployed. Quite a few of these patients had been in therapy for lengthy periods of time before their MPD had been accurately diagnosed, and by then they often had exhausted their mental health insurance benefits.[33] Other therapists in the MPD study group also commented on the financial hardships suffered by many of these patients and the fact that most of the therapists were doing increasingly more work on a pro bono basis. Unfortunately, this arrangement was also creating a financial hardship for many of the therapists, and some questioned whether they could afford to continue to work with this group of patients.

I decided to continue to work in this specialty area despite these difficulties. With time many of the patients began to reveal their accounts of abusive like the layers of an onion. Years of pent-up rage often were released, resulting in increasing self-destructive and suicidal threats and behaviors. At the same time, the patients' financial limitations restricted their capacity to pay for necessary treatment. County and state facilities do not adequately respond to the patient's needs, and I found myself providing more and more services on a sliding scale or pro bono basis and working longer hours to deal with constant crises.

One of the most important things I learned was that many of the patients can be excellent teachers. It occurred to me that that the professional community could learn much from them. Unfortunately, rigid thinking is often difficult to overcome, and many clinicians have shown an unwillingness to rethink their treatment philosophy or modify their professional views in the light of this newly growing body of knowledge.

I consulted with "Sharon," a tall, attractive woman in her late 30s, for almost two years. Sharon had originally come to my office because of violent discord in her home. Her husband accompanied her, along with two of their three daughters. Apparently the older of the two daughters, "Patricia," had, the week earlier, stabbed her younger sister in the hand with a fork at the dinner table. As a part of my evaluation of this family, I psychologically tested and interviewed each family member who was involved in the family conflict. As it turned out, Sharon's psychological testing showed the greatest degree of psychological disturbance. Her testing results indicated that she met the criteria for a diagnosis of borderline personality disorder. It is not an unusual situation in family evaluations when a child is brought in for treatment that another family member is found to be in greater distress and more psychologically disturbed than the child. I recommended that both the family conflicts and the individual problems of the family members be addressed in therapy. Sharon agreed to see me for individual psychotherapy.

She told me that she had felt a need for psychotherapy since she was a child but had also always feared the prospect of therapy. Her parents reportedly discouraged that sort of thing insisting that family business should not be discussed outside the home. When I asked her about her early family life, Sharon, like Susie and Pat, initially said that she had enjoyed a happy and pleasant family life. However, as she continued talking in therapy, she began to relate abusive incidents, inconsistent with her earlier recollections of a happy childhood.

Sharon recounted occurrences of physical and emotional abuse in her childhood, primarily perpetrated by her father. She described him as a cruel and sadistic man whose aggressive impulses were inflicted both on her mother and herself. Sharon characterized her mother as a passive woman who frequently looked the other way, ignoring Sharon's plight. Sharon denied any history of sexual abuse.

As we continued our work, Sharon began to narrate a history of repeated self-destructive acts, including two suicide attempts. She later amended her earlier report that she had not been sexually abused and described an incident with an older man who was apparently a family friend. Sharon explained that this older man had invited both her and another young girl to spend time in his barn, where he offered them both candy. It was there that the two girls were showered with the attention and affection that neither of them was receiving at home. Eventually, he fondled them sexually and required that they do the same with him.

Sharon told me that her girlfriend told her parents what was happening in the old man's barn, but that they did not believe their daughter and accused her of lying. Sharon said that she felt guilty for not corroborating her friend's complaint, but Sharon feared getting into trouble herself. I asked her if she continued to keep contact with this childhood friend, and she said no. Her friend apparently committed suicide before completing high school.

On one occasion, Sharon telephoned from her home to say that she was feeling particularly depressed and self-destructive. It was a Sunday and my office was closed, but I agreed to meet her there. When I drove into the parking lot, I saw Sharon was already there waiting. She was seated in front of the office building, which was locked for the weekend. Next to her were several empty beer bottles. I knew from her history that she frequently drank alcohol before her acts of self-injury. I led her into the building and we walked down the hall to my office.

Once there, Sharon became very quiet. She stared at the floor; her eyes were glazed with a distant expression on her face. She began to murmur under her breath: "I want to see blood. I have to see blood." It was obvious that she was experiencing a desire to cut herself.

Although I had heard this from her before, her words still provoked strong apprehension. I tried to convince her to find some more appropriate alternative to her plans for self-harm.

"I don't think you understand how bad I feel. Well, I'll show you how bad I feel." With that she opened up her purse and took out a razor blade and before I could react, she sliced open the inside surface of her left arm from her elbow to her wrist.

I expected her to wince with pain, but instead, her response to the injury was an expression of ecstasy. Sharon's eyes rolled upward for a moment; her eyelids fluttered. "Oh, that feels good," she moaned.

I tried to wrestle the razor blade out of Sharon's hand, fearing that she might injure herself further, but I could not get it safely out of her grasp. Her expression of elation was gone now, and she looked at me threateningly and in a masculine, low-pitched voice barked, "Back off!" I told her I would let go if she would let the razor drop to the floor. She glared at me for a few moments. Finally, I felt her hand relaxing, and the blade fell to the carpet.

Sharon's mood then changed. She was apologetic. She spoke to me in a gentle, childlike manner, apologizing for bleeding on my office furniture and carpet. Blood was now running down her arm, and I could see that the cut was deep. I asked her to come with me to a nearby hospital where there was an emergency room, and she followed me obediently with her head slightly bowed.

My office was adjacent to a community medical-surgical hospital, and we walked to the emergency room with Sharon dripping blood along the way. Once we arrived in the emergency room, I explained what had happened to the physician on duty. Quickly and efficiently, the emergency room staff strapped Sharon to a gurney and effectively immobilized her. I stayed with her in a quiet corridor while she awaited further medical attention. She appeared subdued and drowsy for a time. Suddenly, Sharon glared at me, her face drawn in anger as she rhythmically repeated in a deep-pitched, hoarse voice, "Kill the bitch. Kill the bitch." I asked her who she was talking about, but she only continued to repeat herself, snarling, "Kill the bitch."

After her wound was stitched, Sharon was admitted to the psychiatric unit of the hospital. Some of those on her treatment team concluded that she had experienced a psychotic episode. Nevertheless, she was an enigma to the staff, with many of the nurses reporting they did not know what to do with her.

While hospitalized, Sharon began to experience lapses in consciousness and memory. At times she would use different names for herself and would behave in different roles consistent with the various names. She would sometimes talk about "Sharon" as a different person, or as if she were not "Sharon." When I addressed this in her staff meeting, none of the other professionals recognized seeing the dissociative symptoms that I was describing. So, with Sharon's permission, I began videotaping some of our sessions. Some of the nursing staff reviewed these videotapes, but Sharon's busy psychiatrist showed no inclination to do so himself. The nursing staff seemed surprised to see Sharon's alter identities revealing themselves in our videotaped sessions. Indeed, this was unlike anything they observed in the time they spent with Sharon on the unit. I asked Sharon why her behavior was so different in our sessions in comparison with her interactions with other staff members. In response to my question, her demeanor suddenly became childlike and she said in a lilting voice, "people inside aren't s'posed to be out." I asked her why, and she took on a serious expression, "Sharon's father said so."

"When did he say so?"
"When the body was little."
"Then why do you talk to me?"
"You won't hurt us."

In her sessions with me, Sharon not only dissociated; she began describing bizarre, sadistic, sexual abuse by her father. When her psychiatrist prescribed antipsychotic medication, Sharon became more passive and less overtly self-destructive such that she was discharged from the hospital.

I continued to follow Sharon on an outpatient basis, but her course in therapy was inconsistent with numerous episodes of very marginal coping. She began to present more alter identities who would identify themselves by name and talk to me in our therapy sessions. Her psychiatrist increased Sharon's antipsychotic medication until she appeared to be showing toxic symptoms. In spite, or perhaps because of being on exceptionally high doses of medication, Sharon's progress was quite limited. In fact, she often appeared to deteriorate and was rehospitalized on several occasions.

Eventually, Sharon's psychiatrist referred her for electroconvulsive shock therapy (ECT). This is a technique in which electricity is passed through a portion of the patient's brain, causing a convulsion (often along with some temporary memory loss and disorientation) and, sometimes, the patient later shows signs of improved mood. Electroconvulsive shock therapy is a controversial method of treatment sometimes used with patients whose severe depression does not respond favorably to more conservative therapies.[34]

Sharon consented to ECT treatments because she was feeling a sense of desperation and hopelessness about her recovery. She admitted being quite fearful of undergoing the procedure. Her mood seemed temporarily improved after each ECT session, but soon thereafter, it deteriorated again. I was very concerned that the extremely high doses of antipsychotic medication and ECT actually might be harmful to her and impede her recovery. When I protested the use of ECT and communicated my concerns regarding the high doses medication to Sharon's psychiatrist, I received an icy response.

Because Sharon was so unstable, her psychiatrist again admitted her to the hospital where he practiced. I continued to express my worries about her high levels of medication and questioned the fruitfulness of subjecting her to protracted ECT treatments. The psychiatrist eventually acknowledged that the patient was showing signs of medication toxicity, and he agreed to begin to gradually reduce her dosage levels. Sharon continued to dissociate with trance states and alternate identities, and her obsession with blood and other morbid topics persisted.

In order to better understand and monitor the progress of my dissociative patients, I often ask them to keep a journal in which they log their various feelings and experiences during the day. One of the curious things about these patients is that their handwriting styles often change depending on which particular alternate identity is present. Such changes in handwriting have commonly been observed by other professionals who work with dissociative patients (e.g., Armstrong & Loewenstein, 1990; Yank, 1991). I also noticed that many of my MPD patients would scribble and draw geometric shapes in their journals (and elsewhere). Sometimes in art therapy, I have observed MPD patients to enter an apparent trance state after looking at another patient's artwork. Surprisingly, this is especially true when the artwork contains some of the stereotypical geometric designs that many of them are prone to draw. Periodically, I ask patients to describe their feelings or to free associate to their drawings or to the drawings of others. Often, in the process, the patients verbalize important information relevant to their recovery.[35] In some cases, the patients say that they remember seeing the geometric designs or symbols as part of bizarre cult rituals in which they had allegedly been present.[36]

Once during one of Sharon's hospitalizations, she seemed unusually mentally unfocused and zombie-like. She complained that she felt "shut down." She said that she felt very depressed but that her mind was blank.[37] Although her mental functioning was already deteriorated, it effectively came to a halt as we began our scheduled psychotherapy appointment. I asked her if she wanted to reschedule for another time, but she was adamant that we should continue. She requested help in becoming more focused, and I responded asking her to free-associate with some geometric shapes because this procedure had been productive with other similar patients.

I drew some simple shapes: a circle, a triangle, a square, and a star, on separate sheets of paper. Sharon looked at them one at a time and described the first thoughts and feelings that came into her mind. Her responses were unremarkable until she came to the drawing of the star. When I asked her what she associated with the drawing of the star, she responded, "Sex."

In free association, a person may normally respond with a variety of different statements, but the association of "sex" to the picture of the star was an unusual one to make, and I asked Sharon to tell me more about it.

"You know," she said.
"No, I don't know. Please tell me," I responded.
"You know — it's what it means."
"It's what *what* means?" I asked.

Sharon was hesitant to talk further and appeared frightened. "My Daddy said to never tell," she whispered in a tiny voice, with tears in her eyes. She appeared to want to communicate something but was extremely fearful of doing so. Eventually she stated that the figure of the star was something she often saw before her father raped her. I asked her how she was able to see a star under those circumstances, and she said that her father used to draw the star in blood on her abdomen. Sharon appeared to switch into the persona of a child alter. Her voice was high-pitched and fearful.

"Who are you?" she asked me. "How did you get me here? I'm not supposed to be here. They will hurt me." Suddenly, her behavior and speech were different. She appeared to be even more apprehensive than before and was initially reluctant to talk to me at all.

Finally, she told me that her name was "Sacrifice" and that she had been given that name because her job was to be the sexual sacrifice at the rituals that occurred in her family's home, usually on Friday evenings, and typically with both of her parents present. I asked her what had made her decide to talk to me, and she said that she trusted me; she knew I would not hurt her. She said I had a bright white "aura" or circular-shaped light around my head and that meant that I would not harm her.

I asked her more about her "aura" experience. For some reason MPD patients sometimes report "psychic" abilities, including a belief that they can see auras. People with such notions sometimes contend that some "gifted" individuals can see lights around others' bodies, and from the color and other properties of the light, make judgments about the other person. This was particularly curious to me, being a skeptic. Although by no means an expert in researching the paranormal, what little I had read in the scientific literature seemed consistently to confirm that there was no evidence for the reality of such phenomena. As I inquired further of this alter, she explained that she was supposed to have the ability to see auras as a result of some of the rituals in which she had been forced to participate. Her father had warned her that these experiences were to remain strictly secret.

I interpreted this "gift" as a probable hallucination[38] or illusion that the alternate identity, "Sacrifice," experienced because she believed that she had been in a ritual that was supposed to produce this ability. Later I encountered other patients whose alters also reported this ability. What I discovered was that the reported shape of the auras was exceedingly similar. Auras were described as being circular or oval shapes around the head of a person, similar to a halo.

This came as a surprise to me because I thought that auras were supposed to be perceived lights around a person's entire body. However, when I asked patients their perception of the color of the aura they saw around me, the colors they reported seeing varied markedly, although most of them saw me as having some kind of light or luminous aura that they interpreted as meaning that I was kind and caring. The patients described color schemes with varying hues associated with differing personality characteristics. For example, one patient gave me an interpretation of the colors as follows: white represented goodness and purity; *gold* indicated saintliness or godliness; *red* designated passion, anger and past suffering; *purple* meant power, authority; and *black*, not surprisingly, symbolized evil. Other patients reporting this experience sometimes interpreted the colors as having a slightly different meaning, but many were essentially in agreement.

Because my patients perceived my "aura" in colors that were not consistent, I concluded that these perceptions could not be interpreted as truly "psychic" experiences. However, the similarity of shape and associated interpretive beliefs described made me wonder if these individuals had been trained to see these "lights" in a particular manner. Curiously, Harner (1990), an expert on shamanism,[39] describes how shamans or witch doctors are trained to "see" visions and learn to have other "psychic" experiences.

One of my patients reporting a history of ritual abuse said that she was also raised Roman Catholic. Once in my office, while in a dissociated state, she took a picture of Jesus out of her purse and, while talking about it, called his halo an "aura." I wondered then if the halos that are seen in some religious art works, especially in earlier times in history, might be related to this perception of "auras" that some people may have been ritually taught to experience.

As therapy with Sharon proceeded, she continued to display dissociated states, different voices, and different names for her different "selves." Finally, one day when she spoke to me, she announced that her name was "Susan." Because Susan was a newly identified identity, I inquired about her own personal history. She was the first alter identity with whom I had ever communicated who said she came into existence during the time I was working with the patient. She said that she had come out the weekend before, when the nursing staff had placed Sharon in protective restraints because Sharon was banging her head against the walls of her room. Susan said that Sharon did not have multiple personality disorder and that the stories about the rituals and the sexual abuse "were all made up." As in the example of Susie, described in Chapter 3, I noted the discrepancy of the patient's denial of having MPD while using a different name for herself, but I chose to not to point this out. Instead, I tried to keep her talking, and she did. She went to great lengths to say that Sharon was going to be okay and that Sharon was ready to be discharged from the hospital. I encouraged her to continue talking. The more she talked, the more difficulty she had maintaining

her façade. Eventually she looked at me sadly as Sharon often did. I
asked her what her job was.

> "To say that the stories are all made up."
> "Why do you want to do that?" I asked.
> "Because Sharon can't take it if she was hurt that way."
> "Well, was she hurt that way or not?" I asked.
> "Yes, it's true," she sobbed.

I continued to protest that Sharon was being over medicated and that
her ECT treatments were not helping and might even be harmful to her.
The response of her psychiatrist, who was also her attending physician,
was to remove me from her case.

A very different outcome was achieved in working with another
patient, "Mary." I began to see Mary in therapy at about the same time I
was working with Sharon. She came to see me at the insistence of her
husband. Mary had reportedly been depressed for as long as she could
remember, but recently, at the age of 41, her depression had increased
dramatically. She felt anxious, nervous, and increasingly emotionally
isolated from her husband and children. Neither her personal nor her
professional life provided her with any sense of pleasure or satisfaction.
Sex, never a particularly strong drive for her, had become an anathema.
Her life simply was not working. Mary had never before sought therapy.
She had briefly attended a free codependency group but recognized that
the solutions to her problems would require a more intensive approach.

My first impression of Mary was of a woman caught up in what
some call a mid-life crisis. She appeared to be very intelligent, highly
articulate, and insightful in many respects. She seemed to recognize the
nature of her problems but felt helpless to do anything about them. As
she proceeded in· the therapeutic process, Mary began to lower her
defenses. However, after a few sessions, Mary began to dissociate, with
altered personality states reporting the now sadly familiar childhood
history of chronic, sadistic, sexual abuse. Mary described her father's
incestuous behaviors and recalled his threats that no one would believe
her. Child alters wept when they recounted how Mary had hoped in vain
for her mother's intervention.

Because of strong self-destructive threats from some of her alternate
identities, Mary entered a psychiatric hospital for a brief stay. However,
during that time it was not only possible to stabilize her, but we were
able to work intensively toward integration.[40] During a ten-day period,
during which no medications were administered, Mary integrated her
alters. I had never participated in such a rapid process of integration and

questioned whether it was genuine. Shortly after her integration she briefly dissociated again with alternate identities. These were newly identified alternate identities that described experiences of ritual abuse. These alter identities recounted their experiences along with the powerful emotions that accompanied them and then reintegrated with the patient. In order to more objectively assess her progress, I readministered Minnesota Multiphasic Personality Inventory (MMPI), and the results showed a dramatic change for the better.

At this point in her therapy there was a remarkable physical difference in Mary, from her posture to her facial expression. As we continued to work in the post-integration phase of her therapy, Mary blossomed. Her self-destructive thoughts and depression vanished. She began taking better care of herself and taking pride in her appearance. She bought a new wardrobe and appeared more relaxed and self-accepting. She took a greater interest in her family, and her marriage reawakened, stronger and happier than ever before. Mary enrolled in graduate school and four years later, she earned a master's degree in counseling and is completing her work on a doctorate in counseling psychology. From diagnosis to integration, Mary had been in therapy for four months. I terminated with Mary following a year of tapering aftercare. She continued telephone contact for several years and reported continued progress. The last time I spoke with her, she spontaneously described herself as a "survivor" of ritual abuse and reiterated that she is coping well. She is basically happy with her life and feeling productive in her work and relationships. I have wondered whether, over time, she would come to think of her memories of abuse as being merely fantasies, but apparently that has not been the case.

To what can one attribute Mary's swift recovery? In spite of the terror she experienced, Mary also had a number of assets that may have significantly helped her. She was fortunate to have been very bright, with a long history of relatively healthy functioning. Her life seemed focused toward realistic goals, and her MPD did not appear to have significantly distracted her from her personal or professional roles. Another advantage was that Mary did not become trapped in the mental health system where she might have suffered the same fate as so many other similar patients who have spent years being inappropriately diagnosed, medicated, hospitalized; in short, continually subjected to useless, if not overtly harmful, procedures. Her favorable outcome may have partly been the result of her father's death while she was still a young child, freeing her from a life of possible continued abuse. Additionally, she was fortunate to have a husband who was emotionally stable, healthy, and supportive.

Mary's case is atypical. Most survivors of ritual abuse require many years of psychotherapy. Unfortunately, many of them are never correctly diagnosed, and they go from one therapist to another trying every possible remedy under the sun without any appreciable relief. For these patients, a repeated series of misdirected and unfruitful therapy efforts can be another revictimizing experience.

NOTES

[22] Horevitz writes that "Little evidence exists of a causal relationship between hypnotizability and dissociative disorders" (1994, p.438).

[23] Additionally, note Weitzenhoffer's (1989, p. 161) critical comments regarding the scientific credibility of Spiel's Hypnotic Induction Profile.

[24] See also Braun (1984).

[25] The concept of resistance in therapy is not a new one. One of the earlier forms of psychotherapy, i.e., psychoanalysis, traditionally focuses on what is called the interpretation of resistances.

[26] I.e., the host, or usually presenting personality was criticized. The "Evil One" was quite happy with "himself" in both cases.

[27] Obviously a real baby could not spell. Alter personalities are not exactly what they sometimes believe or present themselves to be.

[28] Dr. Lefkof developed an inpatient psychiatric program largely limited to patients with dissociative disorders. Patients came from all over the United States to attend his inpatient program housed in a local psychiatric facility. The demand was great, and although the program occupied two separate units in the hospital, there was almost always a waiting list for admission. His work received national recognition when it was featured on CBS television's "48 Hours."

[29] The ISSMP&D changed its name to the International Society for the Study of Dissociation (ISSD).

[30] The journal *Dissociation* is no longer being published. It was discontinued in 1999. Another journal *Trauma and Dissociation* has been planned to replace it.

[31] Although dissociation is commonly conceptualized as a defense mechanism, not all in the field of mental health would agree with this view, which may be overly simplistic. Dissociation may represent a variety of different psychological processes. While dissociation typically disrupts conscious awareness of the events or knowledge dissociated, the process of dissociation is not necessarily itself an unconscious act of psychological defense. Many patients report that they consciously dissociate when they feel overwhelmed. To some extent dissociation may represent the normal breaks of consciousness that occur periodically (e.g., sleep) as well as normal reactions to trauma (e.g., shock).

[32] Some radical behaviorists would go even farther than this, arguing that mental states can never be studied in a truly scientific manner and that psychology should limit itself to observations of the behavior of organisms.

[33] In a study by Putnam, et al. (1986) the authors found that it had taken an average of 6.8 years from the time when the patients first entered treatment before the diagnosis of MPD had been made.

[34] See Laurence & Weinhouse (1994, pp. 282–283) for further discussion of ECT.

[35] Cohen and Cox (1995) have written a helpful guide to the use of art therapy entitled *Telling Without Talking: Art as a Window into the World of Multiple Personality.*

---

[36] The process of asking dissociated patients to free-associate to drawings of geometric figures has often resulted in dramatic trance responses and the presentation of various alter identities. Because of the significant responses of many of these patients to such stimuli, I constructed an assessment device based on this principle called the Picture Association Method (PAM).

[37] Many dissociated patients have alter personalities who are sometimes called "blockers." Many of these blocker alters apparently have the ability to induce a confused state in the patient, especially when the therapy session is to begin. The patient may feel that she is in great distress and needs help, but her mind is blank.

[38] In one of the major textbooks on the subject of hallucinations is a Chapter by anthropologist Weston La Barre (1975) in which the author describes some of the ritual uses of trance and hallucinatory experiences among a variety of pre-industrial cults.

[39] More about shamanism can be found in Chapter 9.

[40] Integration is the process of combining the dissociated alternate identities into a whole and fully functioning person. An excellent paper describing this process and its characteristics has been published by Greaves (1989). This therapeutic procedure may be distinguished from the religious rite of exorcism, wherein inner entities that are considered demonic are ostensibly eliminated through exorcism (see Chapter 5). Integration, on the other hand, serves to unite, rather than discard, the dissociated elements of the personality.

Chapter 5

Possession, Ritual Abuse, and Dissociation

The concept of the devil is an enigma to many people. The results of a large-scale survey conducted in the United States show that 55 percent of the population believe "in the existence of Satan" (Patterson & Kim, 1992, p.204).[41] We are among the remainder of Americans who do not. However, as researchers, we try to keep our personal beliefs separate from those of patients and independent from our professional work. The same principle applies to psychotherapy. A psychologist's goal is not to convince clients to accept the therapist's personal world view, but simply to help them achieve improved functioning and a greater sense of satisfaction with their lives.

There are some mental health professionals who incorporate their religious and spiritual views in their approach to the problem of ritual abuse. Some have expressed concern over the recent idealized portrayals of Satanism and the occult that have surfaced in modern Western culture through movies, books, and rock music, and the possible adverse effects of these influences on vulnerable and impressionable young people.[42]

One of the earlier efforts to educate the public about this phenomenon was *The Satan Seller* (1972), by Mike Warnke.[43] This book was followed by a second, *Schemes of Satan* (1991). Warnke, an evangelist, reports that he was formerly a high priest in a Satanic cult. In *The Satan Seller*, Warnke describes his recruitment and participation in the cult while he was in college, and he describes some of the rituals, beliefs, and practices of this cult, along with his ultimate spiritual deliverance. In *Schemes of Satan*, Warnke describes his experience with

Satanism and other varieties of occultism from a Christian perspective. He notes that multiple personality disorder may occur in individuals who have been exposed to Satanic rituals. Another survivor, Lauren Stratford (1988)[44] reports horrific experiences in a Satanic cult and attributes her recovery largely to her Christian faith.

Other authors have addressed the problem of ritual abuse from a secular perspective. In an article that appeared in *Ms.* magazine, a woman using the pseudonym Elizabeth S. Rose described her ordeals in a multigenerational Satanic cult in which the "leader did not believe in the existence of Satan and told me that I needn't either" (1993, p. 44–45). According to the author, "Belief in Satan is cultivated in order to instill fear and the use of rituals as an emotional straitjacket designed to keep cult members under control" (1993, p. 45).

Another survivor, Margaret Smith (1993), is the author of the book entitled *Ritual Abuse: What It Is, Why It Happens, How To Help.* In addition to being a survivor, Margaret Smith is a researcher and was the founder of an organization and newsletter, *Reaching Out,* that provided information, emotional support, and advocacy for other survivors. Smith describes in some detail her own experiences of ritual abuse as well as reports she has received from other survivors. In addition to having read her book, I have spoken to her by telephone and met with her in person. Her descriptions of ritual abuse are remarkably similar to the accounts I have heard from my own patients. Barbara Jackson (1993), a ritual abuse survivor and Harvard educated biochemist, spoke eloquently regarding her experience of ritual abuse at the National Conference on Crimes Against Children in September of 1993 in Washington, D.C. She addressed the potential for survivors living meaningful and productive lives and the urgent need for our society to seriously recognize this problem.

The first published description of the psychiatric treatment of a ritual abuse survivor is found in the book *Michelle Remembers* co-authored by patient Michelle Smith and her psychiatrist, Lawrence Pazder (1980). The book, which represents a Roman Catholic outlook, includes a comment by the bishop of the diocese of Victoria, British Columbia, who cautiously refrains from validating Michelle's story, per se, but recommends that people be open to what she has to say, stating that this is a subject worthy of further study and investigation.

The books *Breaking the Circle of Satanic Ritual Abuse* (1992) and *Cover-Up of the Century* (1994), by Daniel Ryder, were written by an individual who is reportedly both a survivor and therapist (certified chemical dependency counselor and licensed social worker). Among other things, he advocates a 12-step approach to the treatment of ritual abuse[45], including those elements of spirituality formulated by the original Alcoholics Anonymous groups and expressed in the *Big Book.*[46] Having also come to know Ryder personally, we find him to be an articulate, well-informed and sincere person.

Other Christian therapists have addressed the issue of ritual abuse from both clinical and spiritual perspectives. Holly Hector is the author of *Satanic Ritual Abuse and Multiple Personality Disorder* (1991). In her book, Hector outlines the relationship between multiple personality disorder and what she believes to be a major cause of MPD, Satanic ritual abuse. Hector's message is positive and emphasizes the reality of psychological and spiritual recovery, noting that many individuals who have been abused in such cults erroneously feel unsalvageable. She encourages her readers not to be discouraged and argues that alternate identities who view themselves as loyal to their respective cults are not, in fact, demons.[47]

Another Christian therapist who has published on the subject of ritual abuse is psychologist and pastor James Friesen.[48] Some of his views appear in an article entitled "Treatment for Multiple Personality Disorder: Integrating Alter Personalities and Casting out Evil Spirits" (1989). In his book *Uncovering the Mystery of MPD* (1991) Friesen provides greater detail in describing Satanic ritual abuse as a cause of multiple personality disorder and cites examples of patients' stories of abuse along with his observations of his clients in therapy. In a later book, *More Than Survivors* (1992), Friesen presents case studies of seven clients presenting with this disorder who came from a variety of geographical locations across the United States. Friesen's ideas have generated some controversy because of his strong Christian approach to the problem (that some may view as a kind of bias) and, more specifically, his concept of demonic possession,[49] which he says may occur in some cases of MPD. Friesen believes that individuals with multiple personality disorder may experience both alternate identities as well as possession by demonic spirits and that both kinds of entities are distinguishable.[50] Some other Christian therapists agree. The best-selling author and physician M. Scott Peck writes about patients in his own clinical practice showing signs of what he believes to be possession by demonic entities (1983).

The idea that people can be possessed by demons has been articulated by a number of authors in recent times. Representing the point of view of the Roman Catholic Church is Malachi Martin, a former Jesuit professor who taught at the Pontifical Biblical Institute in Rome. Martin's book, *Hostage to the Devil* (1976), describes the author's research into the reported modern phenomena of demonic possession and exorcism[51] in the Roman Catholic Church, citing specific case examples. More recently, Father Jeffrey Steffon (1992) wrote about this subject in a book that bears the doctrinal approval of the Catholic Church, that is, the *Nihil obstat* and *Imprimatur*. In his book, Father Steffon presents the official position of the Catholic Church regarding the reality of Satan, evil spirits, and demonic possession. How does a person come to suffer possession? Father Steffon answers this question with the following, citing Father Richard McAlear and Betty Brennan who, he says, are experts in demonic possession:

> First, a demonic spirit can attach itself to someone through a wound or trauma. Fr. McAlear calls this a ministering spirit. Secondly, a spirit can attach itself to a person through a repeated sinful action or sinful tendencies. This is a cardinal spirit. One way to remember some cardinal spirits is to remember the capital sins — that is, lust, pride, gluttony, sloth, envy, covetousness, and anger. These sins are against the cardinal virtues of prudence, justice, temperance, and fortitude. These virtues are the hinges of other virtues. Just as other virtues are in some way tied to the four cardinal virtues, so some spirits are tied to, or hinge upon, the cardinal spirits. A third way is through a person's generational heritage. People inherit their make-up from their parents — their physical attributes, mental abilities, psychological makeup, and spiritual characteristics. If parents have been involved in the occult, generational openness for the oppression will be passed along to their children. Exodus 20:5-6 states that a father's wickedness is passed on to his children for four generations, but blessings for a thousand generations upon the faithful. Finally, a demonic spirit can attach itself to a person through involvement in the occult. (Steffon, 1992, p. 169)

Father Steffon further discusses cases of ritual abuse and crime associated with reported cult practices.

Other authors with different Christian backgrounds have also expressed their belief that demonic possession can and does occur (e.g., Koch & Lechler, 1970; Lasalandra & Merenda, 1990; Montgomery, 1976; Olson, 1992; Unger, 1971; Warnke, 1972, 1991).[52] Tom Hawkins, an associate pastor of the Community Bible Church in Altoona, Pennsylvania, not only believes in the existence of demonic possession[53] but provides pastoral counseling to individuals with multiple personality disorder and has written a monograph describing his approach to this problem (1993).

John Nevius' (1964) *Demon Possession* is a book of historic interest on this subject. From 1854 to 1893 Nevius was a Christian missionary in China where he observed what he believed to be demon possession among some Chinese individuals. He also described cases of demon possession from India, Japan Ceylon and Western cultures. He portrayed the victims of demon possession in terms that are very similar to modern descriptions of dissociative disorders. In fact, Nevius admitted that there were a variety of different interpretations that might be made of his observations. However, he seemed to be unaware that trauma might be a causal factor and did not mention this option.

Some Christians may directly or indirectly believe in forms of possession other than merely demonic possession. According to Robert Baker, "many Christians regard glossolalia[54] [i.e., speaking in tongues] as a sign of possession by the Holy Spirit" (1992, p. 206). However, there are a variety of different possession-like religious experiences that are said to occur in a Christian context that have been documented by Garrett (1987) in his book *Spirit Possession and Popular Religion.*[55] The concept of possession, demonic or otherwise, is not unique to Christianity. Many religions and cultures throughout history have incorporated or propounded this belief.[56]

In addition to the notion of possession by an evil entity or the spirit of a deity, is the concept of possession by the soul of another person (living or dead) or an animal's spirit. Perhaps the most exhaustive and scholarly work to date on the general subject of possession is T. K. Oesterreich's *Possession* (1966), first published in 1921, when Oesterreich was the head of the philosophy department at the University of Tübingen. Oesterreich's book has been praised for "containing one of the finest collections of case histories of multiple personality and the phenomena of so-called possession this work has, so far as I know, never been superseded" (Gregory, 1966, p. vii). In his book, Oesterreich thoroughly traces the various accounts of possession around the world from antiquity through his contemporary time.

Among the numerous significant contributions made by Oesterreich's book is his differentiation of voluntary and involuntary possession and the distinction between *lucid* and *somnambulistic* possession. In lucid possession the individual is conscious for the experience and can remember it later. In somnambulistic possession the person is unable to recall his or her behavior or other events while in the possession state. Individuals with DID describe dissociative episodes that can be distinguished along the same lines that Oesterreich outlined for possession states. Some use the term *co-consciousness* to designate the experience of "being present" during the episode and the ability to remember it later. Without co-consciousness, DID patients are simply amnestic when other alternate identities take control of their minds and bodies and many of them describe the experience of "losing time."

In fact, one of the remarkable things about the reports of DID and possession phenomena is their similarity to one another. A list of their shared features is as follows:

1. Both possession[57] and DID[58] are more frequently identified among females than males.
2. Both possession[59] and DID[60] reportedly may occur some time after traumatic experiences, rituals, or ordeals.
3. Both possession[61] and DID[62] have been associated with cults, primitive or pre-industrial on the first hand, or modern Western on the second hand.
4. A sense of secrecy is often a factor in possession[63] and DID.[64]
5. In both possession[65] and DID,[66] the individual may have experiences for that he or she is later amnestic.
6. In both possession[67] and DID,[68] the individual may, at times, experience co-consciousness or a shared awareness with the alternate identity or possessing entity.
7. One characteristic of both possession[69] and DID,[70] is that the afflicted or affected individual frequently acts out behaviors that are uncharacteristic of him or herself.
8. In both possession[71] and DID,[72] there may be strong factors of social control present which some hypothesize to be related to the creation and expression of the inner identities.
9. In both possession[73] and DID[74] the usually present identity is often called the host.
10. In the *Diagnostic and Statistical Manual of Psychiatric Disorders*, fourth edition, (American Psychiatric Association, 1994) both possession and DID are listed as dissociative disorders.
11. In both possession[75] and DID,[76] the inner entities that take control of the body may be characterized as animals, spirits, demons and deities.
12. In both possession[77] and DID[78] there are accounts of individuals engaging in behaviors which defy "the recognized physical limits that define normal embodied existence, particularly with respect to the perception of pain" (Mulhern, 1991a, p. 773).
13. Reports have appeared that a disproportionate number of individuals affected by possession[79] and DID[80] believe they have psychic or paranormal abilities.

14. Mulhern (1991a) also argues that both individuals experiencing possession and DID share a lengthy list of concurrent problems that include psychosomatic and other health complaints, family and marital problems, and explicitly psychological symptoms.

Sherrill Mulhern notes that the socioeconomic problems observed in individuals with possession are not seen in DID patients but, as we explained earlier in this book, poverty is actually prevalent among these patients.[81] Perhaps this dilemma is not widely known to the public or to those therapists whose clinical practices consist of fully funded clients. In fact those therapists who are unwilling to do pro bono work are unlikely to see many DID patients because so many of them are chronically in a marginal state of financial survival.

One could argue that multiple personality disorder is merely a modern, Western, term for what has been known for centuries simply as *possession*.[82]   Possession is a complex socioculturally shaped phenomenon that varies somewhat in its manifestations in different cultures. Is it possible that DID is the prevalent expression of possession seen in modern Europe and the Americas?   One of the differences between possession and DID noted by Mulhern is that in possession cults, many of the rituals are designed to help the follower heal physical and psychological wounds (1991a). This is in contrast to the commonly held professional opinion in America regarding the psychopathology of DID, where it is often viewed as being caused by the trauma or traumatic ritual. However, this distinction is not so clear when one considers the concept of cult *programming*, which will be further discussed later in this book.

Of the patients with whom I have consulted showing signs of both DID and ritual abuse, many describe aspects of cult rituals that are designed to restore some semblance of order to the person's mind after it has been dissociated through the infliction of other traumas.   It is reportedly during the healing phases of ritual abuse that the cult-created alternate identities are often given further definition and programming. As a result, one of the kinds of control that such destructive cults have over an individual is the threat of madness if an attempt is made to leave the cult. The cult leader may attempt to prove that he alone has the power to effect a cure over the raging emotionality present in the cult follower.[83]   Traumatizing rituals may be used to disorganize the individual psychologically and cause amnesia, whereas other procedures may be used which have the effect of organizing (or giving the appearance of greater organization) to the victim's mental functioning and behavior.[84] Thus, we have come to define *ritual abuse* as abuse that occurs in a ceremonial or circumscribed manner for the purpose of creating or manipulating already created alter mental states.

On one occasion, when one of my patients felt a strong desire to harm herself, she was hospitalized. Shortly after her hospitalization she gave me her journal to read. The first page was neatly printed with the following:

> I am being tormented.
> I am crying out all of the time.
> I miss my Daddy.
> I miss my Queen mother.
> I hate myself.
> I am confused.
> I hear demons.
> I see the demons.
> I am breaking.
> We are all breaking.
> The demons are watching us all the time.
> There is not time for anything, not time for love or friends or relationships.
> There is not even time to breathe.
> The demons are demanding us to return to their orchards.
> There is protection in their orchards.
> They are carefully orchestrating our sentencing if we do not return.

Later in her journal there was a page written in a childlike scrawl:

> We are the children and we are afraid. Can anybody help us. [sic]
> Are we going to die?
> We think that they are going to jump through the glass and kill us all.
> They say the numbers [deleted] all the time.
> We don't know what they mean.

Following this, I found a page that was neatly written in script:

> This is ideal [sic] there is so much glass here to break.
> Just remember these people really don't care at all about you.
> If anyone tries to interfere with our plan I will make sure
> that they are taken care of and remember the first opportunity you get to leave this place do it.

Please try to understand that I must impose a strict penalty upon you
for bringing us here.

I should have stopped it but I've been busy with other things.

Is your head starting to hurt? The disorientation will become
more predominant.

You will sleep but feel unrested.

You will wash but feel unclean.

And remember they will probably poison your food and drink.

They all want to bring us down but we won't let them.

And if they try to [deleted] with us there is only one answer.

We must die.

You know that we would like to go on living in the manner
that we use to, but we can't.

Then death is the only way out.

Don't worry it will all be peaceful.

Still later in her journal I found this entry:

Just woke up I guess for the second time.

I'm not sure where I am but I am in a hospital room, because there
are hospital beds, but I am dressed.

Looked out the door and I saw all different kinds of people.

There is no phone in here.

I can't call anyone. Oh God I'm scared.

I think I've been drugged.

I told one of the nurses I was "Sheila" and she said OK yea right —
Get out of here. But it sounded like she was joking or something.
So I came

back here maybe somebody will come in soon
and tell me what's going on . . . Sheila[85]

The ritually abused person often feels a need to continue at least
some of the components of ritual practice in order to stave off mental
disintegration. If actual rituals are not attended, then the cult-abused
individual may resort to bloodletting or other self-inflicted injury in an
effort to prevent internal disintegration.[86] This explanation by my
patients appears to be consistent with the anthropological literature
describing primitive possession cults conducting rituals, sometimes
traumatic, sometimes not, for the purpose of effecting a cure or
improvement in the individual's functioning.[87]

For survivors trying to escape the influence of such destructive
cults, this idea may be very discouraging. However, as many survivors

have demonstrated through their progress in therapy, it is possible to leave these cults and find other more appropriate ways to engage in self-healing and establishing a sense of self-directed inner control. This is a point emphasized by survivors Margaret Smith (1993), Chrystine Oksana (1994), Alexandra Rogers (1994), and others. Survivors can learn to resist tendencies toward self-destructiveness and self-sabotage. But to do so effectively, it is usually helpful to understand the underlying dissociative processes, how they came to be (most "host personalities" are initially amnestic for this information), and how to develop habits of effective internal dialogue with dissociated alternate identities. When the internal communication improves, then the various dissociated inner identities can work in concert rather than in unproductive conflict. Perhaps most helpful of all is the process of learning that many of the perpetrators' messages are simply not true: "You will always be alone. No one will ever love you (if they know what is inside you), etc." Survivors who begin to learn to experience reciprocal trust and affection often report a genuine inner transformation along with improved functioning, self-esteem, autonomy, and satisfaction with life.

NOTES

[41] Another survey of 500 adult Americans showed that 49 percent of the respondents reported belief in the "existence of fallen angels, or devils"; 45 percent denied any such belief. The remainder were reportedly not sure (Gibbs, 1993, p. 61).

[42] For more background regarding adolescent involvement in Satanism and occultism see Dumont & Altesman (1989), Johnston (1989), Larson (1989b), Mercer (1991), Moriarity (1992), Moriarity & Story (1990).

[43] Naturally, Warnke and his published opinions have attracted criticism and controversy (e.g., Alexander, 1990; Trott & Hertenstein, 1992).

[44] Stratford has had some criticism regarding her accounts (e.g., Hicks, 1991; Passantino, Passantino, & Trott 1989). One such criticism is that inconsistencies have been noted in her reports. I have not attempted to investigate whether Stratford's reports are in fact consistent because it is common that individuals who have been subject to such abuse demonstrate clinical signs of dissociation, often resulting in the survivor making different descriptions of a situation at different times because separate and autonomous parts of the patient's mind are able to offer a variety of different opinions and observations. Putnam (1989) has elaborated on this problem, noting that MPDs are often accused of lying when in fact their dissociation has disrupted elements of their memory which often are distorted or incomplete until properly clarified in therapy. It is also common for survivors using a pseudonym to present some fictional biographical data, particularly when it does not distort the substance of their story, in order to protect their confidentiality and reduce the risk of being identified and becoming the subject of reprisals for telling the secrets.

[45] Also see Joe S. (1991), *Out of Hell Again.*

[46] I respect Daniel Ryder (pseudonym) and his work, but I have encountered many complaints from ritual abuse survivors regarding their experiences in 12-step programs. Although some survivors are able to successfully work the 12 steps, many report feeling "triggered" by some of the traditional elements of the program (e.g., standing in a circle

and saying the Lord's prayer). We need to further explore ways of modifying the traditional 12 steps and formulate alternative approaches so that survivors can effectively use these and other support groups.

[47] Some alter personalities consider themselves to be on "the dark side" and bear the names of demons from Christian writings, e.g., Satan, Lucifer, Beelzebub, Belial, Leviathan, etc. Some "dark" alters also have the names of other demonic entities, e.g., Asmodeus, Astaroth, Baal, Kali, Lilith, etc. Others have the names of Christian vices, e.g., Envy, Hatred, Lust, etc. Some of these malevolent alters are identified simply by ordinary human names, e.g., Sarah, Elizabeth, etc. Some of these also consider themselves to demons. Some consider themselves to be the "souls of dead people." Some alters "on the dark side" consider themselves to be merely under the control of an evil inner or external force.

[48] I had the pleasure to meet Dr. Friesen at the First Annual Christian Conference on MPD and Satanic Ritual Abuse, where he and I were both presenters. Additionally, I felt particularly honored to be invited to speak at this conference because it is well known that I am a secular therapist. Perhaps Christians and secular professionals will learn to work together on this problem.

[49] I have never witnessed anything that I recognized as supernatural in my thousands of hours of work with ritually abused patients. To me it is more parsimonious scientifically to consider all the inner entities as alter identities (or as some prefer, to use the terms *alter personalities* — as distinguished from less developed entities called *alter fragments*). I have never observed any miraculous events nor demonstrations of supernatural power whatsoever. Nevertheless, I view this as a fascinating question. Are we observing in these MPD patients the same kind of phenomenon described in the New Testament Christian gospels regarding possessed people who were said to have been cured by Jesus and his apostles? In his book *Jesus: The Evidence*, author and scholar Ian Wilson (1988) presents the argument that many of the people that Jesus was said to have cured may have had MPD. North et al. (1993) cite Miller's (1989) observation that the biblical passage Mark 5:1–3 may be such an example (i.e., "My name is Legion; for we are many.").

[50] I admire his courage in presenting his point of view, which does not appear to be a popular one in the secular intellectual atmosphere of modern times. Unfortunately, some individuals have chosen to ridicule him for his beliefs under the pretense that their theories are more "scientifically" acceptable. This is a kind of intellectual snobbery and has no place in science. Scientists have no special insight into "ultimate truths" and to say otherwise is sheer deceptiveness or naiveté regarding the limitations of science.

[51] The rites of exorcism are not limited to Catholicism. Exorcism has been practiced by Protestants as well as Jews, Muslims, and a variety of pagan sects. Some Protestants prefer what they call *deliverance*, a spiritual act that is briefer and less ritualized than exorcism. Friesen's work (previously cited) very directly advocates deliverance and other modes of spiritual healing. However, some authors are skeptical about the long-lasting benefits of exorcism. Crapanzo (1977) cites Oesterreich (1966) and Huxley (1952) regarding their observations that the effects of exorcism are not often of long or enduring duration. Anthropologist Felicitas Goodman (1988) appears more optimistic about the effectiveness of exorcism. Bowman (1993) reported data on 15 MPD patients and Frazer (1993) described seven case studies of patients who had undergone exorcism. Both authors conclude that exorcism may be harmful to MPD patients.

[52] Also, Thomas B. Allen (1993) provides a fascinating and detailed case study of exorcism in his book, *Possessed*. The author states that he has tried to describe his

findings in an objective manner rather than as an attempt to persuade or convert the reader. He writes that he is an agnostic who was raised as a Roman Catholic.

[53] Hawkins uses the term *demonization* to refer to demon possession.

[54] However, glossolalia has sometimes been viewed as a psychiatric symptom (e.g., Campbell, 1989, p. 307). See Pattison (1974) for a psychiatric interpretation of individuals with glossolalia that is related to their religious beliefs. Also see Maloney & Lovekin (1985).

[55] Many charismatic and Pentecostal Christian congregations espouse a belief in varieties of religious experience that could be accurately labeled as possession states and possession trances (Goodman, 1973). However, such phenomena are not limited to speaking in tongues. The Anastenaria ritual of Northern Greece reportedly invokes possession by St. Constantine, which Danforth (1989) describes. The participants walk on burning coals, sometimes they say, without injury. Similar practices have occurred in the United States according to Danforth's account. Another Christian sect with possession like features involved in its rituals are Shaker sects such as the Indian Shaker cult described by Barnett (1972) and the Shakers of St. Vincent (Henney, 1973). Also worthy of note are the altered states of consciousness associated with the Christian snake-handling cults of the Southern United States described by LaBarre (1962) and Galanter (1989).

[56] See Bourguinon (1973, 1974).

[57] See Kligman (1981), Mischel & Mischel (1958), Ravenscroft (1965).

[58] See Bliss (1980, 1984b), Bliss & Jeppsen, (1985), Coons (1985), Coons and Stern (1986), Horevitz & Braun (1984), Kluft (1984), Putnam, et al. (1986), Solomon (1983), Stern (1984).

[59] See Boddy (1988), Hess (1990), Mulhern (1991a), Oke (1989).

[60] See Friesen (1991), Putnam (1989) — although it should also be noted that Putnam has expressed disbelief in claims of ritual abuse (e.g., see Putnam, 1991).

[61] See Mulhern (1991a), Oesterreich (1966), Oke (1989).

[62] See Friesen (1991, 1992).

[63] See Oke (1989).

[64] See Friesen (1991, 1992).

[65] See Oke (1989).

[66] See Putnam (1989).

[67] See Koehler, Ebel & Vartzopoulos (1990), Oesterreich (1966).

[68] See Putnam (1989).

[69] See Mulhern (1991a), Oesterreich (1966).

[70] See Putnam (1989).

[71] See Lewis (1971), Mulhern (1991a).

[72] See Orne & Bates (1991).

[73] See Mulhern (1991a)

[74] See Putnam (1989).

[75] Curiously, possession is listed as a diagnostic condition, but under the diagnosis, dissociative disorder, not otherwise specified. Even more peculiar is the identification of "possession" in the *DSM-IV* draft specifically with India. Anyone who has researched this phenomenon would be aware that possession is not limited to India; it is a worldwide phenomenon (e.g., see Bourguinon, 1973, 1974; Crapanzo, 1977; Yap, 1960). Furthermore, the *DSM-IV* draft does not seem to recognize the difference between possession states that resemble MPD versus those which resemble DDNOS (e.g., trance possession). The term multiple personality disorder has been changed to dissociative identity disorder. I personally welcome this particular change because it helps avoid the

sensationalism associated with the term MPD and because it may not be appropriate to consider all the inner entities of MPD patients to be actual personalities. On the other hand, this *DSM-IV* taxonomy does not provide a clear rationale for distinguishing dissociative identity disorder from dissociative disorder, not otherwise specified and it does not address the contemporary phenomenon of ritual abuse that is being reported in modern Euro-American cultures. See Appendix A, "A Proposal That the DSM Add the Diagnosis, Cult & Ritual Trauma Disorder, to a Future Revision."

[76] See Hendrickson, McCarty & Goodwin (1990).

[77] See Mulhern (1991a).

[78] Many MPD patients report that some of their alter personalities do not experience pain. Furthermore, some alters report special abilities that the host personality does not have (or does not recognize having). For example, some alters reportedly do not need to wear prescription glasses. Whether this allegation is true or not, I am unqualified to say, but it is clear that some alters believe this. In that my attempts at explaining these phenomena utilize no supernatural assumptions I hypothesize that this occurs because of the mistaken belief of the alters that their vision is different from that of the host or that some other physical explanation accounts for this claim.

[79] See Oesterreich (1966).

[80] See Braude (1991), Ross (1989).

[81] This observation is not only my opinion; I have heard similar comments by a number of therapists who practice in the local environs and in other communities around the United States.

[82] Goodman (1988) notes the similarity between MPD and possession states but remarks that MPD is rarely mentioned in discussions of demonic possession.

[83] Morton (1977) has described a similar phenomenon anthropologically. Ethiopian participants in the *wuqabi* cult are "forced to rely increasingly on the other members of the cult group, and especially the leader around whom the group is organized" (p. 198). This occurs because of the devotees' desperate need of assistance in managing the harmful effects of the possessing "spirits" and the tendency of the family and community to abandon these individuals.

[84] In a very informative report by Gould & Cozolino (1992) the authors explain how self-destructive actions of alters are used to motivate the ritual abuse survivor to stay in communication with the given cult.

[85] This was copied verbatim from the patient's journal, with no corrections in spelling, punctuation or grammar. The only change is the name, *Sheila*, which is a pseudonym for this individual's alter personality who was responsible for writing the note. As in all other discussions of individual patient histories appearing in this book, I did not use the correct name of the alter or of the patient in order to maintain confidentiality.

[86] This may in part explain the commonly reported self-abuse involving bloodletting among these patients. The other common reason for such self-abuse is reportedly enforcement of the cult rules (e.g., as punishment designed to enforce the secrecy). Curiously, the community of psychiatrists seems to be largely unaware of the reported relationship between self-mutilation and ritual abuse. In December of 1992 the *American Journal of Psychiatry* published two letters discussing a previously published article about self-mutilation. Although they both made reference to the reported bloodletting in ceremonies associated with the ancient Mediterranean mystery cult of Cybele, neither made any comment about the current allegations of mutilation in contemporary cults. See Novello & Primavera (1992), Winchell & Stanley (1992).

[87] E.g., Cervantes (1994).

Chapter 6

Empirical Evidence of Ritual Abuse[88]

Although there have been quite a few publications on the subject of ritual abuse, it is surprising how few authors cite the scientific research on the subject. Dr. Colin Ross, a former president of the International Society for the Study of Dissociation and also a member of the False Memory Syndrome Foundation, recently lamented that, at "present there is not a single published clinical research study of Satanic ritual abuse involving a comparison group and statistical analysis" (1995, p. 197). This observation was incorrect at the time it was published and is still incorrect. In spite of his evident unfamiliarity with the literature, he concluded that, "I assume, for the sake of discussion, that 10 percent of the content of such memories could be historically accurate and based on distorted recall of childhood participation in small Christian cults; small, isolated groups of Satanists; deviant elements of the Ku Klux Klan; pornography; or other forms of abuse that a child could misinterpret as Satanic" (1995, p. ix-x). Such statements are fairly common in the literature where unfounded generalizations about ritual abuse are often stated without appropriate reference to the published research.

On the other hand, two publications that discuss and critically evaluate the research are: "Ritual Abuse: A Review of the Research," by Kathleen Faller, Ph.D. (1994) and the section on ritual abuse in the recent book, *Memory, Trauma, Treatment and the Law* by Daniel Brown, Alan Scheflin and Cory Hammond (1998). Most of the empirical studies of ritual abuse can be categorized into six general sub-topics. These are studies of (1) the frequency of ritual abuse disclosures to professionals and their beliefs about such reports, (2) suggestibility, rumor, and iatrogenesis as possible explanations for ritual abuse allegations, (3) children who have made ritual abuse allegations, and (4) adults who have made ritual abuse allegations, (5) legal cases where ritual abuse was alleged, and (6) the hypothesis that there is an international Satanic conspiracy engaging in ritual crime.

The frequency of ritual abuse allegations was investigated in a national survey of 2,709 clinical psychologists with memberships in the American Psychological Association. This study showed that within their sample of psychologists, 70% denied and 30% acknowledged seeing at least one case of "ritualistic or religion-related abuse since January 1, 1980" (Bottoms, Shaver, & Goodman, 1991, p.6). The authors also found that among the psychologists who had worked with at least one individual with allegations of ritual abuse, 93% believed that the harm had actually occurred. This report was part of a series of five studies later published by Goodman, Qin, Bottoms and Shaver (1994). The first study involved a survey of a stratified random sample of clinical members of the American Psychological Association, American Psychiatric Association, and National Association of Social Workers. The second study consisted of a survey of district attorneys' offices, social service agencies, and law enforcement offices. The third study investigated the question of "repressed" and later "recovered" memory based on 490 cases from the first study of which 43 were described as "repressed memory" cases and 447 were "no repressed memory" cases. The fourth study examined children's knowledge of Satanic abuse. The fifth study investigated three types of "religion-related child abuse: abusive acts intended to rid the child of demons, clergy abuse, and medical neglect for religious reasons.

From the data of their first study, these investigators concluded that 31% of the combined sample of psychologists, psychiatrists and social workers had seen at least one case of ritual or religion-related abuse. There were 387 child ritual abuse cases, 674 adult ritual abuse survivor cases, 171 child religion-related cases and 234 adult survivors of religion-related cases reported. The authors concluded that the adult ritual abuse cases "were consistently the most extreme" (p. 4). Of the adult ritual abuse cases 33% reported cannibalism and 28% baby breeding for purposes of ritual sacrifice. Among the adult ritual abuse cases they found that the victims were likely to be diagnosed with DID. They also found that child cases were "far more likely to be disclosed to authorities or professionals, to family members or neighbors and to be linked to corroborative evidence, but were less likely to be disclosed in therapy than adult cases" (p. 4). The authors concluded that the psychologists, psychiatrists, and social workers who responded to their survey "overwhelmingly believed both the allegations of abuse and the allegations of ritual or religious elements of the abuse" (p. 6).

Their second study of district attorneys, social services and law enforcement agencies revealed that 23 % had identified at least one case of ritual or religion-related abuse. "In general, the ritual cases with the most convincing evidence were unlike the satanic ritual abuse stereotype" (p. 6). The authors expressed surprise that "the conviction rate in ritual cases was almost as high as in religion-related cases" (p. 7). In their third study investigating the question of "repressed" and later "recovered" memory they found that the "repressed memory" cases were more likely to be "ritual cases" in comparison with the "no repressed memory cases." However, when they excluded what they called "outlier" cases, the "repressed" versus no "repressed" memory effects disappeared.

The fourth study of children's knowledge of ritual abuse showed that "children have relatively little knowledge of satanic child abuse" (p. 10). Their fifth study considered 271 cases of religion-related abuse. They found that in 94% of the clergy abuse, 48% of the evil ridding cases, and 23% of medical neglect included allegations of sexual abuse. They found that DID and other dissociative disorders were diagnosed in over 20% of the evil ridding and medical neglect cases.[89]

Another survey investigated reports of sexual and ritual abuse made to British psychologists (Andrews, Morton, Bekerian, Brewin, Davies, & Mollon, 1995). The researchers collected data on 810 British Psychological Society practitioners who had seen sexually abused clients. Regarding these psychologists' "belief in essential accuracy of reports of SRA," 3% reported "Never," 54% "sometimes," 38% "usually" and 5% "always." Fifteen percent reported that they had worked with clients reporting SRA. Eighty percent of the psychologists who had seen one or more individuals with a stated history of SRA believed the allegations.

In their national investigation of 270 cases of substantiated sexual abuse of 1,639 children in day care Finkelhor, Williams, and Burns (1988) found 13% of the cases involved allegations of ritual abuse. According to Jonker and Jonker-Bakker, "The National Society for the Prevention of Cruelty to Children in Britain reported in its 1989 Annual Report that seven out of 66 Child Protection Teams in England and Wales were currently working with children victimized by ritualistic abuse" (1997, p. 542). In a survey of the membership of the International Society for the Study of Multiple Personality and Dissociation, Perry concluded that 88% of 1185 "respondents reported belief in ritual abuse, involving mind control and programming" (1992, p. 4).

These studies show that the overwhelming majority of surveyed professionals either believe ritual abuse allegations or are open to them. What would account for such a high degree of concurrence? If ritual abuse allegations are essentially false, then these therapists are at best misguided. Some have argued that false ritual abuse "memories" are implanted or created by inept or unethical therapists. If the patients' allegations are essentially true, then this high degree of concurrence may simply reflect the professionals' accurate assessment of their informants' reports. We hypothesize that patients who make ritual abuse allegations appear to be genuinely traumatized. In a study comparing 34 adult psychiatric patients making ritual abuse allegations with 31 patients making no such allegations, it was found that the group making ritual abuse allegations had significantly higher PTSD scores on the MMPI-2 (Noblitt, 1995). In their study of preschool ritualistic and non-ritualistic sexual abuse, Waterman, Kelly, Olivieri, and McCord, (1993) demonstrated that PTSD criteria were met for 80% of their sample of ritualistically sexually abused children as compared with 35.7% of the non-ritualistically sexually abused children. Other studies finding PTSD to be a significant component of the clinical picture of individuals reporting ritual abuse will be discussed throughout this literature review.

Nevertheless, it has sometimes been argued that ritual abuse is a false construct conceived and spread by individuals who are Christian. McMinn & Wade (1995) conducted a survey of 497 Christian therapists and 100 members of the American Psychological Association. The authors inquired about the therapists' use of dissociative identity disorder (DID) sexual abuse, and ritual abuse diagnoses in their clinical practices. Overall, there was a low rate of diagnosing DID and ritual abuse. Christian psychologists were slightly more inclined to diagnose ritual abuse in comparison with other psychologists, but they were no more likely to diagnose DID or sexual abuse. There were no differences in diagnosing ritual abuse or DID among Christian psychologists, other licensed Christian therapists, nonlicensed Christian therapists, and lay counselors. Licensed Christian therapists who are not psychologists indicated a greater prevalence of sexual abuse among their clients than nonlicensed Christian therapists and lay counselors. These data are interesting because they show a weak relationship between the Christian beliefs of therapists and their diagnosis of ritual abuse. In examining these data we should consider at least three different questions: (1) Do Christian beliefs make therapists slightly more open to considering real cases of ritual abuse? (2) Are ritual abuse survivors slightly more likely to seek Christian therapists? (3) Do Christian beliefs incline therapists to inaccurately look for and confirm the existence of ritual abuse? Hopefully, further research will better clarify these interpretive options.

The question regarding whether individuals with Christian beliefs also believe reports of ritual abuse has been further investigated. Schutte (1994) did not find a relationship between measured religiosity and judgments of guilt regarding ritual and nonritual abuse cases among mock jurors. On the other hand, Bottoms, Diviak and Davis (1997) found small correlations in the measured "religiosity" of mock jurors and their judgments about scenarios where there were elements of ritual abuse reported.[90] Crouch and Damphouse (1991) mailed surveys to police officers whose names were obtained from a mailing list of "a newsletter on cult activity" and "class rosters from several occult seminars" (p. 193). There was only an 11% response to the surveys—a rather significant methodological problem that casts doubt on the interpretability of the findings. The authors address the question in their words, "Who are the 'cult cops'?" They answer their own question with the results of their survey. Regarding the respondents' religious beliefs they state:

> Of particular interest are respondents' religious beliefs and involvements. Almost all believe in God (98%), though fewer report a belief in the devil (88%). Fewer still (70%) definitely believe in life after death, although another 19 percent reported believing that an afterlife is "probable," Most claim to be Protestant (67%), most others, Catholic (21%); none was Jewish. These officers are not, however, particularly active church goers. Over half (51%) report attending church no more than several times a year. Many, however, attend at least weekly (35%), and 17 percent hold a church office. Crouch & Damphouse, 1991, p. 195)

The authors later admitted that they lacked "specific data on strength of religious values" (1991, p. 200), but correlated the frequency of church attendance with scores on a "Satanism Perception Scale" that they developed. Although these data are probably uninterpretable due the serious methodological limitations, Bottoms, Diviak and Davis cite this study and make the following interpretation: "Highly religious police officers are more likely than other officers to believe that satanic activity poses a danger to society and that it results in criminal activity such as child abuse, teen, suicide, homicide, mutilation and drug use (Crouch & Damphouse, 1991)" (Bottoms, Diviak, & Davis, 1997, p. 848).

A number of authors (Bottoms & Davis, 1997; Mulhern, 1991, 1994; Ofshe & Waters, 1994; Spanos, 1996) have argued that ritual abuse allegations are essentially false and the result of suggestibility and social influence. However, this hypothesis appears to be derived from subjective opinion and speculation rather than any research findings. It has never been shown that people who report ritual abuse are particularly suggestible. Nor has it ever been shown that the individuals alleging that they witnessed or experienced ritual abuse were exposed to suggestive influences sufficient to account for their allegations. A study by Leavitt (1997) showed that patients with recovered memories of childhood sexual trauma were less suggestible than psychiatric patients without such recovered memories of child abuse. Furthermore, in another study, Leavitt (1998) found that exposure to media accounts of ritual abuse and inpatient hospital treatment with other individuals reporting sexual abuse histories did not account for the "satanic" word associations found among 43 patients alleging histories of ritual abuse. In fact, Leavitt found that among patients reporting ritual abuse histories, those with lower reported media exposure made significantly more "satanic" word associations in comparison with a group of similar patients reporting a higher degree of media exposure. It has also never been empirically demonstrated that therapists attempt to persuade psychiatric patients to believe that they were ritually abused. Nevertheless, Mulhern argues that therapists who treat these patients develop their own personal beliefs about the reality of ritual abuse by attending conferences on the subject and then pass these beliefs on to their suggestible patients. However, the only study which has attempted to investigate the therapists' beliefs about their patients allegations about ritual abuse longitudinally through the course of therapy show that the therapists were initially skeptical and only later came to believe their patients allegations (Waterman, Kelly, Olivieri, and McCord, 1993).

Nevertheless, several publications present the argument that ritual abuse allegations are more an artifact of suggestibility than actual abuse. Jeffrey Victor (1993) has described what he calls Satanic rumor panics. Victor argues that Satanism is a frightening and provocative subject to the general public and has been the source of numerous rumors for which he cites examples from the popular press. Philip Coons notes: "Unfortunately, it is impossible to tell from Victor's cursory review of the evidence what really did happen at these 61 locations" (1997, p. 108).

However, Philip Coons (1994) contributed a study of his own on this question. He retrospectively reviewed the psychiatric records of 29 patients who had made allegations of Satanic ritual abuse. He concluded that 76% of the patients had either DID or DDNOS but that he was unable to find any external corroboration of the SRA allegations. Three cases he labeled delusional and four were categorized as factitious. He concluded that in all but 2 cases "questionable" therapeutic methods were used. Weir and Wheatcroft (1995) reviewed twenty cases where ritual sexual abuse had been alleged. Based on their evaluative findings they concluded that false allegations of ritual abuse occurred in 75% of the cases and true allegations in only 25%. The primary weakness of these three studies is that they rely entirely on the subjective interpretations of the authors. Whereas the validity of the last two studies would depend on the ability of their authors to accurately diagnose ritual abuse and/or find corroborating evidence; and the extent to which the data they needed to confirm any true ritual abuse was available. With no measure of inter-rater reliability, there is no way to know how reliably or accurately these investigators interpret these data and there is no way of knowing whether sufficient data were available to accurately interpret.

Two other case studies merit attention although they suffer the same methodological problems. Coons and Grier (1990) described a single case where an individual with ritual abuse allegations was instead diagnosed with factitious disorder and Yeager and Lewis (1997) briefly present a single case of a recanter. In the former example one must ask whether the patient's inaccurate reporting of particular events means that they were not abused or ritually abused. In my opinion, the characteristic features of ritual abuse include abuse by ruse and deception. In the latter example it should be obvious that recantation is no more intrinsically credible than an original allegation. It has been found that individuals with well documented evidence of sexual abuse will sometimes later recant and that many recanters, particularly with ritual abuse allegations, later redisclose abuse (Waterman, Kelly, Olivieri, and McCord, 1993).

Ritual abuse allegations have been made by both adults and children. Like other crimes, it is easier to investigate ritual abuse when it has recently occurred. Evidence gathering is hampered by the extensive lapse of time that occurs when adults allege they were ritually abused in childhood. Both the ritual abuse of children and the ritual abuse of adults in childhood have been studied empirically.

The studies of reported of ritual abuse of children may be further subdivided into three categories: (1) cases where ritual abuse was alleged in day care or preschool settings, (2) cases where the abuse allegedly occurred in community based cults, and (3) cases of multigenerational ritual abuse.

Pamela Hudson (1991) assessed 24 children in a case of alleged ritual abuse at Fort Bragg day care center in California. Hudson found five symptoms to be present among many of the children:

(1)   acting out the sexual abuse (n = 13),
(2)   sudden extreme fear of the bathroom, bathing, washing hair (n = 10),
(3)   nightmares, night terrors (n = 12),
(4)   high anxiety disorder, separation anxiety (n = 16), and
(5)   temper tantrums, oppositional behavior (n = 12). (p. 8)

She also noted that among the children's allegations were their being molested by other children (n = 11) and being molested by strangers, day care workers or a parent (n = 11). Hudson identified 16 forms of abuse: (1) being locked in a cage or "jail," (2) being told that their parents, pets or younger siblings would be killed if they told anyone of the abuse, (3) being buried in the ground in coffins which they called "boxes," (4) being held underwater, (5) being threatened with guns and knives, (6) being injected with needles, bled, drugged, (7) being photographed during the abuse, (8) being tied upside down over a "star," hung from a pole or hook, burnt with candles, (9) perpetrators wearing black robes, masks, (10) having participated in a mock marriage, (11) being defecated and urinated upon, (12) having observed animals killed, (13) having observed torture or molestation of other children, (14) having seen children and babies killed, (15) having blood poured on their heads, (16) being taken to churches, other day care settings, people's homes, and graveyards for the ritual abuse. Of these, 13 children acknowledged experiencing at least one of the listed abuses, not counting the 14th. Four children reported number 14, seeing children and babies killed.

Hudson performed a second study. In order to control for the possible contagion effects that may have occurred in her Ft. Bragg case, she conducted a telephone interview of 10 other families, in different locations in the U.S. where ritual abuse had been reported. All but two were day care cases. She collected data from these interviews which she combined with her Fort Bragg data. Thus, she had a total of 11 cases. The following abuses and corroboration were reported:

(1)   confinement in cage (n = 10),
(2)   threats (n = 11),
(3)   live burial in caskets, coffins, boxes (n = 6),
(4)   water torture (n = 7),

(5)   threats with guns or knives (n = 10),
(6)   drug injections (n = 10),
(7)   filming and still photography (n = 11),
(8)   bondage, locked in closets, hung by feet or wrists, spread-eagled over pentagrams,
(9)   tied onto upside-down crosses (n = 7),
(10) abusers wearing masks and robes, carrying candles (n = 11),
(11) mock marriages (n = 6),
(12) defecation, urination, forcible ingestion of human wastes (n = 10),
(13) witnessing animals tortured and killed (n = 10),
(14) fake operations (n = 6),
(15) children's descriptions of the torture and sexual assault of themselves or others (n = 10),
(16) evidential medical examinations: findings commensurate with sexual assault (n = 11),
(17) babies, small children killed, carved up, and parts eaten (n = 9),
(18) transportation elsewhere for abuse; various methods of transport (n = 10),
(19) sexual assault and terrorizing in churches, graveyards, other day care centers   (n = 10).[91]

Susan Kelley (1993) compared three groups of children in day care: 35 allegedly ritualistically abused children, 32 children reportedly sexually abused, not ritualistically, and 67 children without any claims of sexual abuse. She collected data from the abused children's parents and compared the results of for children with non-ritualistic sexual abuse with ritualistic sexual abuse. She found that ritualistically abused children were more likely to report more incidents, types and severity of abuse relative to the non-ritual sexual abuse victims. She also found that ritualistic abuse was more often associated with multiple victim, multiple perpetrator encounters. On the Child Behavior Checklist there were more reported behavior problems and tendency toward internalizing symptoms among both groups of abused children in comparison with non-abused children but the ritualistically abused children scored worse.

Jill Waterman, Robert Kelley, Mary Kay Olivieri, and Jane McCord (1993) did a six year longitudinal study of 82 children who had made allegations of ritualistic sexual abuse (RSA) in the Manhattan Beach, California area in comparison with 37 non-abused (NA) children and 15 non-ritualistically sexually abused (SA) children. A variety of standardized and non-standardized questionnaires and interview instruments were employed. They found that both the RSA and SA group reported intrusive and highly intrusive sexual abuse. Additionally the RSA group but not the SA group reported "terrorizing acts that included killing of animals, death threats to the children or their families, sadistic acts and physical abuse, and ritualistic acts that included Satanic activities" (p. 64). Recantations occurred in 25% of the RSA and 23% of the SA children. This was the case even though the perpetrator in the SA group had given a detailed confession. However, 88% of the RSA group that recanted, later redisclosed abuse. The children alleging RSA had more severe symptoms than SA children with significantly more PTSD, depression, and aggressive behaviors. The RSA group showed less improvement over time in comparison with the SA group.

A case involving 172 children who made disclosures in day care in southwest Michigan has been reported (Bybee & Mobray, 1993; Faller, 1994). Kathleen Faller gathered data from her clinical interviews with 18 of the children and Bybee and Mobray reviewed the records of 106 children regarding interviews by state police, community mental health professionals, and the department of social services. Bybee and Mobray identified 62 (58%) children who disclosed that they had been victimized and 53 (50%) children who reportedly observed others being abused with 92% of the children who were observed being abused also disclosing that they had been abused. They found that children reported experiencing and observing acts of: fondling, penetration, oral sex, sex with children, penetration of an adult, threats of harm, being hit or hurt, being given medicine or bad food, bestiality as well as ritual acts. Among her sample of 18 children, Faller found "sadistic acts (100%), threats of harm and death to children and their family members (100%), use of drugs (56%), confinement (44.4%) and animal killings or injury (22%)" (p. 22). Faller writes that when she compared the 18 children she interviewed with children who were abused by a single perpetrator in a day care center or day care home she found that significantly "higher percentages of ritually abused children were reported to have sexual acting out problems, sleep problems, emotional problems, behavior problems and phobias" (p. 22). Faller also cites an unpublished report by Valliere, Bybee, & Mobray (1988) of scores on the Child Behavior Checklist (CBCL) comparing the abused children with a comparable sample of non-abused children from the community with clinical and non-clinical norms. "The sexually abused children's scores were generally comparable to those of clinical norms, and significantly higher than non-clinical norms. Sexually abused girls demonstrated improvement on the CBCL between times one and two, but the boys did not" (p. 22).

Not all child ritual abuse research is associated with day care cases. Within the professional and scholarly literature on child abuse there are two reports of what Faller calls "community-based ritual abuse" (p. 23). She defines community-based cults as "those whose membership is contemporary and often made up of persons of various ages—children, adolescents, and adults in a particular community" (p. 24).

Snow and Sorenson (1990) interviewed 39 children who described abuse in five neighbor-based cults in Utah. In four of the five cults there were incidents of intrafamilial incest, perpetration by adolescents, and features of an adult sex ring. No adolescent perpetration was found in the fifth group. Also reported was forced sexual behavior, threats of violence, and multiple perpetrators and victims. At least two-thirds of the children described multiple locations of abuse, pornography, ingestion or other use of excrement, the espousal of Satanic beliefs, magical spells and use of occult paraphernalia, animal mutilation or killing, and the use of drugs. The abusers were generally viewed as respected members of the community and many were religious leaders. Two of the accused adult perpetrators were convicted and two adolescents pled guilty.

Ritual abuse has also been reported in the Netherlands. Jonker and Jonker-Bakker (1991, 1997) have described the allegations and their observations regarding a case in Oude Pekela, a small town of 8,000 inhabitants in northeastern Netherlands near the German border. Jonker and Jonker-Bakker initially surveyed the families of 90 involved children six to eight weeks after the initial disclosures. They gathered additional data from the families of 87 of these children at 2 ½ and 7 year intervals after the first outcries had been made. They compared their later findings with clinical information that antedated the abuse and with initial survey results. They found that 20% of the children made spontaneous disclosures. The list of reported abuses included the following elements: sexual abuse, warnings to be silent, taking photographs, making videotapes, tying up children, keeping children in extreme darkness, being scratched, kicked, beaten, being drugged, animals being present, animals being tortured, killed, babies being involved, babies being killed, adults being killed, chanting, forced eating of excrement or semen, and supernatural powers being claimed. "Almost one-third of the parents reported in 1989-1990 profound changes, as if they were dealing with a different child" (p. 550). The symptomatic behaviors of the children included: a poor sleep pattern, nightmares, night awakenings, bedwetting, genital shame, masturbation, inappropriate sexual behavior, swearing, aggressiveness, destructiveness, self- isolation, anxiety, tongue kissing, torturing of animals, fear of being locked up, interest in fire, fear of spiders, interest in devils, ghosts, the experience of words turning around, and interest in death. The three most common symptoms among the boys were: "poor sleep pattern (79%), waking during the night (79%), and aggressiveness toward the surroundings (83%)" (p. 550). Among the girls, "the most exhibited behaviors were poor sleep pattern (67%), anxiety, nervousness (77%), and aggressiveness towards the surroundings (87%)" (p. 550). The authors also noted that "If the Oude Pekela case had been a result of adult community hysteria rather than real children's experiences, then the behavioral changes would be expected to escalate as a function of disclosures to adults. Instead, there was a decrease in the number of changes in behavior following disclosure . . ." (p. 551). In this case two arrests were made but there were no convictions. However, Jonker and Jonker-Bakker noted that the chief of the police investigation team believed that 50% of the 64 children investigated by the police "were certainly involved" (p. 545). A statement by the district attorney on January 21, 1988 is cited:

> A total number of 98 children, 3 to 11 years old were interviewed. The statements of 62 children were used in the further investigation. Finally 48 statements of children remained, speaking of clear sexual abuse, where they had either submitted to or been forced to perform on themselves or others. Many of the children told about strong lights, lamps on poles, and seeing each other on TV. The justice ministry concluded that it was nearly sure that photographs were taken of the children. Against 18 children violence was used. The child abuse took place over a period of several months. The justice Ministry thinks that four people, two men and two women, were involved in the sexual abuse. (quoted by Myers, 1994, and cited by Jonker & Jonker-Bakker, 1997, p. 541)

Faller (1994) cites a study of intergenerational ritual abuse of children by Susan Kelley. This paper, entitled *Ritualistic abuse: Recognition, impact, and current controversy* was presented by Kelley at the San Diego Conference on Responding to Child Maltreatment in January, 1992. Kelley investigated reports of 26 children from 14 families. The accused abusers were parents, grandparents, great-grandparents, uncles, aunts, cousins and siblings. Similar to other reports a significant number of abusers were female (45%). "Sixty-one percent of children were abused by two generations of older relatives, and 57% of cases involved extrafamilial as well as intrafamilial offenders" (Faller, 1994, p. 25). Reported abuses included "terrorizing threats and acts

(89%), including having spiders or other insects placed on them, death threats (77%), making pornography (81%), threats with supernatural powers (89%), satanic reference (92%), animal killings (54%), being made to ingest drugs (92%), songs and chants (69%), and being made to ingest or touch excrement (85%)" (p.25). Scores on the CBCL were in the clinical range for 73% of the children on total problems, 81% on internalizing and 50% on externalizing scales.

Three studies have surveyed the characteristics and experiences of adults who allege to be survivors of ritual abuse (Drisoll & Wright, 1991; Smith, 1993; Young Sachs, Braun, and Watkins, 1991) and three studies have reported psychological test data obtained by adults who believe that they were ritually abused (Leavitt, 1994; Leavitt & Labott, 1998; Noblitt, 1995). These studies primarily appear to have investigated cases of transgenerational ritual abuse.

Lynda Driscoll and Cheryl Wright (1991) investigated the experiences of 37 adult mental health patients who were allegedly survivors of ritual abuse. Eighty-one percent had no memory of ritual abuse before beginning therapy and of the remaining 13%, their memories were incomplete. Dissociation was a commonly reported problem in this sample with 63% being diagnosed with DID, 34% diagnosed dissociative and 17% with "strong ego states" (p. 6.) Eighty-three percent reported involvement in rituals by a relative with their fathers (63%), uncles (41%), mothers (38%), grandfathers (35%) and grandmothers (22%.) Other abusers included "doctors (54%), neighbors (41%), friends of relatives (49%), church members (35%), police (27%), teachers (22%), and morticians (19%)" (p. 6). Eighty percent stated that the ritual abuse began before age six. The mean age was 6. The reported physical and psychological abuses included being "forced to drink blood (84%), tied up (84%), drugged (78%), deprived of food (61%), forced to eat flesh (57%), forced to eat or drink body waste (57%), deprived of sleep (54%), and given electric shock (38%)" (p. 8). Ninety percent reported being exposed to confusing and degrading experiences. "Seventy-five percent reported being isolated, 61% ejaculated on, 54% urinated on, 38% defecated on, 50% put in coffins (46% with corpses), 44% buried alive, and 39% put in graves" (p. 8). They were allegedly coerced into silence "by threats of harm (84%), of abandonment (76%), death or mutilation of themselves (73%), death of parent or relative (57%), Most victims reported they were threatened with supernatural powers (62%), and they were told they had been magically altered (51%) in a way that would end their lives if they 'talked' or disobeyed" (p. 8). Seventy-four percent said they were forced to perpetrate.

Ninety three percent were allegedly sexually victimized including oral sex (89%), vaginal (84%), object penetration (81%), anal (78%). They reported sex with adults (89%), group sex 84%), with animals (62%), other children (54%), and corpses (38%). Eighty-four percent reported human sacrifice, 14 % claimed they were breeders for sacrifices.

The alleged affects of ritual abuse included problems with trust (100%) and emotional intimacy (97%). "Eighty percent mistrust family members, peers, males, and authority figures in general . . . . Over ninety percent reported chronic depression, anxiety attacks, obsessions and suicidal behavior" (p. 9). Over 80% described feelings of "worthlessness, inferiority, lack of assertiveness, and dirtiness" (p. 10). Roughly 70% state they feel "helplessness, difficulties making decisions, embarrassment about themselves, humiliation and hopelessness" (p. 10). Reported physical symptoms include headaches (90%), insomnia and chronic back and abdominal pain (75%), acute unexplained weakness (76%), catatonic spells (33%) episodic paralysis (37%), and blackouts (50%). Eating disorders included: anorexia (30%), bulimia (30%), and consistently over 20 pounds overweight (70%).

Another study conducted by Margaret Smith (1993) presents data on 52 adults who reported being survivors of childhood ritual abuse. Ninety-seven percent reported that "at some point in their lives, they were amnestic of their ritual abuse experience" (p. 20). Smith found that perpetrators were reportedly fathers (67%), mothers (42%), grandfathers (31%), grandmothers (23%), aunts (21%), uncles (27%), non-family member physicians (33%), non-family member clergy (17%), and non-family member teachers (17%). In her study of the occupations of the family and non-family alleged perpetrators there were physicians (35%), teachers (25%), clergy (22%) and police (15%). Sixty five percent reported that the abuse began before age 4. The following experiences of abuse were allegedly perpetrated against the respondents: molestation or intercourse (100%), forced participation in group sex with adults (96%), being tortured (94%), witnessing or forced participation in animal sacrifice (90%), witnessing or forced participation in human sacrifice (88%), sodomy (88%), being drugged during the abuse (88%), witnessing or forced participation in cannibalism (82%), being forced to torture others (75%), child prostitution (52%), child pornography (52%), being forced to breed children who were later sacrificed (36%). Smith also lists "other forms of abuse mentioned by ritual abuse survivors:" mental programming (21%), bestiality (17%), torture by electric shock (13%), witnessing or forced participation in dismemberment or mutilation of bodies (12%), being hung upside down (10%), being forced to kidnap children from playgrounds (8%), hypnotism (8%), having pets killed (4%), having psychic surgery (4%), and being lent to other cults (4%).

Walter Young, Roberta Sachs, Bennett Braun and Ruth Watkins (1991) collected data on 37 patients who reported victimization by transgenerational childhood ritual abuse. They found that all patients reported sexual abuse, witnessing and receiving physical abuse or torture, witnessing animal mutilation or killings and experiencing death threats. Ninety-seven percent indicated forced drug usage. Other abuses included witnessing and forced participation in human adult and infant sacrifice (83%), forced cannibalism (81%), marriage to Satan (78%), being buried alive in coffins or graves (72%), and forced impregnation and sacrifice of own child (60%). All of the patients had severe PTSD and experienced dissociative states with Satanic characteristics. Other psychiatric sequelae included survivor guilt (97%), indoctrinated beliefs (94%), unusual fears (94%), sexualization of sadistic impulses (86%), bizarre self-abuse (83%) and substance abuse (62%). The authors also described corroborating evidence.

Studies of psychological test data from individuals claiming to be ritual abuse survivors are being investigated (Leavitt, 1994; Leavitt & Labott, 1998; Noblitt, 1995). Leavitt (1994) found that with the exception of the Paranoia scale there were no significant differences between MMPI scores for a group of adults claiming to be ritual abuse survivors and a group of adults reporting childhood sexual but not ritual abuse. However, Leavitt noted that adults claiming to be ritual abuse survivors scored significantly higher on the Dissociative Experiences Scale in comparison with the reportedly sexually, but not ritually, abused control group. Leavitt and Labott (1998) have gathered data on word association test responses for adults who allege they are survivors of satanic ritual abuse. It is perhaps no surprise that individuals who report that they were ritually abused would produce characteristically "satanic" associations to a word association test. What was more surprising was that, in spite of making significantly more overall responses, the SRA group produced significantly fewer normal or "normative" responses than either of a group of non-ritual sexually abused individuals and a non-abused group.

In another psychometric study, the PTSD scales of the MMPI (PS, PK) were compared between a group of adult outpatients who reported being RA survivors and a group of adult outpatients who made no such ritual abuse allegations (Noblitt, 1995). The results showed significantly higher PTSD scores for the alleged ritual abuse survivors.

Legal cases involving ritual abuse allegations have had varied results in both civil and criminal actions. It is important to recognize that civil and criminal trials use different standards of evidence. Civil cases rely on the preponderance of evidence in making determinations. Criminal cases require that the evidence be beyond a reasonable doubt. Thus, criminal cases demand a more stringent standard of evidence.

Civil cases involving ritual abuse allegations have included child custody disputes, lawsuits by survivors claiming damages from their alleged abusers, and malpractice lawsuits against therapists for purportedly implanting false memories of abuse. To my knowledge there is no published review of these cases regarding outcomes. Because some of these cases involve children and matters of family privacy some of the cases have been "sealed" by the court. Some malpractice claims have settled out of court with an agreement that the terms of settlement may not be disclosed by any of the parties.

Criminal cases have been easier to study empirically. However, even this area is not without difficulties. The fact that a crime involves ritual practices may never be disclosed. Most states do not have laws specifically prohibiting ritual crime and therefore the crime is prosecuted under some other defined crime (e.g., murder or child abuse). We discovered that the rumor that the FBI has been studying ritual abuse is untrue when we communicated directly with the FBI about this question.

In spite of these limitations, some data has been collected particularly in cases of ritual abuse of children. Faller (1994) whose review of literature was already cited includes data on convictions associated with the various studies of ritual abuse that she reviewed. Michael Newton (1997) has accumulated data on the sentencing of 145 defendants for crimes in which the ritual abuse of children was alleged. He found that only 17 (11.7% were reversed on appeal). Sixty-four or 44% of the 145 defendants made guilty or nolo contendere pleas. Newton has argued that these reversals do not necessarily that the defendants were innocent. Newton found that in most instances the reversals were based on legal technicalities rather than factual indicators of innocence. Although we have been unable to find any publications with quantitative data on ritual abuse involving adult victims the research of Carl Raschke (1990) and Kahaner (1988) has provided narrative accounts of many of these cases.[92]

Another curious area of research concerns the question of whether there is an "international Satanic conspiracy" that is engaging in these alleged abusive practices. Two research efforts have addressed this particular question: (1) the studies conducted by Bottoms, et al. (1991), and Goodman, et al. (1994), in the United States (previously cited), and (2) the research of J.S. LaFontaine (1994, 1998) in England.[93] Neither found any evidence of such a Satanic conspiracy. Should one then conclude that there is no Satanic conspiracy? Unfortunately neither study disproved this hypothesis; they merely did not find evidence that met their criteria. (It is our contention that neither study adequately tested this hypothesis.) A serious problem in studying an alleged conspiracy is that the usual methods of investigation are often not sufficiently sensitive to identify it when it is present.

A case in point is the study of organized crime in the U.S. The terms *Mafia* and *La Cosa Nostra* have been commonly used to describe one such alleged Italian-American criminal conspiracy. However, for decades the FBI denied the existence of the "Mafia" or "Cosa Nostra." Although the FBI recognized that organized crime existed they had accumulated no evidence that linked any crime to any group that called itself the "Mafia" or "La Cosa Nostra." As far as the FBI was concerned the talk on the street about the Mafia and Cosa Nostra was simply the reflection of contemporary legend. Curiously, an advocacy group arose calling itself the Italian American Civil Rights League. This group claimed that the rumors about the Mafia and Cosa Nostra were really efforts to defame Italian-American people by spreading these supposedly spurious rumors about Italian-American organized crime. The primary organizer of the Italian-American Civil Rights League was Joseph Colombo, who ironically, was the head of one of the "five families" of New York. Finally, in 1989 the FBI surreptitiously tape-recorded a Mafia initiation ceremony in which the words, "Mafia" and "La Cosa Nostra" were during the ceremony. Later when the participants were arrested, not one admitted that there was such an organization as the "Mafia" although some admitted to other accusations of serious crimes including murder. (Pistone, 1992).

This example of the investigation of organized crime in the U.S. illustrates how difficult it may be to demonstrate evidence of what is a genuine criminal conspiracy. In my opinion, neither of the two earlier cited research efforts studying the question of "Satanic conspiracy" was sufficiently sensitive to adequately test that particular hypothesis. To say that there is *no evidence* of an international Satanic conspiracy misrepresents the facts. There are many people who allege that they have eyewitnessed elements of such a conspiracy. Eyewitness reports do constitute evidence. The question is not whether evidence exists. It does exist. The question is to what extent are these alleged eyewitness reports true. This question requires further study and corroboration. It is more accurate to say that the question of the existence of a Satanic conspiracy has not yet been settled in the scientific and legal literature, and that further investigation and research is needed.

NOTES

[88] This chapter has been adapted from *Accessing Dissociated Mental States* (Noblitt, 1998a).

[89] Curiously, some of these authors have written commentaries that are skeptical that ritual abuse occurs very often and blame therapists for many of these "false memories." This position is taken even though there are no objective data in existence to warrant such statements which are potentially damaging toward therapists who are currently being threatened by civil lawsuits for treating individuals who allege that they are survivors of ritual abuse. In some instances these patients will recant and they or their families will blame the therapist for the memories of trauma. This has occurred even in cases where the trauma memories predated any treatment by the therapist in question. More curious is the failure of these researchers to integrate their own and others' research findings with these speculations. Their citation of other studies appears to be highly selective and their interpretation of their own outcomes is inconsistent. See Bottoms, Shaver, & Goodman, (1996), Bottoms & Davis, (1997).

[90] Otherwise the authors report that "it would appear that jurors are as likely to believe allegations of sexual abuse involving occult and ritualistic activities as nonsatanic allegations" (Bottoms, Diviak, & Davis, 1997, p. 854). This particular finding is consistent with a study reported by Schutte (1994).

[91] Adapted from Hudson, 1991, pp. 11–21.

[92] Also see Chapter 10.

[93] One reported case was from Wales.

Chapter 7

Breaking the Code

"Leslie" was one of the first borderline personality disorder patients who came to me for professional help after I established my private practice in Richardson. Although she made gradual progress in her therapy, she continued to have episodic experiences of explosive anger and strong self-destructive urges. After a while, Leslie began to dissociate in therapy with alternate identities who talked with me during our individual therapy sessions. At first, it was not obvious to me what was happening. Initially, Leslie's alternate identities did not announce their names when talking to me. However, her tone of voice and facial expression changed, and she frequently complained that she was unable to remember what happened in our sessions. On one occasion when I said that our time had come to an end, Leslie looked at me incredulously, exclaiming, "I just got here." I motioned toward the clock and when she looked at it, she expressed amazement that her entire therapy time had elapsed. I asked Leslie's permission to videotape our next session, and she agreed.

During our next meeting, Leslie again "lost time." As the video camera recorded the session, she became overtly dissociated and identified herself as "Carol." Leslie responded with shock as she reviewed the video recording of our session. She observed a child alter, Carol, talk about Leslie's collection of teddy bears. Leslie and I had never before discussed her having teddy bears but, as she watched her videotape, she admitted having a rather extensive collection. Leslie watched the tape with a stunned expression, hardly able to believe what she was seeing. As she viewed her image and heard herself speaking in a child's voice and using a childlike vocabulary, she finally had external evidence of her elusive, tumultuous, but dissociated inner world. Leslie said that, prior to this session, she did not understand why she felt compelled to invest so much money and energy in collecting teddy bears. However, Carol provided the explanation. There were several child alters within Leslie's system who were very attached to these stuffed animals.

Eventually, during the course of therapy, other alternate identities emerged. I made it a practice to videotape Leslie's sessions so that she could view them later. This procedure assisted her in recalling the events that had transpired while she was in a trance state. Each time Leslie reviewed the taped sessions, she seemed surprised at what she saw on the television screen. Eventually, her alters described a history of cruel childhood abuse. Some of these memories she acknowledged as real because she could remember them herself, but others sounded unrecognizable, like events that had possibly happened to some other person. She wondered about these reports of abuse for which she had no memories and watched herself in state of bewilderment as she saw her own videotaped image describing traumas for which she had no recollections nor any memory of discussing in therapy.

Leslie sustained an injury at work that required surgery, extensive medical treatment, and physical therapy. She again felt a sense of hopelessness, as if she were powerless to stop this unending series of torments. She was also feeling increasingly self-destructive. At my recommendation, Leslie reluctantly agreed to enter a psychiatric hospital where, at the time, I was providing intensive psychotherapy for patients with dissociative disorders. Arrangements were also made for Leslie to continue to receive physical therapy and biofeedback-assisted therapy[94] for pain reduction as ordered by her surgeon.

Because Leslie's multiplicity had just recently emerged in therapy, I directed one of my staff, with Leslie's permission, to contact the biofeedback therapist to explain the nature and implication of Leslie's psychiatric diagnosis and to relay my request that Leslie not be allowed to go into trance states while in biofeedback therapy. As my staff explained, some of Leslie's alters could be violent, and the biofeedback therapy environment was an inappropriate place for them to present themselves. The biofeedback therapist exhibited some understanding of multiple personality disorder and agreed to comply with my request.

After returning from her first session of biofeedback, Leslie described an awkward meeting in which the biofeedback therapist reportedly indicated a disbelief in the MPD diagnosis. Leslie thought this was unprofessional because the biofeedback therapist had never examined her psychologically, nor was she qualified to do so. After

Leslie's next biofeedback session, she reported that the appointment had gone very strangely. Leslie told me that her biofeedback therapist took considerable time to discuss Native American Indian religions and inquired about Leslie's own spiritual beliefs.

After Leslie's third session of biofeedback therapy, she reported that had been "out" for at least 15 minutes while undergoing biofeedback. Leslie said that she entered into trance so deeply that her biofeedback therapist told her that it had taken an unexpectedly long time to bring her back to a conscious state. I was dismayed at this news. This was precisely what the biofeedback therapist had been asked to avoid. Leslie and I spent our individual therapy time trying to explore what had occurred and to discover what had caused her to go into such a deep trance. Leslie told me that the last thing she could remember was that her biofeedback therapist said something, but Leslie could not remember what it was.

Immediately following our session, Leslie and I went to the scheduled session of therapy group. I was conducting this group for dissociative patients who were hospitalized on the adult psychiatric unit. The four patients present in group on this particular day were also all participating in individual psychotherapy under my care. Leslie was somewhat reluctant to talk about her biofeedback experiences in the group, but I encouraged her to do so. She began to remember some of what the biofeedback therapist said to her before she went "out." Leslie recalled, "She kept saying 'feel the feelings,' and 'deeper and deeper', and 'you will soon be cured.' "

One of the patients in the group, "Karen," expressed anger toward me for my continued questions of Leslie about what had happened. Karen said to me, "Don't say that. Don't say that."

I didn't understand her. "Don't say what, Karen?"
"Those words!" She said angrily.
I was still confused, "What words?"
"Deeper and deeper."

But by now, Karen was no longer visibly angry. She was, in fact, in a trance. I looked around the room. Everyone present was in a trance, everyone but myself. The room was completely quiet. The four group members stared, glassy-eyed, with their gaze directed downward toward the floor. I was amazed. In my eleven years of doing group therapy, I had never witnessed anything like this.

I decided that if the group therapy were to continue, the participants would have to come out of this trance. It should have been easy to accomplish because, I was an experienced hypnotherapist and had never failed to bring a patient out of a trance that I had induced. Although I tried a variety of standard methods, I was unable to bring even one of the group members out of the trance state. The group session was discontinued. Two of the four patients were so dazed that they could not sit upright, and I had to call nursing staff to assist them to their beds. The other two patients were able to walk and went to sit in the unit's day room, but they were too mentally foggy to make sensible conversation.

Several hours later, all four patients appeared to have returned to a relatively normal state of consciousness. I went to each of them individually and privately to inquire about what had happened in the group. None of them seemed to know what had caused the group trance experience. Two of them could not even remember much of what had happened shortly before or after the trance took effect. Only one of them, Karen, appeared able to recount the events with some accuracy. She reiterated her anger at me because of what she interpreted as my interrogation of Leslie. The words that Karen said bothered her were "deeper and deeper." She also indicated that she felt very sleepy when she heard those words repeated.

I wanted to test what Karen was saying to me, so I asked permission to use those words. She was initially reluctant but eventually agreed. I told her that I would use the words but that she would not go into a trance. I would simply use the words in conversation, not in a hypnotic induction. I talked to her about her concerns about her financial condition and how she was getting *deeper* in debt. I inserted the word *deeper* into the conversation this way several times. Before I knew it, she was out.

What caused this reaction? I had clearly given her the suggestion that she would *not* be hypnotized, yet when she heard the words in question, she did enter a trance state. I wondered if she had previous experience in hypnotherapy where a therapist had trained her to respond to those words with a trance. I asked her if she had ever participated in hypnotherapy. In a groggy monotone she replied, "No." "Why are you in a trance now?"

She was silent for awhile. Her eyes rolled upward and her eyelids fluttered for awhile. I repeated my question. She spoke in a different voice identifying herself as four-year-old "Kathy." Kathy said she could see people inside a house. The house was very dark. There were other people there who were wearing black robes with hoods covering their heads. She saw herself on a table, tied down. She was wearing a flimsy white cotton robe without a hood. She said someone was cutting on her arm with a razor blade saying the words "Deeper, and deeper, and deeper" with each painful stroke of the blade across her skin. She expressed an unmistakable feeling of terror. She said she could see herself passing out not so much from the pain, but mostly as a result of her overwhelming fear. Kathy told me that this had happened several times. She also reported experiences of sexual abuse in which her tormentors spoke the words "deeper, and deeper, and deeper" as she was sexually penetrated. She indicated that whenever Karen heard the words repeated over and over, she would automatically enter a trance state as a reaction to this experience, which she called "training."

What Kathy described was not hypnosis as it is normally conceptualized, being a result of repetitive suggestion to produce a trance. Instead, she revealed what appeared to be the results of classical conditioning[95] in which a trance response produced by trauma was paired with the words "deeper, and deeper, and deeper" until the words alone were able to elicit the trance response.

I asked Kathy to help me bring Karen out again because my last effort had failed. Kathy said she was willing to help me. She offered, "All you need to do is say, 'Karen I will count you down from 10 to zero, and when I reach zero, you will be fully awake, pain free and relaxed.' " This sounded like a standard hypnotic countdown procedure. Earlier when attempting to bring the group members out of the trance state, I had tried several similar methods but none of them had worked. Kathy explained that I had to use the exact words as she had stated them to me. Kathy said that Karen had been trained to respond specifically to those words and might not respond to other phrases that were worded too differently. I followed Kathy's instructions, and Karen reappeared and resumed executive control of her mind and body.

I asked to see her arm where Kathy had said that cutting had occurred. Little scars were visible, but it was not clear to me whether the scars were necessarily caused by the abuse that Kathy described. This patient had engaged in some self-mutilation in the past, and it was possible that the scars were self-inflicted. I asked Karen what had caused the little scars on her arm, but she said she did not know. I asked her if she had ever cut herself there, and she said, "Not to my knowledge."

I asked Karen if she would not discuss what Kathy had said to me in the session that day with anyone else. She asked why, and I explained that I wanted to find out what each group member had experienced in session, and I did not want their views contaminated or influenced by one another, and so for that reason I wanted all to refrain from discussing it with each other. I especially did not want the other patients to know what Kathy had said to me because that might influence their reaction to a similar test of their responsiveness to the words and phrases. Karen agreed to my request. She also said that she did not remember much of what Kathy had revealed.

I met with each patient individually and requested permission to investigate what had earlier occurred in the group and each person agreed. I did not tell any of the individuals that I had talked to Karen's Kathy nor what Kathy had discussed with me regarding the manner in which these words had been paired with trauma to produce a trance response. However, in each case, the patient in question went into a trance when I introduced some of the words and phrases into our conversations, but the patients each appeared oblivious to what was happening to them and could not initially explain why they were re-experiencing altered states of consciousness while we conversed.

Karen had specifically responded to the word *deeper*, particularly when it was used in repetition. Another patient responded most strongly to the phrase, "feel the feelings" when it was used repetitively, and to a lesser degree, she responded to "deeper" and " you will soon be cured." One of the individuals became agitated when I used the phrase, "you will soon be cured." I asked her why, and she did not know. At a later date, an alternate identity in her system said that in her abuse history the perpetrators would sometimes repeat the expression "You will soon be cured of your false virginity" in a sexual abuse ritual. All four patients responded with trance to either one or a combination of these terms and phrases and, to my surprise, they all awoke from the trance when I utilized the procedure described by the alternate identity, Kathy. However, when one of the four individuals emerged from trance, she was in a panic state. With tears in her eyes and a look expressing her mental anguish she said, "Don't say *pain free*." "Why?" I asked.

At first she seemed puzzled as if she did not know. Then she blurted out, "Because that means we've been hurt." With further inquiry, only two of the four patients could tell me why they were going into a trance (i.e., identify which words and phrases that they appeared to be responding to).

I was frankly astonished at what I witnessed, but I thought that in spite of these results, I should further cross-validate these findings. Science is based on the idea that valid knowledge can be acquired through careful observations that can be repeated or replicated. When replicated results can be found with at least some consistency and they defy the chance or random variations in nature, then one can say that there is scientific support for a particular hypothesis. However, in order to properly test these initial findings, I had to insure that some alternative explanation could not account for the observed results. For example, if I had told the other three members of the group what Kathy had told me about the various effects of the words and phrases, it might have implanted the idea in their minds that they were supposed to respond in a particular way. By not telling them what I was doing or what I was looking for, I was getting results that were more likely to be free of the effects of suggestion.

I decided that in order to continue to test this particular effect, I should do so in an unobtrusive manner and with other individuals to observe their reactions. In the process I also discovered a variety of other specific signals that resulted in producing altered states of consciousness, physical immobility, and other peculiar responses in some patients. I found that most of these could be surreptitiously introduced into a normal conversation resulting in mild to profound trance responses and other anomalies. On some occasions these methods would bring out specific alternate identities, some of whom would appear ready to do anything asked of them. On some occasions, the patient would go into such a deep trance as to appear in a coma-like state.

Once, during a therapy session, a female patient, "Jenny," went into such a deep trance her speech was barely audible. While in this state, her body was limp and she drawled, "You can have me." I asked her name and she identified herself as "Natasha." She indicated that it was her job to sexually please any male who had the ability to access her. I told her that she would not have to do this anymore and that the decisions about her sexual behavior should not be made or carried out by any individual alternate identity but should be made by herself as a whole person.[96]

The incident in the group therapy session illustrates what some survivors call a response to *programming* (as I later learned). The term *programming* is used in at least two ways in the context of cultism and mind control methods. Most commonly, the term refers to any *coercive persuasion* whether it is experienced in a destructive cult, an established religion, the armed services, or any other group or organization. A second usage for this word is more specific. I have defined programming as "the manipulation or traumatization of alter personalities, fragments or other dissociated mental states or entities for the purpose of mind control" (Noblitt, 1993a). Some patients and therapists refer to the stimuli that bring out particular and often programmed behaviors, moods, and states of consciousness as "triggers."[97] These reported stimuli may be words (as previously described), sounds (e.g., tones, rhythmic patterns, a particular pitch, or sequence of pitches, etc.), visual cues (e.g., hand signals, colors, etc.), or tactile stimulation (touch patterns or designs on the skin). Some survivors state that virtually any stimulus can be used for the purpose of eliciting a preprogrammed response if that particular stimulus has been used previously as a signal for a repetitively traumatizing procedure.[98]

Could this really be possible? This is essentially the theme of the fictional novel (Condon, 1959) and motion picture (Axelrod & Frankenheimer 1962), *The Manchurian Candidate,* in which a United States serviceman is programmed to kill the president.[99] But is there any nonfiction description of this phenomenon? In his book entitled *A Criminal History of Mankind,* Colin Wilson (1984) writes about a case that may illustrate this process. He described an account of a woman who traveled by train to Heidelberg, where she planned to consult with a physician regarding pain she was experiencing in her stomach. According to Wilson, she entered into a casual conversation with a man named Franz Walter, who was reportedly a nature healer and who claimed he could cure her of her ailment. Apparently, Walter persuaded the woman to leave the train at one of the stations, purportedly for coffee.

> She was unwilling, but allowed herself to be persuaded. As they walked along the platform he took hold of her hand 'and it seemed to me as if I no longer had a will of my own. I felt so strange and giddy.' He took her to a room in Heidelberg, placed her in a trance by touching her forehead, and raped her. She tried to push him away, but she was unable to move. 'I strained myself more and more but it didn't help. He stroked me and said "You sleep quite deeply, you can't call out, and you can't do anything else." Then he pressed my hands and arms behind me and said: "You can't move any more. When you wake up you will not know anything of what happened." .
> . . Later, Walter made her prostitute herself to various men, telling her clients the hypnotic word of command that would make her unable to move. And when she married, he made her attempt to kill her husband by various means. The latter became suspicious after her sixth attempt at murder — when his motor cycle brake cable snapped, causing a crash — and when he learned that she had parted with three thousand marks to some unknown doctor. The police came to suspect that she had been hypnotized, and a psychiatrist, Dr. Ludwig Mayer, succeeded in releasing the suppressed memories of the hypnotic session. In due course, Walter received ten years in prison. How did Walter bring her under his control so quickly and easily? (Wilson, 1984, p. 29)

Although Colin Wilson poses the above question, he offers no conclusive answer. He speculates that paranormal processes accounted for the apparent ability of Walter to induce such a powerful trance in this woman, presumably against her will. However, one of the "rules" of the logic of science is called parsimony. In science we are required to explain phenomena in the simplest terms necessary to account fully for them. In other words, if we can explain these events in purely naturalistic (rather than supernatural) terms, we are obligated to do so. The procedure that I have already defined as programming can easily account for these trance states. In fact, the scenario described by Wilson is very similar to many of the reports made by survivors of ritual abuse.[100] Their programming reportedly begins in early childhood and continues as long as the survivor is unable to resist being accessed or otherwise controlled by the programmers. Others who know how to access the survivor can then use triggering stimuli to induce a trance or call out alternate identities to do their bidding.

This may make sense to the reader except for the fact that Wilson's description of this case does not indicate that Walter previously knew the woman he met on the train. For this reason, how could he know of her possible previous programming? According to my patients, some programming methods are commonly used in a variety of abusive groups (e.g., in the example I described earlier where all four members of the therapy group went into a trance). However, it is possible for an individual who understands the concepts underlying programming to identify cues that would affect the programmed person simply by talking to that individual and by observing his or her eyelid and other responses. Patients with programming will often initially respond with eye blinks and a lowering of their gaze when effective accessing stimuli are presented. When the accessing method is repeated, susceptible individuals will often experience involuntary eye closure sometimes with fluttering eyelids. Sometimes there will be dissociative switching to an alternate identity for the purpose of complying with the commands of the person who initiated the access procedure.

There are old legends that tell of men who make a pact with the devil for the purpose of having relatively extensive sexual access to women (e.g., the story of Faust). The concept of programming with potential for access may explain how there may be some truth to this legend. As cult members do the bidding of their cult leader, they can, in turn, be taught more about the procedures for accessing others and thus may be rewarded with increasing power and control over the minds of others who have also been programmed.

There have been other reports that may illustrate this phenomenon further. In another book Colin Wilson (1988) describes a criminal trial in 1865 in which a beggar by the name of Timotheus Castellan was sentenced to 12 years in prison after being found guilty of raping a 26-year-old peasant woman named Josephine:

> Castellan had begged a night's lodging from her father, a poor peasant, claiming to be a healer. . . . Over the midday meal Castellan made a sign with his fingers, as if dropping something on the girl's plate, and she felt her senses leaving her. He carried her into the next room and raped her; she said she was conscious but unable to move. Later Castellan departed, taking her with him. At one farm where he stayed the night he demonstrated his power over her by making her crawl around on all fours like an animal and burst into peals of laughter. He was eventually arrested. (Wilson, 1988, p. 201)

Brian Inglis (1989) describes a 1988 court case in Wales, where an uncredentialed hypnotist, Michael Gill, used a device with flashing lights to hypnotize women who, while in this state, were allegedly raped by him.[101]

The three cited criminal cases illustrate instances in which women were sexually abused while in trance states that were induced powerfully and quickly causing the women to lapse in their normal, self-protective behaviors.[102] Professional hypnotists and hypnotherapists have no such technology at their disposal.[103] Although I know of no large-scale study that has proved it, it is commonly believed by hypnotists that one cannot hypnotize another individual to do anything against that person's will or which violates that person's conscience. In cult programming, however, the loss of the individual's normal sense of executive control is commonly reported by survivors. Not only are such uncharacteristic responses reported; they can be demonstrated in the consulting office. Although it would be unethical to deliberately provoke patients sexually, it is possible to generate the powerful trances with rapid onset and also to investigate other atypical behaviors that can be accessed by such techniques. Such phenomena have occurred on numerous occasions and have been witnessed by other therapists and by other patients when they have occurred e.g., in group therapy sessions.

Another criminal case that involved a man exerting bizarre control over others occurred in Singapore. In this case three individuals, Adrian Lim, his wife, Tan Mui Choo and his mistress, Hoe Kah Hong were all convicted in a capital murder case where Lim confessed to the ritual murder of two children (John, 1989). However, at his pleading Lim told the magistrate that his two female accomplices "are not to be blamed. They are under my control" (1989, p. 51). It was found that Lim had used bizarre methods of mind control that included sexual abuse, beatings, electric shock, drugs, occult rituals, and trickery with Tan and Hoe as well as with other individuals who experienced dissociative states and identity alteration in response to his methods. It was noted that even Lim had experienced periodic trance states and what appeared to be dissociation of identity. At their trials Tan and Hoe attempted to plead insanity but even with appeals that went to their national Supreme Court, Lim and his two assistants were convicted and executed. The details of this case showed significant parallels to the reports of alleged to be ritual abuse survivors and in this case included perpetrator confessions and physical evidence.

How does such mind control work? The perpetrator uses traumatic methods to create or control dissociated states in his victims. While in these dissociated states, the victim is taught to take on a new identity. Later, this particular dissociated identity can be accessed by a triggering stimulus, often a stimulus or cue that is similar to some ritual element of the trauma procedure. One patient wrote in her therapy journal an example of the process whereby some of her alters could be accessed:

Dim the lights
implement the countdown
insert information
repeat information several times (6)
anoint the sense points (forehead, cheeks, throat) w/Blood
enter
this may cause anger if not done in a proper way
have others stand by
Speak the words
"restrain thyself — show no resistance" (may need to be repeated)
Breathing will slow
When inputting information breathing will increase.
Administer Nitro 1 tab will create headache to assure confusion and block all other thought
processes except for the one in which you wish to implement.
"We offer our minds to you (our leader). Please accept our offering of sacrifice — ourselves [sic][104]

For several years now, I have unobtrusively introduced stimuli (as I described earlier in Leslie's case) into my consultations with patients in an effort to cross-validate the results described earlier[105] and in order to provide some objective procedure for assessing a given patient's possible history of ritual abuse. I have found that some patients respond in a predictable way to specific triggering stimuli. I have observed similar behavioral and trance responses from patients in my practice who grew up on the East Coast as well as the West Coast. I have, of course, had patients who did not respond to any of the techniques I used and on other occasions, some of the techniques have worked with some individuals whereas other methods did not. I have also supervised other therapists who have used such techniques with their patients with similar outcomes. Other therapists refer patients to me for evaluation to assess the possibility of such cue specific dissociative responses. Typically, I videotape these sessions so that the referring therapist, as well as the patient, can later observe the results of the evaluation.

In addition to observing these unusual dissociative responses, these patients have recounted similar histories of tormented childhoods involving sadistic and ritualized abuse. These individuals typically have had no previous interactions with one another, coming as they do from different geographical locations, cultural backgrounds, religions, socioeconomic strata, and different generations. Yet, despite the differences, they have described histories of the same or similar ritualized traumatic events, and they present with similar internalized systems of alternate identities.

Although the majority of my patients typically have no conscious memories of having previously known one another, it is curious that several of these patients have switched to alternate identities and identified one another by reputedly secret cult names when speaking to me privately and individually. For example, on one occasion I was saying good-bye to a male patient diagnosed with DID and inviting the next patient, "Alice," into my office. Once inside my office, Alice switched to a child alter who very fearfully inquired, "Why do you have Robert James coming to see you? Don't you know he's very dangerous?" Because of patient confidentiality, I could not say anything about the male client with whom I had just visited. I could not even identify him as a patient. However, his real name was *Robert Dale*. He had confided in me that *Robert James* was one of his secret cult names. How was it that Alice recognized him at all, much less identified him by his cult name, *Robert James*? To my knowledge he had not told that name to anyone else — that is, no one outside his cult — and to my knowledge, he had never seen or met Alice before. He neither greeted her nor recognized that he knew her when they passed each other in the waiting room. Alice also identified three others of my patients, allegedly from rituals she had attended in childhood, two of them by secret cult names that were only known to me and, presumably, the cults where these individuals reportedly had been abused. Alice has also been recognized by the alter identities of two other patients who, in private session, revealed that they had known each other from past cult experiences.

Some of my patients have complained of being "accessed" by other people whom they believe to be involved in destructive cults in which programming methods are understood and utilized. Some of my patients report experiences in which they received telephone calls or patterned knocks on their door that have caused alter identities to emerge who were allegedly trained to acquiesce to anyone using that particular signal. This point leads us to the story of "Maggie."

Maggie was estranged from her mother whom she claimed was the high priestess of a Satanic cult in a distant state. When she occasionally received mail from her mother, she would bring it to my office to open in the presence of staff because she feared that the mail could be provocative. Sometimes communications with her mother had reportedly caused her to experience strong suicidal urges. One day, Maggie came to the office with a bulky envelope that was sealed and bore an out of state postmark. The return address on the envelope was the same as her mother's. Maggie asked one of my staff to open the envelope because she feared what it might contain. The staff member could feel a cylindrical object through the paper and cautiously opened the envelope, allowing the contents to spill onto the surface of her desk. The contents included a folded piece of notebook paper, four photographs, and a hypodermic syringe containing one cc of a red, viscous liquid that appeared to be blood.

The four photographs looked like candid, amateur photos taken of a man, woman, and two children, in four different poses. The letter appeared innocuous. It was a chatty letter addressed to Maggie from her mother, full of mundane items regarding family news. There was no explanation for the syringe. When Maggie saw the syringe, she appeared to go into a trance state. When she heard my voice as I stepped from my office, she lunged for the syringe and attempted to stab me with it. It took several staff members to subdue her and remove the syringe.

Eventually, Maggie dissociated as several alternates who explained that the pictures and the syringe were all triggers designed to influence or coerce Maggie to kill me. She subsequently received other syringes through the mail, each with different levels of the unidentified liquid. Unfortunately, we were unable to obtain any assistance from the police. The local police claimed there was no law against sending syringes with what appeared to be blood products through the mail. The postmaster concurred. No one within the city, county, or state government was even willing to analyze the liquid; and at the time neither Maggie nor I could afford to do so through a private laboratory. We were advised that we could consult the Federal Bureau of Investigation, but Maggie was terrified of the prospect of FBI involvement because she feared it would mean her death. I dropped the matter in deference to Maggie's fears. Ultimately, with appropriate treatment, Maggie no longer responded to those particular triggers. However, she reported an additional disturbing situation that had occurred earlier.

Maggie said that she was abducted and tortured with electric shock, during which time she was instructed to kill me with a knife, mutilate my body, and take selected parts of my anatomy back to her cult. According to her story, Maggie had attended a group therapy session with me and was prepared to stab me when the session ended. Maggie recalled that during the course of the group, another patient said something that effectively canceled the alleged assassination program. Later in individual therapy, we discovered that Maggie's programming could temporarily be interrupted by using the word, *disarm.*[106] Knowledge of that word became an important element in dealing with this highly volatile and violent patient. One of the undesirable side effects of working with these patients is that some have a potential for violence. On some occasions I have been threatened and on others physically assaulted. Many other therapists who work with this patient population report similar threats and assaults.

Reports of exposure to deliberate and traumatic methods for inducing dissociation, and what I have described as programming, have been a near-universal characteristic of patients who report ritual abuse. They describe programming procedures as occurring in a variety of different environments including destructive cults. Many of the cult experiences that have been described appear characteristic of demon worshipping groups,[107] but this is not always the case.[108]

NOTES

[94] Biofeedback therapy is a procedure in which the patient is attached to a device that monitors one or more physical functions (e.g., skin temperature, muscle tension, etc.). The patient is given instructions regarding how to change that particular function while observing the change on the monitor device. Biofeedback therapy has been found to have a limited degree of effectiveness with some pain patients and patients with certain vascular disorders. Some researchers and clinicians have questioned whether biofeedback's effectiveness is due to "nonspecific factors" such as the placebo effect.

[95] Classical conditioning is a term that describes reflexive or spontaneous learning that occurs when certain stimuli are paired together in the presence of the person or the animal expected to do the learning. The original work was done by Ivan Pavlov (e.g., Pavlov's dogs). Razran (1971) has presented an interesting theory describing a variety of similar forms of conditioning or learning that he believes may occur in different organisms with differing levels of neural complexity. In any case there may be a variety

of different techniques for instilling learning and these techniques do not all require the voluntary cooperation of the subject exposed to those techniques. Kroger & Fezler (1976) have described a combination of hypnosis and conditioning techniques for clinical use that they call "imagery conditioning."

[96] This incident was not unique. Quite a few of these patients have had alter personalities emerge in therapy reporting that it was their job to sexually please the person who had accessed them. A near universal observation by psychotherapists is that they encounter psychotherapy patients who sometimes become overtly seductive during therapy sessions. Freud was so perplexed by this phenomenon that he invented the term *transference* to explain it. However, we also need to consider the possibility that some patients are behaving seductively because they have programmed mental states which are seductive in nature and which are sometimes accessed in therapy.

[97] See Smith (1993).

[98] I presented a paper on the subject of programming at the annual 40th Annual Meeting of the American Society of Clinical Hypnosis (Noblitt, 1998b) and in more detail in a monograph (Noblitt, 1998a).

[99] Declassified CIA documents show that the Manchurian Candidate phenomenon was considered as a possible explanation for the assassination of President John F. Kennedy. Because all the relevant investigatory documents have not been declassified, we cannot be sure precisely what the CIA's findings or conclusions were on this question.

[100] I have had several patients who have described similar scenarios. They recall being raped or sexually abused by an individual who incapacitates them after saying a certain word, phrase, or other similar signal including hand grips and facial touching. When exploring this phenomenon in therapy, these patients are initially unable to explain the event or the apparent power of these signaling stimuli. With further interviewing, however, it frequently happens that an alter personality is able to emerge and explain the process and even give an accounting as to how the programming was originally established, e.g., as Karen's alter, "Kathy," did. In other cases as in Jenny's, alters emerge and explain their sense of obligation to be a sex object for the male.

[101] Flashing lights and other illuminated images and figures are frequently used as accessing stimuli according to ritual abuse survivors. These stimuli reportedly acquire the ability to incapacitate the victim after the stimuli have been paired with trauma in the same manner as has been explained in this book regarding other such programming.

[102] According to Ashe, Aleister Crowley, the British occultist, "had hypnotic powers which he used freely for seduction" (1974, p. 235).

[103] Unless they also know how to use this technology of programming and accessing.

[104] This was copied verbatim from the patient's journal notes. Although I frequently attempt to test such alleged accessing procedures, I did not in this case, in part because it involved blood and a drug that should only be used by prescription. I have found that some accessing procedures are generic, that is, the procedure seems to effect survivors from different backgrounds, cults, and geographical regions. Other access procedures appear to be more idiosyncratic or specific to a particular survivor. The effects of such signals can be tested by introducing them unobtrusively (and testing to see that the signal was in fact unobtrusive to the person witnessing it).

[105] Although it is often helpful to introduce these stimuli unobtrusively, it is not necessary to do so on all occasions. In some instances the examiner will want to observe how the patient responds when there is no effort to disguise the procedure.

[106] Some patients report they experienced abuse in cults that forcibly involved them in training violent behaviors (e.g., martial arts) because the cult wanted "warriors." In order to provide for the safety of the "trainers," those being trained under such conditions

would often learn to cease violent behavior on the command of a particular cue or triggering word.

[107] Some survivors have alters who purport a sincere devotion toward a demonic entity such as Satan or Lucifer.   These alters sometimes claim that they have voluntarily endured horrible rituals as a means of expressing their profound commitment to these "demons," whom they sometimes revere as gods.   However, in the majority of the cases I have encountered there is a more agnostic and skeptical view of these demons' existence or status as gods.

[108] Margaret Smith (1993) also makes this point.

Chapter 8

The African Connection

Like Leslie, "Sarah" entered into therapy with me shortly after I established my private practice. Sarah was a Caucasian woman of medium height with dark brown hair and penetrating dark brown eyes. When we first began to work together in an inpatient therapy group, she said that I intimidated her. She also frequently complained about what she perceived to be my critical attitude toward her. She initially made this complaint before I had ever said anything to her. Actually, she was her own worst critic. Sarah felt that she was a bad and incompetent person and often flew into rages when she recognized some minor mistake she had made. Her anger was even more intense when she perceived that someone else was making similar critical judgments of her.

Sarah was initially referred for psychological counseling by her gynecologist and was assigned a female therapist for individual psychotherapy. She was diagnosed with borderline personality disorder and when her condition deteriorated periodically, she was rehospitalized for suicidal acting out and self-mutilation. During her inpatient stays, she participated in group therapy sessions that I facilitated. On an occasion between hospitalizations when her individual therapist was out of town, Sarah called my office in a panic for an emergency consultation. She was experiencing a strong desire to cut herself. I agreed to see her but recommended that we videotape our meeting so that her individual therapist could later review our taped session. Sarah arrived at my office a short while later. The video camera was in place and ready to run. We began the session.

Sarah told me that she had a strong urge to cut herself. She recognized that this desire was irrational, and she knew that if sufficient cutting occurred, she would be hospitalized. She asserted loudly and in no uncertain terms that she did "not want to go into the hospital!" She was unable to justify her compulsion to harm herself other than saying, "I hate myself." I thought that there must be more to the story, but she appeared unable to elaborate.

I asked Sarah to close her eyes and tell me what she could see inside her mind. She instantly complied and told me that she could see "confusion."

"What does the confusion look like?" I asked her.
"People."
"What do you mean, people?"
"I see people in my head."
"Tell me about the people."
"They're arguing."
"Who are the people? Do you recognize them?"
"No, I don't recognize them, but they've always been there."
"Have you told your individual therapist about the people?"
"No. She didn't ask and I was embarrassed to bring it up."
"Why embarrassed?"
"She would think I was crazy!"
"What are the people arguing about?"
"Whether to kill me or not."
"Do some of them want to kill you?"
"Yeah, especially one."
"Tell me about the one who wants to kill you."
"He's really mean. He says he wants to cut me. And then he just laughs at me."
"Who is he?"
"He says his name is 'Damon'."

Before I knew it Damon assumed control of Sarah's speech and began talking to me. I felt relieved that the video camera was on because I didn't know if Sarah would later remember this session. (Some patients are evidently co-conscious for experiences similar to this although others are not). Damon told me that "he" enjoyed hurting Sarah and that "she deserved it." Damon took credit for other occasions when Sarah had been cut and was later rushed to the hospital emergency room.

As we talked, I learned that Damon was a male alter, a teenager, who first came into existence when Sarah was being sexually abused earlier in her life. According to Damon he had been created by Sarah's mind[109] to protect her from this abuse. However, Damon had reportedly been unable to effectively fight off Sarah's assailants and since that time, Damon had taken out his rage on Sarah rather than on Sarah's perpetrators. It was eventually possible to create something of an alliance with Damon and he agreed to a temporary moratorium on the self-mutilation. I was very happy with this outcome. Together, we had been able to avert another psychiatric hospitalization while keeping Sarah safe from self-injury.

When Sarah watched the videotape she was astonished. Although she had the name Damon in her head, she had no memory of Damon taking control of her speech. She invited her husband, who was in the waiting room, to come into my office and view the tape along with her. Upon viewing the tape, her husband did not appear to be surprised. With the numerous instances of strange and bizarre behaviors that Sarah had displayed throughout their married life, he believed that they had never gotten an adequate psychiatric explanation. The strange events on the videotape seemed to reflect other incidents that he had observed at home and so, ironically, he received some consolation that progress was finally being made. Sarah said that she wanted to transfer her therapy to my care. I told Sarah that I would rather she talk to her usual therapist and get her therapist's recommendation before she made any sudden decisions.

I provided the videotape to Sarah's individual therapist, who was not pleased. She said she had no experience with clients who dissociated and therefore could no longer follow this patient. I offered to provide occasional consultation to assist them in their work together, but Sarah's therapist decided instead to terminate her relationship with Sarah.

I talked to Sarah's psychiatrist, and he was also unhappy with what had happened. He also refused to view the videotape of Sarah's session with me. He insisted that Sarah did not and could not have a dissociative disorder. Sarah's psychiatrist was in training to be a Jungian analyst. He told me that it is normal for people to have "inner people" and he mentioned the book *Subpersonalities: The People Inside Us*, by John Rowan (1990), and he also discussed some other concepts regarding dissociation from a Jungian point of view. I was grateful for the information he provided to me, but disappointed that he was unwilling to consider that this patient might really have a dissociative disorder and that he would not even take the time to consider the evidence.

I did not know much about Carl Jung's thoughts regarding dissociation, so it was helpful to be exposed to a new perspective that might provide a broader understanding of this phenomenon. I purchased a copy of Rowan's book.   From it I learned that the idea of subpersonalities could be traced, in part, to Carl Jung's theory, as well as to the Italian psychiatrist Roberto Assagioli (1975).   Rowan presented the concept that people normally have a variety of inner roles or identities that may be, to some degree, dissociated from one another. Rowan indicated that the presence of subpersonalities was not indicative of multiple personality disorder, which he described as being a more severe manifestation of personality dissociation.   However, from reading his book, it was not clear to me where one would draw the line between the two.   Furthermore, it was not entirely apparent that subpersonalities were, as Rowan hypothesized, normal facets of one's personality.[110]   For example, he cited another author (Schwartz, 1987) who was impressed with a bulimic patient partly because the voices she described in her head were somewhat like the voices in his own head.   Richard Noll has described "the all-too-real, almost audible, internal dialogue that babbles incessantly on and on in many of us, and is especially pronounced in times of great moral conflict" (1993, p. 250).

To what extent is it normal for people to experience some sense of dissociated identity?   Is it normal for people to hear voices in their heads?   My psychological training had emphasized that hearing voices was symptomatic of relatively serious psychological problems.   I had never met any psychologically healthy people who admitted to hearing voices.   I was determined to learn more about this way of thinking about dissociation and found a variety of resources that were helpful (e.g., Noll, 1989; Ribi, 1990; Sliker, 1992).   Unfortunately, Jungian concepts did not help my understanding of Sarah's predicament.[111]   As I was later to learn, Sarah would describe problems of an entirely different sort.

With the passage of time, Sarah dissociated as a variety of different alternate identities in our sessions.   Like the other patients diagnosed with DID, Sarah had quite a few different alters that would periodically take executive control of her body.   Sometimes she would have conversations with me in these dissociated states. Before too long, some of Sarah's alter identities began to describe sexual abuse by an uncle. Some of the abuse reportedly occurred in an abandoned house not far from where she lived during her childhood.   Over time, Sarah reported that during the abuse, other people wearing robes and chanting to Satan were present.   She began to have alters emerge who fit the category sometimes called *enforcers*.   These alters typically do injury to the patient's body or threaten harm, particularly when the perpetrators' rules (e.g., to keep the secrets) are not followed by the patient.[112]

It took considerable negotiation to deal effectively with the numerous alternate identities that emerged in therapy.   There were children, teenagers, and adults, both male and female. A couple of animal alters were identified. An alter who believed herself to be a 17th-century witch presented herself. There were a variety of Satanic alters, those who felt abused by the rituals, those who believed they were the abusers, priests and priestesses, and entities who believed that they were demons. The purpose of Sarah's therapy was not to convince her that these experiences were all accurate representations of actual events. Instead the goal was for her to become more consciously aware of her dissociated functioning, and to develop more control over her feelings, impulses and behaviors. To accomplish these goals it was necessary to learn more about her dissociative functioning.

However, I eventually encountered an entirely different category of alters and themes of abuse. Sarah began to describe abuse that she attributed to the label, *Voodooism*. Although Sarah denied having any knowledge of Voodooism, she presented with a number of alters who claimed extensive knowledge and experience with the subject. They explained to me that Sarah had been forced to participate in rituals in three different Voodoo cults. The first one, they said, was of Dahomean origins. The second was associated with a cult that followed the traditions of the Yoruba tribe of Africans (who reside in present-day Nigeria). The third was what the alters called "Haitian Voodoo" which, they explained, was an amalgam of the first two combined with other influences. These alters described the various pantheons of gods and goddesses associated with these groups in detail. Much of the information was written in Sarah's journal. In it she discussed rituals that were as grizzly and shocking as those that she had previously reported as Satanic abuse.

When the alternate identities were no longer present and Sarah resumed executive control, I asked her what she thought about the alters' allegations. Sarah said she had no idea what to make of them. She reiterated that she knew nothing about Voodooism and seemed skeptical that her alters could have so much detailed knowledge about a subject that was basically alien to her.

Voodoo was also something about which I knew little. It appeared that I needed to become more familiar with the subject, and so I began to read about the topic. In the meantime Sarah made a trip to New Orleans, where she purchased some books in order to check the accuracy of what the alters had written in her journal. She was, however, too anxious to read the books in New Orleans and waited until she was back in the Dallas area to do so. To her dismay, the books corroborated what the alters claimed about the rituals and gods of this Afro-Caribbean religion.

Through my own research I learned that some authors prefer the term *Vodoun*[113] as a more accurate or more respectful name for this religion. To further confuse things, people sometimes incorrectly use the term *Voodoo* or *Vodoun* in referring to any "primitive" (or, preferably, the less value-laden term, *pre-industrial*) magic or sorcery-oriented religion.[114] Vodoun specifically refers to a syncretism of French Catholicism superimposed over a core of African and other beliefs. Among the many beliefs inherent in Vodoun some originated from the Fon people of Dahomey (who currently reside in the African nation of Benin).[115]

Although Vodoun is historically derived from Africa, it is not an indigenous African religion. The indigenous religion of Western Africa is sometimes referred to as *juju*[116] (Oke, 1989) and is a parent religion from which Vodoun evolved. Vodoun has thrived primarily in the Americas in areas that were colonized by the French and where Africans were subjected to slavery, for example, Louisiana (Tallant, 1990) and Haiti (Deren, 1991; Rigaud, 1985). However, Vodoun is also reportedly practiced in other parts of the world, including other islands of the Caribbean; the southeastern United States, including the environs of Charleston, South Carolina; and cities in the North where African-Americans emigrated to escape slavery, racial hatred, and violence. According to Rigaud (1985), Vodoun rituals have also been practiced in Galveston, Texas. My own patients have described Vodoun rites occurring in Louisiana and East Texas. Luhrmann (1989) reports that Vodoun ceremonies have occurred in London. Elsewhere in the United States, especially within some African-American communities, there can sometimes be found what is called *hoodoo*, which is essentially an eclectic mixture of magical beliefs derived from a variety of different African tribes (Haskins, 1978).

A number of highly reputable scholars have investigated Vodoun and similar related phenomena. For example, the eminent Harvard physiologist Walter B. Cannon researched this subject and reported his findings in a paper entitled "Voodoo Death" (1942). Cannon was interested in investigating claims that Voodoo practitioners could bring on a person's death through ritual magic (e.g., bone pointing). Unfortunately, Cannon incorrectly used the term *Voodoo* in reference to several different sorcery religions that existed in a variety of pre-industrial, or "Third World," communities, including African and Polynesian cultures. However, Cannon did record sufficient accounts from people he believed to be reputable witnesses and concluded that some victims of Voodoo curses did die afterward. Nevertheless, Cannon, in the tradition of modern science, was unwilling to seriously consider the possibility that supernatural forces were responsible. Instead, Cannon offered a variety of more conventional explanations for these deaths, including the possibility that some individuals who had been cursed may have deeply believed that death was imminent and may have stopped taking proper care of themselves.[117]

Wade Davis (1985) presents a more recent investigation of Vodoun practices in the book, *The Serpent and the Rainbow*. In this book, Davis describes his trip to Haiti and his attempts to study the pharmacology of substances associated with Vodoun rites and the alleged power of Vodoun priests to resurrect dead persons as zombies. Davis examined the hypothesis that the so-called zombie phenomena were the result of ingested drugs that produced deathlike symptoms and appearance but did not, in actuality, kill the victim. Continuing with this premise, such a "dead" person could later be revived, and supernatural power might then be attributed to the individual doing the "healing." Davis did find some evidence for his hypothesis, but he also discovered mystical, ominous, and secretive subcultures that practiced these rituals and ceremonies.[118]

A curious observation about Vodoun is cited in two publications (Spiegel, 1974; Spiegel & Spiegel, 1978). The focus of these reports is not primarily concerned with Vodoun. Instead, the authors' writings discuss some personality characteristics that they believe are associated with highly hypnotizable subjects. They identify one such characteristic as "a fixed personality core," which is defined as the subject's entrenched ideas that cannot be easily negotiated or challenged by logic or observation. They go on to relate an anecdote about a Haitian native:

> An amusing illustration in a sociological aspect was provided by a Haitian native. When asked what the distribution of the different religious beliefs in Haiti is, he replied without hesitation: " 70 percent Catholics, 20 percent Protestants, and 95 percent Voodoo." In sum, this is an illustration of the hard core non-negotiability. (Spiegel & Spiegel, 1978, p. 320)

Unfortunately, the Spiegels may be missing the point. Vodoun is apparently practiced by individuals who also consider themselves to be Christians.[119] How is this done? It is accomplished through syncretization and dissociation on the part of the Vodoun follower. It is the same with Santeria, and Brujeria in which Catholic ceremonies are overtly followed and saints are ostensibly prayed to, but in actuality some element of the worship is really directed to the pagan (indigenous African or Mesoamerican) gods.

Vodoun is a possession cult with a formal liturgy and a specific terminology for its gods, priests, and ritual paraphernalia. The gods could be referred to either by their African derived names or by the name of particular Catholic saints that were treated as representing the respective African gods. The names of the gods varied with the different African tribes. The Dahomean, Yoruban and other African cultures contributed syncretistically with Catholicism in the origins the New World Vodoun beliefs. The Vodoun religion incorporates a belief in a supreme being who created the universe. However, this supreme being is considered both unapproachable and uninvolved in human affairs. Thus humans are left to deal with a pantheon of lower level gods called loa or mystères. Different Vodoun sects may emphasize rituals devoted to particular loa. The father of the loa is Danbhalah, the serpent god. Rosemary Guiley writes:

> According to the creation myth, Danbhalah, the Serpent, and Aido-Wedo, the Rainbow, taught men and women to procreate, and how to make blood sacrifices so that they could become the spirit and obtain the wisdom of the Serpent. (1989, p. 350)

Vodoun ceremonies are officiated by a man who is called the *houngan*, the Vodoun priest. The female counterpart of the houngan is a *mambo*. The houngan is generally said to work in benign magic for the purpose of assisting those present in becoming possessed by the gods. On the other hand, the *bokor* is the sorcerer who can perform either benign or malevolent magic rituals. The Vodoun temple is called an *oumphor* and its altar or altar stone is the *pé*. The *peristyle* is a partly enclosed courtyard that in the middle has a center post, the *poteau-mitan*. According to Rigaud (1985), the oumphor "closely resembles the design used by Moses to build the Ark of the Covenant and the tabernacle described in Exodus" (p. 14). Furthermore, according to Rigaud:

> In the Voodoo tradition Moses was initiated into Voodoo and perfected his knowledge as a student of the black Midianite teacher Ra-Gu-El Pethro (Jethro). The Tradition relates that Moses became the husband of Pethro's daughter Sephora, who bore two mulatto sons by him: Gershom whose name means *I dwell in a foreign country*, and Eli-Ezer, whose name means *Help of God*. The tradition goes on to say that Aaron and Miriam, the brother and sister of Moses, complained that he never should have married a black, and so to please them Moses finally repudiated Sephora. When Moses built the first Hebrew temple, according to the Voodooists, he planted his staff in the place occupied by the poteau-mitan in the oum'phor. The gods of Voodoo were so angry at Moses' repudiation of Sephora and

> Voodoo, according to the tradition, that they "struck Miriam
> with white leprosy." (1985, p. 14)

There has been some controversy as to whether or not human torture
or sacrifice ever occurs in any Vodoun rituals. According to Tallant
(1974), there is not much evidence that human sacrifice has ever been
performed in *Vodoun* rituals in Louisiana. Nevertheless, my patient
Sarah reported that she had been present at rituals in Louisiana involving
torture, human sacrifice, and ritual cannibalism. Other patients
subsequently validated Sarah's claims in that they also described abusive
and traumatizing Vodoun rituals.

Rigaud's (1985) account indicates that some Vodoun followers in
Haiti do practice ritual acts of human violence in what are called the "red
sects." Like Christianity or any other religion, Vodoun consists of a
variety of smaller sects that differ from one another in some particular
aspects of belief, ritual, or tradition. One of the larger of the red sects is
the Petros sect (Deren, 1991; Gersi, 1991; Rigaud, 1985), which
apparently is known for its violent rituals. The specific subgroups of
Vodoun practitioners who engage in abusive rituals are also likely to be
more secretive and represent a more closed society.[120] Tannahill (1975)
cites a report by Sir Spenser St. John, the British consul general in Haiti
during the 1860s, who witnessed a criminal case in which eight people
were convicted for participating in a human sacrifice ritual.

Efforts to learn about New World Vodoun also led to the
exploration of the subject of indigenous African religion. We found E.
E. Evans-Pritchard's book, *Witchcraft Oracles and Magic Among the
Azande* (1980), to be useful and instructive. This work presents a
methodical and detailed account of the beliefs, customs, and rituals
associated with an African tribal confederacy in East Africa. *The Worlds
of a Maasai Warrior,* by Saitoti (1986), illustrates the spiritual beliefs
and life experiences of the author as he grew up in an East African
herding community. Lucy Mair's (1971) *Witchcraft* and Parrinder's
(1970) *Witchcraft* discuss aspects of sorcery and witchcraft associated
with African native religions and offer some comparisons with European
lore, traditions, and accounts of witchcraft. *Parallel Worlds,* by Gottlieb
and Graham (1993), presents a personal account of the authors'
experience living in a West African village, observing the culture,
spiritual beliefs, and rituals while coping with the secrecy, distrust, and
ambivalence of the local villagers.

However, of all the literature available on indigenous African
religions, *Blood Secrets,* by Isiah Oke (1989), most directly addresses the
question of ritual abuse. The author recounts his upbringing as the

grandson and successor of an important *babalorisha,* or juju high priest, in West Africa. Oke describes the traumatizing procedures he underwent in his training to be a high priest and the ordeals he was required to inflict upon others, including an act of ritual torture and murder. He relates what appear to be common experiences of dissociation (although he does not use that term) in the community as he illustrates instances of significant memory loss as well as accounts of spirit possession among his fellow villagers.

According to Oke, "Our rituals are designed to appease the most horrid of our gods. And — because those gods are so fearsome — so must be the rituals: We believe that nothing better appeases the fierce spirits of juju than blood" (p. 19). Oke explains that although the religion of juju is practiced openly in West Africa, there is a side to it where the "secrecy is so complete that one might almost say there is another religion, unknown to the outside world, *inside* the religion of juju" (p. 19).[121] He describes the open and relatively benign *ceremony* which occurs in the public *Temple:* "But there is another sacrificial place, usually well out in the forest, far from prying eyes and ears, that we call the Shrine. It is usually no more than a hut in a hidden clearing in what we call the igbo-awo (the secret forest). What is performed here is not the innocuous *ceremony,* but rather the gruesome and bloody *ritual*" (p. 19).

Oke explains that blood rituals are a common aspect of juju, and he speculates that the prevalence of these rituals may have something to do with the high incidence of AIDS among the entire African population (not just among gay males and intravenous drug users). Although Oke does not mention it, it may not be a mere coincidence that AIDS is also prevalent in Haiti,[122] given that Haiti is a center for the related cult of Vodoun. Oke indicates that among his countrymen, there is a practice of infant sacrifice, but there is an even more prevalent custom of discarding unwanted babies to die of exposure or fall prey to predators. This typically occurs not for ceremonial purposes, but simply to free the mother from the burden of caring for the child. According to Oke, Western demographers have mistakenly over attributed Africa's high infant mortality rate merely to poor dietary and health conditions when the problem of "baby dumping" and sacrifice are also significant factors.

Another author who validates some of Oke's observations regarding African religion is Malidoma Somé (1993, 1994). Somé is a West African whose books indicate that he is a scholar in the Western sense, reportedly holding doctoral degrees from both the Sorbonne and Brandeis University. Although Somé appears to be an advocate for his religion, he emphasizes its use of secrecy and fear. He describes rituals in which people appear to be speaking in different voices with different identities. He notes that the priests who conduct the rituals are able to affect the minds of others present so that they are typically unable to recall the events that transpire. He describes the case of a tribesman who offered to reveal secrets of the cult to outsiders but, before being able to do so, reportedly experienced a psychotic episode and committed suicide.

Such accounts are similar to those of survivors of ritual abuse in the United States who indicate that they feel their mind is blocked or "shut down" as they try to remember the rituals or who feel particularly self-destructive when they are about to tell, or have already told, some of the secrets. This enforcement of inner secrecy may be accomplished by the procedure called programming.[123] As previously mentioned, this conceptualization of programming has nothing to do with the supernatural. Survivors describe programming as a form of classical conditioning that involves creating and manipulating conditioned responses to trauma.[124]

Sargant (1974) describes the personality transformation, dissociation, amnesia, and programming associated with an *orisha*[125] cult whose ritual practices were carried out in what the author calls a "convent":

> Pierre Verger himself has become a priest of the Orisha cult, so he could not tell me about many of the secret ceremonies that took place in the convent. But he was able to say that it was a severe brainwashing process in which the normal personality is replaced by a new personality. The postulant is never permitted to remember his normal personality, what he was like and how he behaved as his former self. But when he leaves the convent he is given back his old personality by a special process, and has little memory of what happened during his time in the convent. People go back into the convent from time to time and by the same hypnotic process revert to their god-like personality, to emerge once more with their ordinary personality when they return to the outside world. (p. 149)

A variety of other cults have evolved from African juju. In the Spanish-speaking cultures of the Caribbean and North and South America there are sects that go by such names as Santeria, Abaqua, Palo Mayombe, Palo Monte, and Obeah. Native to Brazil is Macumba, which is a general term that can be subdivided into Candomblé, Umbanda, Batuque, and Quimbanda. It would be beyond the scope of this chapter to attempt to describe them all in detail but some brief comments about

Santeria, Palo Mayombe, and Macumba should be made along with a few words about Brujeria, even though it is not technically of African origin.

In *Santeria: An African Religion in America* (1988), Joseph Murphy describes his experiences observing and participating in Santero practices in the Bronx, New York. Murphy presents his view that the sensationalized media reports of cruel ritual practices sometimes associated with Santeria are inaccurate and reflect cultural biases and prejudices. He says that ceremonies involving blood sacrifice of animals are always conducted in a humane manner and that the animals are killed quickly and later eaten. He makes no mention of any rituals where humans are harmed but describes an emotionally warm and supportive sense of community among these people. However, Murphy admits that he is both a neophyte and an outsider who is not immersed in the beliefs and inner traditions of Santeria. As mentioned earlier, other authors have described incremental levels of secrecy with increasingly higher involvement in violent rituals in some of the African and African-derived cults. Warnke (1972) also makes the same contention regarding increasing levels of secrecy and malevolence in reference to his experience in a Satanic cult.

Garrison (1977) notes that in New York City, the traditions of the African-derived Santeria have become intermixed with the beliefs and practices of *curandismo* and *Espiritismo*, the latter two reportedly being of more Euro-American derivation. However, the "great majority of those who attend spiritist *centros* in both area surveys and in the *centro* client sample report their religion as Roman Catholic" (1977, p. 395). This parallels what was previously stated regarding Vodoun practitioners who typically consider themselves Christians. Garrison also notes how experiences of possession are categorized and interpreted in this amalgamous sect.

Migene Gonzalez-Wippler (1984, 1987, 1992) also writes about Santeria, describing it as another possession cult, primarily derived from the African religion practiced by the Yoruba tribe of Nigeria. It is noteworthy that previously cited author Isiah Oke, a Yoruban and former high priest of his native African religion, describes ritual murder as an intrinsic component of his cult. However, Gonzalez-Wippler's accounts of Santeria deny that any element of such "black magic" practices are normally a part of Santeria.[126] The author does concede, however, that abusive and violent acts are common in Palo Mayombe, a possession cult derived from the Bantus of the Congo tribes. The alleged malignancy and violence associated with Palo Mayombe has been reiterated by Detectives Pat Metoyer of the Los Angeles Police Department and Jim

Bradley of the Washington, D.C., Metropolitan Police Department in interviews conducted by Larry Kahaner (1988).

The practices of Santeria and Palo Mayombe have been associated with the drug cult led by Adolfo Constanzo at the Santa Elena ranch outside Matamoros. There is evidence that ritual murders occurred in the vicinity, and the remains of fifteen bodies and numerous artifacts of Santeria and Palo Mayombe (Kilroy, 1990) were discovered. In a thoroughly researched account by Carl Raschke (1990), the author also points out that the sadistic and ceremonial murders committed by Constanzo showed the influence of *Brujeria,*[127] an Hispanic form of black magic derived from Aztec blood rituals. In addition to the material evidence, some of Constanzo's accomplices confessed, providing eyewitness accounts of their ritualistic activities and descriptions of the occult beliefs.

> The Hernandezs' confessed to the murder of Kilroy and began to reveal all about the workings of the cult and its leaders. They fingered Adolfo de Jesus Constanzo, as well as a Brownsville college student named Sara Villarreal Aldrete. She acted as the "high priestess" of the group. . . . Aldrete was an honors student by day at Texas Southmost College and a *narcotraficante* by night. At her home in Matamoros, police came across an assortment of "voodoo" paraphernalia and a blood-splattered altar of sacrifice. Aldrete's neighbors, her classmates, and her teachers naturally expressed astonishment and dismay . . . . Aldrete, however, had fled the scene of the crime along with Constanzo and there was much talk about her . . . "multiple personalities." (Raschke, 1990, p. 11)

Despite the abundance of evidence,[128] some (e.g., Green, 1991) have chosen to discount the occult religious practices of Constanzo and his accomplices. However, the nature of the murders, the mutilations, the confessions of the perpetrators, the use of ceremonial paraphernalia and even the manner of the victims' burials were clearly ritualistic.

At least one of my other patients reports experiencing cult abuse while living in Brazil. Sarah also alleges abuse by a group located in Louisiana that reportedly used the term *Macumba* to describe its practices. Macumba, or *Santuario*, is a general term for the Brazilian version of Santeria. Both belief systems are primarily traceable to Yoruban religion. They have essentially the same gods with the same legends. There are only minor differences in spellings of their names along with the expected regional variations in status and idiosyncratic characteristics that the particular gods have to the local believers.

According to Guiley (1989), Macumba is sometimes erroneously equated with black magic, but such malevolent practices are more correctly specifically associated with the sect of Quimbanda.[129] The French author and photographer, Serge Bramley, writes about the secretiveness that Brazilians have about Macumba, yet reports on its prevalence. For example, Bramley states that on December 31, 1975, there were an estimated one million participants in the festival for the Macumba goddess Iemanja in the city of Rio de Janeiro alone (1977). Seth and Ruth Leacock (1975) describe the *encantados,* who are believed to be important spirits of the Batuque religion, an Afro-Brazilian cult. When a person is possessed by an encantado, harm is sometimes self-inflicted while in the possessed state if that person has broken any of the rules of the cult.[130]

Sarah was the first patient who told me that she was ritually abused in some form of African derived cultism. However, after her a number of other patients reported similar experiences. Were these individuals actually abused in Afro-Caribbean cults? Were these reports fabrications of overly suggestive women? Do some Afro-Caribbean cults actually engage in ritual abuse in modern times? With time, effort and care hopefully these questions will be better understood.

NOTES

[109] Previously we have described patient reports of having alter identities created by cult programming. Many patients also believe that their minds are capable of creating alter personalities when under great duress.

[110] Although we agree that people normally assume many roles, we do not believe that these sometimes disparate roles exist in a state of dissociation or amnesia for one or the other without a history of profound trauma.

[111] It is not our intention to present a critical attack on Jungian and similar views of dissociation but simply to make the point that this theoretical outlook would not have helped to understand what the patient was later to report about her alleged experiences of ritual abuse.

[112] In part, "Damon's" role was that of an enforcer.

[113] There are a variety of different spellings for vodoun, a term which is preferred by authors such as Wade Davis (1985, 1988), Maya Deren (1991), and Rosemary Guiley (1989). Sometimes the terms Voodoo or Voodooism are more commonly used in Louisiana and East Texas.

[114] We use the term *sorcery religion* or *sorcery-oriented religion* to refer to religious belief systems and practices in which sorcery or witchcraft plays an important role. To modern Westerners this concept may sound incomprehensible, i.e., to merge any magical practices with religion; but many historians of religion have argued that magical beliefs are common, especially in the early stages of the more traditional Western religions including Judaism and Christianity (e.g., see Neusner, Frerichs, & Flesher, 1989; Thomas, 1971; Vetter, 1973). However, the notion of combining religion with evil magic is even more difficult for modern Westerners to grasp but it is important to understand

that the Western notion that sacredness is exclusively associated with goodness is not universally accepted by all religions in every culture (see Cervantes, 1994).

[115] According to Gersi (1991), who indicates that he lived for five years in Haiti studying and participating in Vodoun ceremonies, Haitian Vodoun has also been influenced by the occult practices of the indigenous Arawak Indians and a variety of traditions from Europe including "many aspects of Freemasonry, as well as esoterism, the Kaballah, occultism, alchemy, astrology, metaphysics and Theosophy" (p. 127).

[116] In this book we generally capitalize the names of religions. However, Oke writes about *juju* without capitalizing the word and we follow his convention.

[117] Although Cannon did not mention it, it is certainly possible that some Vodoun deaths have been self-inflicted by alters who were signaled to do so by the "bone pointing" or other triggering acts.

[118] Gersi (1991) provides a similar but supplementary description regarding the creation of zombies. He also argues that zombies are drugged to reinforce the illusion that they have died and that they are later revived by the *bokor,* or sorcerer. In the process of their revival Gersi describes severe abuse and what he calls "brainwashing" of the revived individual.

[119] Gersi (1991) describes it thus: "Ninety percent of Haitians are Voodoo worshippers; the great majority of them are also devout Catholics" (p. 128). Metraux (1959) states that the Vodoun follower thinks "of himself as a good Catholic" (p. 323).

[120] Wade Davis (1985, 1988) describes what he calls the secret societies within the general community of Vodoun worshippers which Haitians generically and interchangeably call *Bizango* or *Sans Poel* (i.e., "those without skin"). According to Davis, the initiation into one of the Bizango secret societies leaves "the clothes on your back in shreds" (1988, p.262).

[121] Compare this with M. Smith's (1993) citation of the British occultist, Aleister Crowley's observation that "behind the exterior of the church is an interior church, the most hidden of all communities. . ." (p. 19). See Crowley (1979, p. 16) for the original source cited by Smith.

[122] It is noteworthy that while AIDS has been a significant problem in the nation of Haiti, it has not been prevalent in the adjacent nation of the Dominican Republic, both of which share the same island of Hispaniola in the Caribbean. See Cantwell (1988, p. 129).

[123] And as previously mentioned, the alters who inflict the harm are often called *enforcers.*

[124] The point that programming is based on classical conditioning has also been made by Gould (1993a, 1993b) and Gould & Cozolino (1992).

[125] *Orisha* is the Yoruban expression used to denote their gods. This term is used in Yoruban juju and New World Santeria, which is influenced by the Yoruban culture. In Macumba, which is roughly the Brazilian variant of Santeria, the similar word *orixa* is often used in reference to the Yoruban gods.

[126] However, one should note that Gonzalez-Wippler (1992) admits that there is great secrecy associated with Santeria and that as a result she has not described it in its entirety. In this same publication, the author describes an incident that occurred when she was a child. She was taken to the seashore by her caretaker and stripped of her clothing in a manner that was so frightening that it caused her to cry. The author was apparently being introduced to the Santero ocean goddess, Yemanya (also identified as Iemanja in discussions of the Macumba cult). Gonzalez-Wippler also states that the Santeros drink the blood of their sacrificial animals while possessed by the *orishas,* or gods.

[127] Although the term *brujeria* is normally reserved for malevolent witchcraft, especially incorporating Aztec traditions the term is occasionally (but rarely) used to denote "white" witchcraft as well (e.g., see Devine, 1992).

[128] During the excavation of the burial site accomplished under police guard by Constanzo's accomplices, they volunteered information that there were other burial sites on the property. The police already feared the ramifications of their discovery and decided to abandon their search for more victims. The sites identified by Constanzo's accomplices were bulldozed and leveled.

[129] The notion that Quimbanda represents the dark side of Macumba practice is also expressed by anthropologist Esther Pressel (1973, 1977).

[130] Earlier in this chapter the concept of *enforcer* alter personalities was mentioned. Enforcers punish the host person when the "secrets" are divulged or whenever any other infraction of inner "rules" occurs.

Chapter 9

Other Cultures

Coincidentally with these efforts to learn more about African derived cults, we also investigated a variety of other cultures and studying their history and anthropology. Some patients reported abuse in rituals associated with other cultural groups, including Native Americans, Hawaiians, and Australian Aborigines, which appeared similar to Sarah's accounts of traumatizing Vodoun ceremonies. Researching the relevant literature was necessary to adequately understand these apparent survivors' claims. The patients describing these incidents substantiated their possible residency (albeit sometimes temporarily) in the locations where the abuse reportedly occurred.

One of the classic anthropological works by the eminent scholar Clyde Kluckhohn (1962) addresses Native American occult practices. Kluckhohn was, by the way, president of the American Anthropological Association in 1947, following the publication of what many considered to be his finest work, *Navaho Witchcraft* in 1944 (republished in 1962). Kluckhohn noted the extreme degree of secrecy associated with Navaho occultism and the reluctance of these Native Americans to discuss the subject. After extensive time was spent collecting data from interviews with the Indians, Kluckhohn concluded, "There seems to be clear evidence that witchcraft *is* practiced — we as yet have no scientific certainty as to frequency or as to whether all the types which are described in words are indeed actualized in deeds" (Kluckhohn, 1962, p. 56).[131]

We were both surprised to learn the extent to which abusive rituals have been described throughout among diverse cultures. Patrick Tierney writes about the practice of ritual human sacrifice in Peru in *The Highest*

Altar (1989).   He identifies this practice with the ancient Incan civilization and cites modern cases of human sacrifice, two of which he personally investigated.   Tierney describes some of the "occupational hazards" associated with his research: "You want the natives to tell you their most intimate secrets, secrets they've pledged not to divulge — and which could incriminate members of the community if learned by authorities.   The protagonists who performed the human sacrifice in secret make no secret of the fact that they'd like to sacrifice the prying journalist" (p. 20).

Tierney questions why it has taken anthropologists so long to acknowledge the existence of human sacrifice in a variety of New World cultures, even when there has been ample evidence of these practices.   In addition to the Moche (Davies, 1981), the Incas, the Mayans (Davies, 1981; Lemonick, 1993; Schele & Miller, 1986, Tompkins, 1990), and the Aztecs (Davies, 1981; Markman & Markman, 1992; Tompkins, 1990) demonstrated a propensity for ceremonial acts of violence.   Tierney suggests that many people, including scholars, tend to be in denial regarding the prevalence of human sacrifice.   If one honestly scrutinizes the subject, it becomes apparent that human sacrifice is also part of Europe's heritage as well.[132]   It is a shared legacy that many prefer to deny.

Tierney attributes the two recent ritual murders that he investigated, at least in part, to the shamanistic practices of that region.   Shamanism is an occult practice that ritual abuse survivors will occasionally broach and discuss.   Three of my patients have alleged being abused in what they believed were Native American ritual ceremonies.   One of the patients identified a specific cult using the term *Shamas*.

A review of anthropological literature has addressed the subject of Shamanisms.   The article, "Shamanisms Today," by J. M. Atkinson (1992), appeared in the *Annual Review of Anthropology*.   Atkinson states that "Just a few decades ago, shamanism appeared to be a dead issue in American anthropology" (p. 307).   Atkinson cites Taussig, who writes that "shamanism is   .   .   . a made-up, Modern Western category, and artful reification of disparate practices, snatches of folklore and overarching folklorizations, residues of long-established myths intermingled with the politics of academic departments, curricula, conferences, journal juries [and] funding agencies" (Atkinson, 1992, p. 307).   In spite of Taussig's criticism of the subject, Atkinson presents a scholarly account of this subject.   She concurs with Holmberg's (1983) observation that there really is no single unified shamanism per se but that there exists a plurality of *shamanisms*, each with its own individual variations.

Two other works discussing shamanism have provided a sympathetic but scholarly perspective on the subject: Harner's (1990) *The Way of the Shaman* and Eliade's (1964) *Shamanism*. According to Harner and Eliade, shamans are essentially equivalent to what Westerners call "witch doctors" and "medicine men." Shamanism is basically a very old system of healing, spiritual revelation, and the exercise of "spiritual power"; existing from prehistoric times. It is distinguishable from witchcraft and sorcery (e.g., Guiley, 1989) and the possession cults (e.g., Oesterreich, 1966)[133], although Harner (1990) specifically identifies some as "warrior shamans" who may also be correctly called sorcerers. The shaman is an individual who is able to attain a ritual trance state, often with the aid of drums, chanting, and ceremonial dancing. Sometimes sleep deprivation and/or the ingestion of mind-altering drugs facilitate these trance states.

While in the trance state, the shaman purportedly enters a "parallel" spirit world. In this state the shaman has visions, and from these he makes diagnoses of health conditions and may offer interpretations or make judgments about other problems including legal disputes. In shamanism, cures are not usually effected by giving the person seeking treatment drugs as much as the shaman himself may take a drug to alter his own consciousness. In such a state the shaman believes himself able to confront and negotiate with spiritual forces or to recover the sick person's lost soul in the "spirit world" to effect the desired cure. Within this belief system, these tasks are accomplished with the aid of spiritual entities. Each shaman is assisted by what is sometimes called a "guardian spirit" and one or more "spirit helpers."[134]

Not all shamans limit their craft to benevolent activities, and some may also dabble in sorcery or witchcraft involving the "dark" or malignant forms (e.g., in the cases mentioned previously by Tierney). Huxley (1989) distinguishes between what he calls "black" shamanism and "white" shamanism, which deal with evil versus benign practices. Wright (1957) presents a similar argument regarding the benevolent healers, *corandeiros,* and the malevolent *feiteceiros* among the Native American Amazon witch doctors. Drury (1987) observes a variety of similarities between traditional shamanic practices and selected features of modern ritual magic such as may be seen in the modern occult, quasi-Masonic organization called the Hermetic Order of the Golden Dawn, in his book, *The Shaman and the Magician.*

How do shamans obtain their "spirits?" We have hypothesized that these "spirits" are actually dissociated inner identities. Because most of the literature on multiple personality disorder indicates that the DID patient's alternate identities are caused by severe trauma, it was hypothesized that this might also be the case with regard to the spirits of shamanism. This notion has been supported by the reports of several patients reporting abuse in possession cults (e.g., Sarah's abuse in Vodoun cults) wherein possession by alter personalities (including some in the form of Vodoun "spirits") occurred as a result of traumatizing rituals.

In his book *The Way of the Shaman*, Harner is not entirely clear how these spiritual entities come to be part of the shaman's inner psychological world. According to Harner, the guardian spirit may come to the shaman after a serious illness, or this spirit may be deliberately encountered during a ritual exercise he calls a *vision quest*. In his book, terms like "another identity" (p. 43), "alter ego" (p. 43), and "another self" (p. 59) are used in reference to the guardian spirit. De Martino (1972) uses the expressions "dual personality" and "second personality" (p. 85) in describing the experience of coming in contact with such an entity. Obviously, these terms could also appropriately be used to describe the alternate identities associated with dissociative disorders.

However, one observable difference between DID and possession cults on the one hand, and shamanism on the other, is that in shamanism there is allegedly no complete "possession" by the spirit. Shamans may experience a possession trance, but the possessing entity does not necessarily "take over" the entire body's functioning. The experience is often described as an "inner journey" wherein the shaman attempts to communicate with one or more spirits. This kind of mental functioning may be more similar to the *DSM-IV* category dissociative disorder, not otherwise specified. This diagnosis is associated with individuals who may experience trances and alternate inner identities but where these identities do not completely assume executive control and where there is not necessarily extensive memory loss as in DID or somnambulistic possession states.[135]

Harner also states that there are "involuntary ways" (p. 43) whereby a person may obtain a guardian spirit although he does not specify how this is accomplished. Later in his book, he explains that the Jivaro tribe commonly gives their newborn infants a hallucinogenic drug for the purpose of assisting in the process of the child's producing a guardian spirit. After briefly mentioning the practice of drugging newborns, he indicates that there are other involuntary ways whereby children may acquire guardian spirits, but he does not describe these methods either.

In his book *The Occult: A History*, Colin Wilson (1971) argues that traumatization is part of the shaman's training. "The *shaman* himself has achieved his priesthood through the most terrifying ordeals, an initiation through pain" (p. 147). According to Gersi, "Becoming a shaman takes years of painful initiations. I have heard that many neophytes die from the hardships involved. The neophyte experiences the worst physical and psychological torments — even madness" (1991, p. 45). Eliade (1964) also presents the view that shamanistic initiation involves traumatizing ordeals in which the initiate returns to the village with what appears to be memory loss to the extent that basic living skills must be relearned and the individual is given a new name.[136]

Ritual cannibalism has also been attributed to some shamanic practices. Ritual cannibalism is presumably a traumatizing experience both for the victims before they die, as well as for those who perpetrate it. According to R. D. Jamison (1984):

> The generally reliable account of the Cambridge expedition to the Torres Straits reported that sorcerers ate the flesh of corpses or mixed the flesh of corpses with their food when they were out to practice their art. The consequence was that they became violent and, when angered, committed murder. Too little is known of the steps taken to induce the shamanist trance except to note at cannibalism in this instance promoted the consumer to an inhuman or superhuman state. (p. 189)

The motion picture from some years ago entitled *A Man Called Horse* (Silverstein & Howard, 1985) also addresses the question of traumatizing shamanistic practices. This movie depicts the story of a captive white man enslaved by a Sioux tribe. Once he proved his prowess as a hunter and earned sufficient respect from the tribe, he is allowed to participate in a torturous tribal ritual initiation. The ceremony entails his suspension by ropes attached to claws inserted into his pectoral muscles. In this fictional account, the white man enters a trance during this torture, apparently in response to his suffering, and in this trance state, he sees spectacular and majestic visions. According to Kurath (1984), Powers (1977), and Yenne (1986), such practices have actually occurred in the past and continue in the present among some tribes of Plains Indians. White Americans sometimes call this ritual the sun dance. However, according to Powers, the Indian phrase describing this ceremony is better translated as the "sun gazing dance" (p. 95). John Lame Deer (1972) describes the ritual as follows:

> The dance is not so severe now as it once was, but even today it asks much of a man. Even today a man may faint for lack of food and water. He may become so thirsty blowing on his eagle-bone whistle that his throat will be parched like a cracked, dry riverbed. He may be blind for a time from staring at the sun so

that his eyes see only glowing spirals of glaring whiteness. The pain in his flesh, where the eagle's claw is fastened in his breast, may become so great that a moment arrives when he will no longer feel it.   It is at such moments, when he loses consciousness, when the sun burns itself into his mind, when his strength is gone and his legs buckle under him, that the visions occur — visions of becoming a medicine man, visions of the future. (Lame Deer, 1972, p. 189)

The author continues to say:

The difference between the white man and us is this: You believe in the redeeming powers of suffering, if this suffering was done by somebody else, far away, two thousand years ago. We believe that it is up to every one of us to help each other, even through the pain in our bodies. Pain to us is not "abstract," but very real. We do not lay this burden onto our god, nor do we want to miss being face to face with the spirit power. It is when we are fasting on the hilltop, or tearing our flesh at the sun dance, that we experience the sudden insight, come closest to the mind of the Great Spirit. Insight does not come cheaply, and we want no angel or saint to gain it for us and give it to us secondhand. (Lame Deer, 1972, p. 197)

In another account of Native American religion, Lemonick describes the manner in which the traumatizing rituals of the Mayans (who inhabited Southeastern Mexico and Guatemala) induced altered states of consciousness that had religious significance to them. The author states that "The gruesome ritual of bloodletting accompanied every major political and religious event in ancient Maya society . . . . The intense pain of such rites led to hallucinatory visions that allowed participants to communicate with ancestors and mythological beings" (1993, p. 49).

Other shamanistic and primitive cultures also allegedly performed painful or abusive rituals. In *Kingship and Sacrifice*, Valeri (1985) describes numerous episodes of ritual human sacrifice performed by Hawaiians prior to 1819, when such ceremonies were officially abolished. Valeri notes that sacrifices were also used in rites of sorcery. Steiger (1971) indicates that among the Hawaiians (as elsewhere) male circumcision has been a kind of blood ritual. Without anesthesia it is also presumably a very painful ritual experience that may cause an altered state of consciousness. Similarly, Cowan (1992) describes the shamanistic practices of the Australian Aboriginals:

> The idea of bloodletting or blood sacrifice is rooted in
> Aboriginal ritual practice. There are few ceremonies that do not
> involve the cutting of some part of the body to release blood. . .
> . In the strict sense a boy cannot become a man until he has
> undergone initiation. Until he is initiated, it follows that he lives
> only a part life as a child. Ritual initiation allows him to be
> 'reborn' into a more complete life as an adult. Prior to European
> contact young girls often underwent ritual deflowering by men
> of the same class as the intended husband. This also involved a
> clitoral cut with a stone knife, followed by intercourse with the
> men concerned. (p. 55)

According to Cowan, Aboriginal boys also experience painful rituals that result in a transformation of identity:

> During the ceremony a boy's personality undergoes an abrupt
> and permanent change. Not only must he experience pain in the
> act of submission to his Elders, he must learn obedience. . . .
> Sworn to secrecy about the rites he has witnessed, the initiate
> finds himself transformed by the nature of his experience into a
> man on whom the burden of cultural continuity is already
> beginning to fall. (pp. 56–57)

The practice of ritual infanticide and keeping the embalmed body is reportedly practiced by some Eskimo shamans as a means of gaining a "familiar" spirit (Ahmed, 1968). This procedure is presumably traumatizing to the shaman perpetrator, who then may dissociate (further) as a result of this experience. This ritual act is similar to a practice observed in some of the Caribbean islands in which, according to Beck (1979), a "familiar" spirit called a *bolum* can be acquired. Ritual sacrifice of children is attributable to a variety of shamanistic and other cultures (e.g., Potter, 1984). Repeated ritual murder is reportedly a characteristic practice of "sorcerers" from the Cebuano culture of the Philippines (Lieban, 1967):

> To become one who can practice *hilo*, it is said that a man must
> first kill a member of his own family, and from then on one or
> more victims each year. One sorcerer said that the sorcerer's
> obligation to kill grows with time; the longer the sorcerer
> practices, the more frequently he has to kill. All informants
> agreed that once a sorcerer assumes such obligations, if he does
> not victimize others according to schedule, he himself will
> become a victim, struck down by his own instruments of sorcery
> that turn against him. As one sorcerer expressed it, "If he does

not kill, he gets seriously ill, and he only gets well when he kills.
If he does not kill, he will die." (Lieban, 1967, p. 23)

It is our hypothesis that repeated experiences of trauma are a necessary precedent to the development of intrusive experiences of dissociated identity. Furthermore, certain rituals that include blood sacrifice and the ritual eating of the sacrificial victim increase the probability of mentally internalizing the conceptualization of the victim, or the entity that the victim symbolizes, creating dissociated identities or alter personalities. Tierney makes a similar point:

> When the shamans have finished the kill, there is a double sensation — relief and guilt. There's the infinite relief — "He's dead but I'm still alive." Then there is the guilt — "He died instead of me." And in this mingled guilt and pleasure a sense of incorporation takes place, the commingling of the victim with his killers. "He lives on in me," I feel. I am grateful to the dead victim, so grateful, in fact, that I feel as though he could never die — that I will never let him die. This heartfelt emotion embraces all the participants, and seems, in a moment of drunkenness, like an intimation of immortality. (1989, p. 23)

Painful rituals may have been an early characteristic of shamanism. Certainly it is possible that these early healers came upon suffering people who appeared to be in a state of psychological shock as a result of their physical pain. Because of the unresponsiveness often seen in people in a state of shock, it would be easy to understand how shamans could conclude that these people's souls had left their bodies. The return of a person's soul to his or her body might be inferred when a suffering individual returned to consciousness. Certainly the capacity to regain consciousness after a brief lapse would be a favorable sign in the individual's recovery, and presumably, shamans did typically try to assist their patients' return to consciousness as expeditiously as possible. This may explain the shamanistic belief that although brief vacancies of one's soul could be harmless, more prolonged losses of one's soul (i.e., lengthy unconsciousness) could result in death.

It is possible that as shamans gained experience in healing, they were able to generalize the idea of loss of soul to phenomena beyond the simple loss of consciousness induced by trauma or sickness. For example, illness may also result in less obvious departures in a person's normal states of consciousness. An effective healer would need to be observant to such subtle changes, particularly as they related to illness and health. Shamans probably also noted that there are other altered states of consciousness that are adaptive, such as sleep. When early shamans themselves became very sick or accidentally ingested certain drugs, especially hallucinogens, these practitioners may have believed that they had entered a spirit world much like the parallel worlds where they believed their patient's souls had become lost. At other times, shamans may have noticed that trances could be induced through certain repetitive sounds and activities: a drum beating, chanting, dancing, sleep deprivation, or the like.

In taking such a perspective, it is easy to see how shamans may have developed their characteristic approach to healing. Their primary goal was to negotiate in the spirit world or otherwise return their patients' souls to their bodies. What better way to do this than for the healer to go into the "world" of lost consciousness (i.e., the "spirit world") to find and recover these "lost souls"? As absurd as this may sound to modern Westerners, it is a concept that is sacred and treated reverently in shamanism. Furthermore, there must have been some effective cures, or the practice would probably not have continued. But how could such an unscientific approach to treatment have any useful effect? Even today in modern Western medicine, one of the most potent kinds of treatment is often said to be the placebo effect.[137] Because the placebo effect seems to depend on the patient's belief in the practitioner's ability and the patient's own capacity for recovery, it would seem reasonable that in some cases a dramatic ritual might exert a more powerful placebo effect than routine office practices in a modern clinic.[138]

How does one orchestrate such a dramatic ritual? A ritual killing, although gruesome, might provide a particularly emotionally provocative method. To symbolically trade the life of one (e.g., an animal or person of lesser value to the tribe) for the life of the "benefactor" might be enacted as an impressive spectacle wherein the expectancy of an effective cure would be maximized. In some cases where patients got well, it seems reasonable that the recovered patient attributed the "cure" to the shaman's prowess. The patient might even describe his or her descent into the fearful spirit world simply by reporting the imagery and hallucinations experienced while in that altered state of consciousness.[139]

But what would happen if the patient recovered, but was in a state of confusion, disorientation regarding his or her own identity, and unable to recognize family or friends or the immediate environment? Such cases do occur in modern Western hospitals and emergency rooms where an individual is so ill as to be disoriented. In such cases where the shaman was unable to assist in recovering the patient's soul through the other means already described, it may have seemed necessary to give the patient another soul (identity), possibly a helper soul, and presumably rituals evolved in which people could effect this alternative kind of cure. The effects of hypnosis are typically short-lived. Something stronger might be needed to ensure that this helper soul did not leave as well. Some people might be able to keep their helper soul alive by repetitive rituals equivalent to ongoing hypnosis sessions. However, to produce a truly lasting helper spirit, some sort of extremely powerful ritual might be needed. The effects of trauma may be psychologically buried, sometimes emerging as nightmares and flashbacks, but this kind of dissociated state simply does not easily go away of its own accord. It leaves a psychological scar that can usually only be removed after lengthy therapy or some equivalent emotionally healing process. What if the flashback experience could be molded into taking the form of an alternate identity?

It is at this point, the discovery of more powerfully dissociated states produced through traumatizing rituals, that shamanism was likely to have given birth to a new kind of "spiritual" tradition: sorcery and black magic. Such a diabolical craft would have some obvious disadvantages (i.e., painful rituals, the abandonment of normal morality, and so on). On the other hand, these methods of sorcery could probably produce more powerful and lasting experiences of possession.

In many pre-industrial communities, there may have been a desire to have the immediate presence of their gods among them. Such a spectacle would be possible after the gods had suitably taken possession of one of the local villagers. The traumatizing techniques were probably more effective in creating possession by the gods than other less enervating methods. Valeri observes that the "gods who no longer receive human recognition in the form of sacrifices and prayers die" (1985, p. 104). However, in most cultures the traumatic rituals for inducing this kind of possession would have to be secret. In order for the dissociation of identity to work most effectively, the victim (or recipient) of the possession, would be amnestic for the details of the traumatizing rituals. It has been demonstrated that in working with modern dissociative patients, psychological recovery, including a lessening of the effects of dissociation, is facilitated by as the patient recalls experiences blocked by amnesia. Observant sorcerers probably learned that they could also create other kinds of possessing entities including familiars (e.g., the spirit guardians mentioned earlier) and a particular kind of familiar which is a helper to the sorcerer, not the victim, of the ritual. Oke (1989) calls this entity an *iko-awo,* or "spirit slave." The spirit slave is a dissociated identity within the individual who, at some level of awareness, remembers being traumatized by the sorcerer and will do anything the sorcerer commands, often including suicide. The enforcer alters previously discussed would likely be related to the spirit slave.

We propose that this is how black magic works. When a spell is cast, or a curse, or a signal is given, the "spirit slave" is effectively called out.[140] The spirit slave may be commanded to carry out a specific task for the sorcerer. Often this command is expressed merely in the form of a signal. If the dissociation is great enough, this can be done without the victim's conscious awareness.[141] If the sorcerer does not know the victim's programming or if the victim has no such programming, then the sorcerer's efforts may fail altogether. However, if the sorcerer has successfully programmed several individuals in the tribe without their awareness, then the community may have great fear and reverence for him or her, particularly after such "magical powers" may later be demonstrated.

Sorcerers, who themselves had inner dissociated entities, would probably more accurately be considered "witches" because of the anthropological distinction which is sometimes made between sorcery and witchcraft. Anthropologists have responded in large part to E. E. Evans-Pritchard's observation (1931) that the African Azande have different words to denote witchcraft versus sorcery.[142] Although this anthropological distinction is not universally accepted[143], we find it useful to make a differentiation for purposes of clarity. Sorcery may be defined as the use of ritual magic and cues that are designed to cause psychological changes in others by triggering or accessing dissociated mental states in such individuals. Witchcraft may be defined as a more specific form of sorcery in which the practitioner believes that he or she has made a pact with a spiritual entity (actually a dissociated alternate identity within the witch). The witch may then use ritual magic or other cues to cause mental changes both within the witch as well as within the external person who is "bewitched" (i.e., accessed or triggered). Witches purportedly perform black magic with the aid of an evil deity or "demon," but they are also indebted to that malignant entity.[144] In other words, true witches may have undergone some ceremonial procedure whereby one or more dissociated entities have been created in themselves. Such a dissociated entity could view itself as a demon or malevolent god (depending on the procedures by which the entity is created and the beliefs of the cult).[145] Such a practice could be passed down through families, thereby facilitating the secrecy of the procedures.

It is noteworthy that in many cultures, witchcraft is considered to be hereditary.[146] In the United States, the incidence of ritual abuse is also frequently associated with multigenerational practices.[147] Another perplexing characteristic of witchcraft in many cultures is its association with incest and other behaviors typically taboo in most organized societies. This feature of witchcraft also parallels the American reports of ritual abuse. Euro-American Satanism is often described as a kind of possession cult or sorcery religion similar to the preindustrial rituals that I have described. Thus, Satanism may be construed as a particular form of witchcraft wherein the evil deity is, of course, Satan. This is not to confuse Satanism with Wicca, which is not, in an anthropological sense, actually witchcraft, but is, instead, a syncretized form of modern nature worship combined with elements of shamanism and influences of Western ritual magic.[148] (Wicca is discussed further in chapter 12). It should also be noted that the term Satanism might sometimes be incorrectly used for other occult (see Chapter 12) and non-occult beliefs and practices.

With the advent of sorcery and witchcraft, possession cults may have been able to formalize effective but secret rituals for creating possession states. As has been noted elsewhere in this book, some religions have evolved around these practices including African and African-derived sorcery religions and some similar rituals of Australian Aboriginals, Polynesians, Native Americans and Eskimos, some of which would be considered primarily shamanic. Similar cults and religions also emerged in Asia (e.g., Thugees and worshippers of Shakti), the Middle East (e.g., devotees of Baal and Molech), the Mediterranean (e.g., mystery cults), and Northwestern European cultures (e.g., Druids,[149] Berserkers[150], etc.) throughout history.

NOTES

[131] Also see Simmons (1980), *Witchcraft in the Southwest*, for additional information about Native American witchcraft along the United States Rio Grande Valley along with discussion of possible Spanish and European influences on Indian beliefs.

[132] See Burkert (1983), Davies (1981).

[133] Couliano (1991) argues that the distinctions are often blurred in reality.

[134] The term *familiar spirit* is a comparable expression often used in reference to the dissociative experiences of witches and sometimes, mediums and shamans.

[135] The *DSM-IV* lists "possession trance" and a variety of specific "examples" under the diagnosis dissociative disorder, not otherwise specified (American Psychiatric Association, 1994). However, it is not clear that all of the examples listed in the *DSM-IV* are truly indicative of possession trances and in some cases may actually represent somnambulistic possession states. Curiously, Asian Indian possession is also listed under the diagnosis dissociative disorder not otherwise specified.

[136] See Eliade (1964), p. 65.

[137] The placebo effect is a nonspecific treatment response presumably due to the expectation by the patient that he or she will get well.

[138] E. Fuller Torrey (1972) has made an interesting comparison between witch doctors and psychiatrists.

[139] In most shamanistic cures it is the shaman rather than the patient who is drugged or otherwise in an altered state of consciousness.

[140] The "spirit slave" is merely a dissociated part of the victim's mind, comparable to an alter personality. The "spirit slave" was originally created by the witch or sorcerer in a traumatizing ritual most likely during the childhood of the victim, who is also amnestic for the ordeal and for the existence of the spirit slave. Such a process could occur in the same manner in which MPD patients are typically amnestic for the abuse that created their dissociation and initially unaware of their alter personalities

[141] This is why the individuals who were triggered in group therapy described in Chapter 6 were unable to identify the cause of their disorientation.

[142] However, Musopole (1993) indicates that the terminology used by Africans to describe practices associated with magic, witchcraft, and sorcery may not coincide with Western notions, and there may be glaring or subtle misunderstandings as a result.

[143] Anthropologists, historians, and other scholars sometimes distinguish witchcraft from sorcery. According to Keith Thomas (1971), witches are often (falsely) believed to posses psychic powers by which they are able to harm others whereas sorcery simply involves the knowledge and use of spells or incantations. The distinction made by Thomas is essentially a restatement of Evans-Pritchard's (1980) in *Witchcraft, Oracles and Magic Among the Azande*. In an earlier article, Evans-Pritchard (1931) differentiates witchcraft, magic, and sorcery. However, Macfarlane (1970) argues that distinctions such as sorcery versus witchcraft and "white" versus "black" witchcraft should take into consideration both the means and ends of these practices in an effort to understand how they are different. Occult historian Colin Wilson (1971) distinguishes witchcraft and sorcery by characterizing witchcraft as based on a passive approach to using psychic abilities from an enlightened or benign frame of reference. Sorcery, according to Wilson, is more active, systematized, and self-serving. Wilson's distinction would probably be welcomed by Wiccans, white witches who view their craft as essentially an enlightened and humane nature-worshipping religion. See Chapter 12 for more about Wicca. Hoyt (1989) argues that the distinctions made by scholars between witchcraft and sorcery are not particularly meaningful and that the terms are essentially identical.

[144] As per the distinction between witchcraft and sorcery made by Robbins (1981).

[145] For example, Mulhern (1991) cites Gibbal, who compares the relatively peaceful prepossession experiences of some Brazilian possession cults in comparison to a cult in Mali in which the possession experience results in significant physical damage to the person possessed. Gibbal notes that the latter cult commonly subjects girls to the traumatizing practice of infibulation. Is it possible that the potential for violence in a dissociated state is somehow related to the degree or extent of violence perpetrated on the victim during the "training" rituals? Within the field of psychiatry many professionals believe that there is a relationship between self-mutilation and a history of child abuse. In fact, in a study by Walsh & Rosen (1988) the authors found that the presence of child abuse was among the most highly correlated with self-mutilating behavior in comparison with five childhood conditions that they investigated.

[146] See Kluckhohn (1962), Mair (1971), Marwick (1982).

[147] This coincides with the research findings that child abuse in general has a multigenerational quality. See Belsky (1993) for a recent review of the literature and critical analysis.

[148] Larner (1974) argues that what is called modern Western witchcraft does not resemble historical and anthropological accounts of witchcraft.

[149] See Piggott (1987).

---

[150] The Berserkers (from which the term *berserk* derives) were reputedly a cult of Odin worshippers. When they went into battle they supposedly demonstrated superhuman stamina, strength and savagery. The word Berserker may derive from "bear shirts."

Chapter 10

1990: The Year of the Awakening

I noticed seasonal and chronological variability in some of my patients' moods and behaviors. A few of my patients seemed to get worse at certain times of the year. Curiously, some of them seemed to deteriorate in a pattern that coincided with the phases of the moon. At least one of these patients expressed frustration with me because seemed to I ignore her repeated observations that she became more self-destructive when the moon was full. She was right. I had ignored her reports, thinking she was merely telling me about some of her superstitious beliefs. Obviously, the moon does not exert control over people's lives.

When I was in graduate school, I wrote my doctoral dissertation on the subject of astrology (Noblitt, 1978/1979). I conducted an empirical study that showed there was no relationship between selected astrological predictions of personality and the results obtained from objective personality testing. Nevertheless, in reviewing other published research, I found some studies that did show occasional significant relationships "between the moon's phases and state hospital admissions (Osborn, 1968; Weiskott & Tipton, 1975), psychiatric ward admissions (Blackman & Catalina, 1973), criminal offenses (Tasso & Miller, 1976), and homicides (Lieber & Sherin, 1972)" (p. 19). However, a number of studies showed no significant relationship: "in comparing lunar periodicity with patterns of suicide (Lester, Brokopp, & Priebe, 1969), homicides (Porkorny & Jachimczyk, 1974, suicides and homicides (Porkorny, 1964), psychiatric emergencies (Bauer & Hornick, 1968), mental hospital admissions (Porkorny, 1968), telephone calls to a counseling service (Weiskott, 1974), and "acting out" behavior on a psychiatric ward (Shapiro, Streiner, Gray, Williams, & Soble, 1970)" (p. 19).

Although there is no substantial scientific evidence supporting the claims of astrology, it is safe to say that self-fulfilling prophecies can and do occur. Bok (1975) suggests that such self-fulfilling prophecies play a role in validating people's belief in astrology and in keeping them dependent on an ineffective methodology for solving life's problems. Such dependency further fosters a magical style of thinking.

Could some of these patients be responding with distress to the phases of the moon (typically the full moon) because of their own expectations? When this possibility was explored, an altogether different explanation began to present itself. In response to such inquiries, the patients would at first typically say that they had no idea why they had emotionally deteriorated during these particular times. However, alternate identities would sometimes emerge and recall traumatizing experiences that coincided with a full moon. Sometimes these recollections occurred along with flashbacks of horrible rituals.

As their recollections were pieced together, these patients often came to the conclusion that they had undergone horrible experiences in the past that were perpetrated as deviant practices of a cult that had certain celestial or season factors as determinants. Such clinical manifestations are common in traumatized individuals who can be triggered into flashbacks or states of panic or depression by some event or occurrence that reminds them of their original abuse. One such example is called the "anniversary reaction," which occurs when patients relive some traumatic experience on the same date but a later year than when the painful event first occurred.

Many patients report having been abused in cults that allegedly held meetings at the time of the full moon. We have investigated this claim by asking other therapists about their observations among their clients and by researching the literature. The information from both our colleagues and the literature paralleled these patients' reports.[151]

Furthermore, some patients produce calendars listing what they call "cult holidays." Although the calendars presented are very nearly the same, there are often minor individual variations. Some patients explain that because a variety of cults exist, they do not all have the same traditions or goals, nor do they adhere to identical dates and holidays. These holidays appear to correspond to the times that many patients demonstrate diminished functioning. Other mental health professionals confirm that they are discovering in their patients the same things. A review of the relevant literature provides additional confirmation that many occult groups have special designated days for particular ritual observances.

Of the various calendars of cult holidays that I received, the most detailed one was provided by a patient, "Elaine," with a notation that the year of 1990 was "the year of the awakening." When I questioned Elaine about what she had written, she said that she had primarily been abused in a Satanic cult that had taught her that 1990 was the year when all the members of her cult were to "awaken," or start to recognize the presence of their cult alters, in preparation for the arrival of Satan.

I told her that I did not understand her, and asked, "What arrival?" She told me that in her cult, the members had been taught that Satan was supposed to make a presence on earth for the Apocalypse in the manner described in Revelations. However, according to her cult, Satan and his followers would be victorious in the final battle against God and the forces of light. She told me, "1999 is the year of the arrival."

This was news to me. I had heard of apocalyptic religions that prophesied the "final days." Many of these groups predicted dates that later uneventfully passed. However, the change from the year 1999 to the 2000 had many people speculating that the world as we knew it would come to a disastrous end. Some in particular speculated that industry, banking and electrical power services would come to a sudden standstill. This doomsday message received some serious attention because not all computer programs were able to distinguish the year 2000 from 1900 and were said to be not Y2K compliant. This feared computer problem was referred to as the *Y2K bug*. It was also called the *Lucifer bug*. The two of us took the position that the problem was more hype than a genuine threat, and the benign passage to the year 2000 seemed to have proven us right.

On the other hand, we were concerned that some fanatics might seriously entertain such beliefs, which, even if false, could be dangerous. Such a belief might provoke potentially volatile people toward acts of violence. Indiscriminate acts of violence have occasionally occurred because unstable people thought the end of the world was near.[152] Certainly we have seen violent and threatening groups emerge in the final decade of the twentieth century.

In the years preceding 1999, I tried to explore this idea with other individuals who said they were cult survivors. I was told by some that they thought Satan was indeed coming to do battle on earth. Again, some specifically mentioned the year 1999. What could be the origins of such a strange belief? The patients were unable to explain it.

In the course of researching this question, we came upon a series of verses by 16th-century French occultist Michel de Nostredame. Better known as Nostradamus, his quatrains were supposedly predictive of major events in history. According to Wilson, "one of its most disquieting prophesies declares":

> Like the great king of the Angolmois
> The year 1999, seventh month,
> The Great king of terror will descend from the sky,
> At this time, Mars will reign for the good cause. (Wilson, 1971, p. 265)

Apparently this poetry was sometimes interpreted as predicting that an Armageddon would occur in the year 1999. Obviously no such event has transpired.

Elaine further explained that she believed that the reason that so many individuals with DID were "coming out of the woodwork" in recent times was because those who had been abused in such cults were preparing for this "arrival." Although 1990 was supposedly the "year of the awakening," some were apparently awakening even earlier. A number of other patients indicated that they had alternate identities that were preparing for an apocalyptic return and victory for Satan or Lucifer. Some even used the phrase *Armageddon programming* to describe the training that they had allegedly received for this purpose.

Several patients stated their belief that a number of the mass killers of recent times had been trained by such cults, in which these grand acts of evil were looked upon as sacrificial events. By increasing human suffering, there is supposed to be a magical augmentation of the power of evil (or as some would argue, specifically, Satan's power). For other cultists, their goals have been described as establishing a "new world order" along the lines of a totalitarian police state. Some ritual abuse survivors state that they had been trained in military style combat in remote areas of the United States. A number of such individuals have told me that they believe that the bombing of the federal building in Oklahoma City was one such undertaking.

In the course of our investigating patients' reports regarding recent, allegedly cult-inspired murders, it became apparent that a number of convicted killers had actually confessed or made allegations of Satanic involvement or other cultic influence over their criminal acts, including Charles Manson, Henry Lee Lucas, Charles Gervais, and Richard Ramirez. Several books have been written regarding the subject of frequently brutal criminal activity associated with destructive cults (Kahaner, 1988; Mandelsberg, 1991; Newton, 1993; Raschke, 1990; St. Clair, 1987; Terry, 1987).

Cult-related crime is in itself a curiosity. Do the police believe that such crimes are really occurring? In a survey of 125 Chicago police officers by Connie Fletcher, the author concludes that "Satanic cult murders are out there. It is not to say that it is everywhere. But people are doing these things" (1990, p. 90).[153]

In order to understand these allegations better, it seemed necessary to review the early literature within the field of mental health. We hoped that such information would provide some historical background to the current psychiatric reports of ritual abuse. One of the earliest professional references to the subject of ritual abuse, is a comment in Dr. Karl Menninger's (1930) popular book on psychiatry entitled *The Human Mind*, which mentions the Black Mass, Satanism, and devil worship as real events that occurring large cities in Europe and the United States — although in great secrecy. Thirty-five years later there appears an entry in the *Encyclopedia of Aberrations*, edited by Edward Podolsky, M.D., entitled "Devil Worship":

> In the twentieth century in England black magic is practiced and taught in secret schools both at Oxford and at Cambridge. The Black Mass is still celebrated in the drawing rooms of Mayfair and in Chelsea studios under conditions of almost absolute secrecy. There are at least seven active chapters of Satanists, each with an initiated membership of nearly fifty men and women, who meet at stated intervals and have their hidden chapels devoted to the worship of the demon. ("Devil Worship", 1965, p. 186)

The article describes a variety of incidents involving the desecration of churches in Europe and a case in Helsinki where a group of cultists[154] were discovered "meeting in a cemetery and that more than thirty corpses had been disinterred and indescribably mutilated" (p. 186). The article further describes abusive acts towards children that were reportedly perpetrated by other Satanic[155] cultists along with the ubiquitous threat of death for "those who spill the secrets" (p. 187).

It was surprising to find such an unequivocal statement about the existence of modern devil worship at a time when there was practically no other professional literature on that topic. Furthermore, *The Encyclopedia of Aberrations* is a respectable professional publication authored by a prestigious group of psychiatric experts with the foreword written by Alexandra Adler, M.D., the daughter of Alfred Adler.

When Sigmund Freud wrote: "I have an idea shaping in my mind that in the perversions, of which hysteria is the negative, we may have before us a residue of a primaeval sexual cult which, in the Semitic East

(Moloch, Astarte), was once, perhaps still is, a religion. . . . I dream, therefore, of a primaeval Devil religion whose rites are carried on secretly, and I understand the severe therapy of the witches' judges" (1966b, p. 243), he seemed to be expressing a view that malignant cult practices did exist and that somehow there was a connection between such practices and his patient's symptoms. In *The Assault on Truth*, Jeffrey Masson argues that Freud abandoned one of his major theories after a patient, Emma Eckstein, described to him mental images in which the Devil "sticks pins into her finger and puts a piece of candy on each drop of blood" (1992, p. 103).

The theory Freud dismissed was his "seduction theory," which postulated that hysterical neuroses were caused by the trauma of sexual abuse in childhood. According to Masson, Freud's decision to abandon his seduction theory occurred after he wrote a letter to his friend and colleague Wilhelm Fliess dated January 17, 1897:

> What would you say, by the way, if I told you that my brand-new theory of the early etiology of hysteria was already well known and had been published a hundred times over, though several centuries ago? . . . But why did the devil who took possession of the poor things invariably abuse them sexually and in a loathsome manner? Why are their confessions under torture so like the communications made by my patients in psychological treatment? (Masson, 1992, p. 104).[156]

Were some of Freud's patients survivors of ritual abuse? Was this such a terrifying possibility that Freud chose to ignore his patients' reports that they had been sexually abused in childhood? Was this what motivated Freud to create a new theory wherein he argued that children tend to create fantasies of sexual traumas?[157]

Masson does not address the possibility that ritual abuse occurred among Freud's patients. Instead, Masson argues that the memories of diabolical experiences were screen memories for the actual sexual abuse that was usually perpetrated by the child's father. However, many of my patients describe ceremonies in which they were sexually abused by someone costumed as Satan or some other demonic entity in the manner described by Freud's patient Emma Eckstein.

The mental image of being stuck with pins and having candy placed on the drops of blood certainly paints a bizarre picture for any modern, civilized person, but similar abuses are reported by individuals who say they have been ritually traumatized. The activity is often explained as programming in a ceremonial cult. Pins stuck into a child in an occult ritual are likely to cause the child to dissociate, to go into a trance.

Candy placed on the child's wounds might be used to bring out a newly created alter identity, to define particular characteristics of that alter being programmed, or to direct the manner by which accessing that alter may occur. Later, the newly created alternate can be accessed or brought out by a cult member who simply provides the particular relevant signals (which could include the kind of candy used in the ritual and/or stimulation of that part of the body where the pins were inserted). Such a process would not have any basis in supernatural events or phenomena but would simply be a matter of classical conditioning with dissociated trauma responses.

In another letter to Fliess, dated January 24, 1897, Freud notes the following: "Imagine, I obtained a scene about the circumcision of a girl. The cutting of a piece of the labia minora (which is still shorter today), sucking up the blood, following which the child was given a piece of the skin to eat" (Masson, 1992, p. 105). Masson says that Freud is still referring to the same patient, Emma Eckstein. The scenes reported by Emma Eckstein are consistent with the accounts of patients describing ritual abuse in contemporary America. Such rituals increase the individual's likelihood of experiencing an altered state of consciousness, dissociating into fragmented identities, and responding with obedience to the cult leaders.

Pamela Hudson also makes the observation that Emma Eckstein may be a ritual abuse survivor. Hudson writes:

> One hopes that by 1996, one hundred years after Freud's initial paper on Hysteria, we shall have adopted the more logical view that previously repressed rape memories are, in the words of one ritually abused child, "no fun" to recall. I submit that it is "no fun" to fantasize ritual abuse and that 3 or 4 year olds could not possibly invent identical reports across the United States, Canada, and Europe. (1991, p. 65)

In order to understand these contemporary patients' allegations of ritual abuse, it is also necessary to have some knowledge of occult lore and traditions. Such information was not part of the university curricula that either of us had studied. We found that we had a lot more reading ahead of us.

NOTES

[151] Also see Smith (1993), p. 60.

[152] For example, regarding the Branch Davidians, the Solar Temple Lodge or Aum Supreme Truth. Televised reports of the Japanese cult, Aum Supreme Truth indicate that

this cult had an Armageddon date of 1997 and like the cult survivors that I have talked with in the U.S., they planned a military style revolution with genocide of those who were not useful to them.

[153] Because Fletcher did not provide any quantitative data we did not discuss this in Chapter 6 that addresses empirical research.

[154] I used the expression "cultists" here, but the original author used the term "Satanists" at this point in the article. I wanted to make the point that not all cultists, nor all devil worshippers, are necessarily Satanic. Some cult survivors describe "organizations" in which apparently demonic rituals transpire but in which no particular reverence or regard for Satan is shown (e.g., in some Luciferian-inspired fraternal organizations and secret societies).

[155] See the previous note.

[156] Masson's quotation of Freud leaves out a sentence. It is as follows: "Do you remember how I always said that the medieval theory of possession, held by the ecclesiastical courts, was identical with our theory of a foreign body and a splitting of consciousness?" (Freud, 1966a, p. 242).

[157] Ritual abuse survivors frequently say that in their cults they were told that if they attempted to tell any outsiders about their abuse that none would believe them and that instead of helping them others would blame them for the outcry possibly putting the complainant in jail or a psychiatric hospital. See Smith (1993).

Chapter 11

Investigating Western Occultism

Who can say for certain where and how occult beliefs and practices began? Some authors speculate that such practices originated long ago in prehistoric times among the first shamans and folk healers (Wilson, 1971). Lissner (1961) argues that shamans were originally monotheistic but later regressed into polytheism and a belief in magic, but it is not clear that this notion is prevalent among scholars in this field.

The term *occult* may be unclear to some readers. For the purpose of this book, *occult*, is defined to mean "relating to hidden, mystical or purportedly magical phenomena in which secrecy and often, ritual, is reportedly an important feature" (Noblitt, 1993a).

So where did it begin? The previously cited authors have theorized that occultism began with the early folk healers, prehistoric and ancient people who utilized magical beliefs and practices in their work. Although such thinking is speculative, it is consistent with archeological findings that lend evidence to the existence of magical beliefs among the prehistoric and ancient peoples of the world.

In ancient times, ritual magic, witchcraft, and sorcery were ubiquitous facets of everyday life. Many ancient sources describe these practices as commonplace within diverse cultures. Shamanism, possession cults, sorcery, and witchcraft, having all taken place in a variety of pre-industrial cultures, have been discussed in previous chapters.

Although the origins of Western occultism are obscure, the records of ancient religions often depict the prevalent beliefs in magical and secret practices. However, occult themes were particularly characteristic

among certain ancient religions.   Such were the mystery cults of the
Mediterranean and Middle East.

Walter Burkert's *Ancient Mystery Cults* (1987) compares five of
these cults associated with Eleusis, Dionysus, Meter, Isis, and Mithras.
Burkert emphasizes that these mystery religions were not *religions* in the
sense of modern monotheistic faiths where there are mutually exclusive
traditions of worship.   The mystery cults were each merely one part of
the ancient panoply of beliefs and rituals available in the pagan world.
According to Michael Howard:

> The Mystery cults used elaborate initiation ceremonies, arcane
> symbolism and theatrical rituals to provide the initiate with the
> revelation of the spiritual reality hidden behind the illusion of
> the material world.   During initiation, the neophyte was placed
> in a trance and experienced contact with the gods through a
> symbolic journey to the Underworld.   Initiates symbolically died
> and were reborn as perfected souls. (1989, pp. 21–22)

Howard's account is interesting, particularly because of the obvious
similarities between the mystery cults and shamanism, possession cults,
sorcery, and witchcraft.   The importance of trance states, a ceremonial
"journey," and rituals of death and rebirth, are repeated themes.
Furthermore, these are phenomena described by modern survivors in the
context of their own reported experiences of ritual abuse.

Were the mystery cults abusive?   This is difficult to determine with
great certainty, primarily because of the imposed secrecy.   According to
the ancient Roman historian Livy (1976) the mystery cult of Bacchus
was investigated by the Roman Senate.   It was determined that these
Bacchic rites included sexual transgressions and murder as well as
promoting a variety of other criminal acts:

> all sorts of corruption began to be practiced.   .   .   .   The
> corruption was not confined to one kind of evil, the promiscuous
> violation of free men and of women; the cult was also a source
> of supply of false witnesses, forged documents and wills, and
> perjured evidence, dealing also in poisons and in wholesale
> murders among the devotees, and sometimes ensuring that not
> even the bodies were found for burial. Many such outrages were
> committed by craft, and even more by violence; and the violence
> was concealed because no cries for help could be heard against
> the shriekings, the banging of drums and the clashing of cymbals
> in the scene of debauchery and bloodshed. (1976, p. 402)[158]

But did these cultists also experience possession states? In Plato's dialogue, *Ion,* he makes a passing reference to the female followers of Dionysus while making a more general commentary about great poets and their inspiration. He writes that the inspiration of such poets is like "the Bacchant women, possessed and out of their senses, [who] draw milk and honey out of the rivers" (Warmington & Rouse, 1956, p. 18). Plato's statement would seem to indicate that he believed that these cultists were possessed or could be possessed, but it is not clear whether his opinion was based on fact or rumor. However, Burkert states that "Plutarch declares himself convinced that ghosts, daimones, take part in the mystery celebrations" (1987, p. 113) and, further, that the madness associated with these ceremonies to some ancients represented possession by the god.[159]

The cult of Mithras is another that has attracted the attention of scholars. Unfortunately, and partly because of its secrecy, we have little information about it. In fact, there is some controversy over whether it was of Roman (e.g., Ulansey, 1989) or Iranian (e.g., Cumont, 1956) derivation.   However, Benjamin Walker writes about a Mithraic initiation ceremony:

> There followed a few days abstinence from food and sexual relations, then a ceremonial ablution, after which the candidate's hands were bound behind his back and he was laid on the ground as if dead. After certain solemn rites his right hand was grasped by the hierophant and he was raised up.   Then followed the baptism of blood. He was made to stand naked in a pit covered with a grating, and over this an animal as sacrificed, so that its blood flowed over him.   Whatever the animal was, it was regarded as a surrogate of the bull of Mithras. Prudentius (d. AD 390), a Christian poet writing in Latin, gives a vivid description of this rite, of which he may have had a personal recollection. 'Through the open grating the bloody dew flows into the pit; the neophyte receives the falling drops on his head and body, he leans back so that his cheeks, lips and nostrils are wetted; he pours the liquid over his eyes and does not even spare his mouth, for he moistens his tongue with blood and sips it eagerly.' Symbolically the initiate has been raised from the dead and washed in the vitalizing blood of the bull, and is regarded as 'born again into eternity.' He is received into the community of initiates as a brother, and is allowed to participate in the sacramental meal of bread and wine which establishes his status as one of the elect. (1989a, p. 155)

Several authors note a strong resemblance between the mystery cults and the lodges and fraternal organizations that appeared later in Europe.[160] Some authors even argue that the Freemasons and other similar organizations have patterned themselves partly after these traditions.

The rise of Gnosticism was another significant movement in the overall evolution of Western occultism.[161] Recent literature has also attributed a major role to Gnosticism in the history of Satanism and ritual abuse.[162] Scholarly accounts of the history of the devil[163], Satan[164], Lucifer[165], witchcraft[166], and secret societies[167] have also appeared in which Gnosticism is mentioned as a significant related historical movement.

The term *Gnosticism* is sometimes used in slightly different ways by different authors. In its narrowest sense, the term refers to a variety of sects which appeared beginning in the first century, C.E., Roman Empire. These congregations subscribed to beliefs that were declared to be heretical by the established Christian church. Some attribute the founding of Christian Gnosticism to Simon Magus, who is mentioned in Acts 8: 9–24.[168] The early Gnostics and their later derivative sects typically considered themselves to be the *true* Christians in opposition to what they viewed as the inferior, if not downright evil, organized churches of Rome and, later, Constantinople.[169] However, in its broader usage, Gnosticism also refers to other parallel and related religious movements including: (a) the Persian-derived Manicheanism and post-Manichean dualisms as espoused by the Bogomils of Southeastern Europe and the Cathari of Southern France and Italy, (b) pagan Gnosticism such as Hermeticism, and (c) modern variants of Gnosticism, some of which are active in present-day Europe and America.

These various sects differed in some respects but tended to have several features in common. Most were based on a dualistic concept of good and evil as eternal and sometimes sacred spiritual forces. This dualism was more extreme than the qualified dualism of Christianity in which good and evil have been construed as existing in opposition to one another, but where the good is considered to be infinitely more powerful and is predicted to ultimately prevail. Judaism, in contrast, has presented a more monistic position on this question whereby good and evil are usually both subsumed as normal features of God's creation, where Satan is a relatively unimportant figure and not necessarily God's adversary.[170]

One of the prominent Gnostic themes was that the creator of the universe, sometimes called the Demiurge, was an inept, or overtly evil, spiritual being.[171] The Demiurge arrogantly and falsely believed himself to be the god who ruled heaven and earth but was actually a spiritual entity of lower rank in comparison with the true, ultimate god[172] of the Gnostics. The human spirit was viewed as a spark of this ultimate deity trapped within the inferior and evil material body created by the Demiurge.[173]   Many Gnostics equated the Demiurge with the God of Israel, whom Christians call God, the Father.   Conversely, the serpent mentioned in Genesis (and considered by Christians to be Satan) was viewed by many Gnostics as a benevolent and wise being who had come into the world to help humanity learn the desperately needed knowledge of good and evil.   In the Gnostic treatise *The Testimony of Truth* the author quotes from Genesis:

> It is written in the Law concerning this, when God gave a command to Adam, "From every [tree] you may eat, [but] from the tree which is in the midst of Paradise do not eat, for on the day that you eat from it you will surely die." But the serpent was wiser than all the animals that were in Paradise, and he persuaded Eve, saying, "On the day when you eat from the tree which is in the midst of Paradise the eyes of your mind will be opened." (Robinson, 1988, p. 454)

The Gnostics observed that Adam and Eve did not die the day they ate the forbidden fruit, but that their eyes were opened.   Thus, they concluded that the serpent was correct and the God of creation was in error or had been lying.[174]   The author of *The Testimony of Truth* goes on to write:

> And he cursed the serpent, and called him "devil." And he said, "Behold, Adam has become like one of us, knowing evil and good." Then he said, "Let us cast him out of Paradise lest he take from the tree of life and eat and live for ever." But what sort is this God?   First [he] maliciously refused Adam from eating of the tree of knowledge. And secondly he said, "Adam, where are you?"   God does not have foreknowledge; (otherwise), would he not know from the beginning? .   .   . Surely he has shown himself to be a malicious grudger.[175]

Thus, one can plainly see that some Gnostics had essentially reversed what orthodox (or "straight-thinking") Christians regarded as the holiest of beings with the one who was regarded as most evil.   In some instances, from a Gnostic point of view, Christianity was Satanism, and from a Christian point of view, Gnosticism was Satanism.   However, many Gnostics did consider themselves to be Christian, and although they had adverse opinions about God the Father, they were usually favorably predisposed toward Jesus, whom they considered to be (along with the serpent) a savior figure who had come to earth to convey knowledge.

Gnosticism also differed from orthodox Christianity on the subject of spiritual salvation. The Gnostics believed that humanity was in its deplorable spiritual condition because of a lack of knowledge (i.e., *gnosis*).[176] They did not consider Adam and Eve in the Genesis story to be sinful as a result of their eating the fruit of the tree of knowledge of good and evil. The Gnostic view was that the Demiurge unfairly wanted people to remain ignorant in order to control and dominate them. With the appropriate knowledge, the Gnostics argued, an individual could reunite with the ultimate god by becoming the god. This knowledge was not readily available to all because (1) it was a kind of mystical knowledge or "enlightenment" and (2) much of it was secret.[177] Additionally, the Gnostics held that this enlightenment and the process of becoming the deity were accomplished by magical operations or ritual magic, sometimes called theurgy, or high magic.

Some Gnostics alleged that they possessed secret knowledge from Jesus that had been passed down to specially chosen individuals citing Mark, 4:11, "To you has been given the secret of the kingdom of God, but for those outside everything is in parables; so that they may indeed see but not perceive, and may indeed hear but not understand; lest they should turn again, and be forgiven."[178] The secrecy of some Gnostics included a ritual handshake[179] that is similar (or identical) to a modern Masonic grip and a handshake to which some modern survivors of ritual abuse often respond with an altered state of consciousness, frequently without awareness of why they are doing so.

Ritualism was another source of contention between orthodox Christians and Gnostics. The Gnostic *Gospel of Phillip* states: "God is a man eater. For this reason men are [sacrificed] to him" (Robinson, 1988, p. 147). Allegations were made that some Gnostics performed religious ceremonies that involved ritual cannibalism and communal sex acts. Some of these activities would clearly be viewed as ritual abuse. Among the more believable reports of bizarre Gnostic ritual practices are the accounts of Epiphanius, a monk who allegedly witnessed orgiastic rituals among a Gnostic group that he called the Phibionites.[180] However, a number of authors have commented that the criticisms of Gnosticism may have been religious propaganda intended to defame the Gnostic belief system.

Nevertheless, it is evident that there are historians[181] and modern occultists who consider at least some of the accusations of immoral Gnostic practices to be true.[182] In his book *The Gnostics*, Jacques Lacarriere (1991) argues that the Gnostic violations of sexual and other conventions betrays a "Luciferian" (p. 70) conviction of the believer's indestructibility and incorruptibility.

Lucifer literally means "the bringer of light." Although Christians traditionally define Lucifer as Satan before his fall,[183] some Gnostics associated the notion of Lucifer with Prometheus, the Titan of Greek mythology who was said to have given fire to mankind in defiance of the will of the Olympian gods.[184] Spence (1993, p. 123), argues that pure Satanists have been historically rare but suggests that there is more known about the cult of Lucifer.

Western occultism was also influenced by Jewish occult lore, notably the Kabbalah, and also alchemy. The development of the Kabbalah[185] was another extension of ideas similar to Gnosticism, but within the context of Jewish mysticism.[186] The lore of the Kabbalah is found in a variety of writings, the most important, being the *Zohar* and *Sefer Yetsirah*. These texts provide a secret mystical interpretation of traditional Jewish scriptures and relate the concept of an absolute and unknowable deity identified as En-Soph[187]. From En-Soph there were ten emanations or *Sephiroth*, which are the ten "spheres" representing aspects of the universe and essential characteristics of humanity (both reflecting the image of God). The ten Sephiroth have been depicted as part of a mystical Tree of Life that occultists often use to conceptualize their spiritual and mystical journey to know God, the self, and to discover the God within the self. Such "journeys" may involve altered states of consciousness resembling the trance journeys of shamans.[188] According to Bakan (1965), Freud himself was influenced by the Kabbalah.[189]

Alchemists were known for their search for the philosopher's stone, which supposedly could change other metals into gold, but some occultists interpreted this as a metaphor representing the spiritual processes involved in an individual being transformed into a higher spiritual being. The alchemists' search for the elixir of life and fountain of youth also may have shown their desire to escape from the normal limitations of mortal existence something that Gnostics generally deplored. Some Gnostic traditions had promised that the enlightened individuals could advance spiritually to a higher or immortal plane.

Additionally, alchemists had interest in creating homunculi[190], or artificially created people-like entities. *The Sorcerer's Handbook* (Baskin, 1974) explains that a "golem" (p. 285) is an example of a homunculus. Within the traditions of the Kabbalah and Jewish mysticism, a golem referred to an automaton, or living being (either with or without a physical body), that could be created by the magician. One might consider the possibility that alchemists and Kabbalists were actually referring to dissociated states of mind, which could, of course, be created by ritual acts. Knapp (1977) argues that golems were created in the phenomenal or experiential world of these occult practitioners while in an altered state of consciousness.

Thus, alchemists may have known how to create alter identities. Through the experience of having alternate identities, one might be able to achieve one of the alchemist's other dreams, to feel young and childlike even in old age. Such an experience could certainly occur when child alters take control of the individual. One could also produce the illusion of immortality by creating what appeared to be immortal alter personalities whose identities were kept relatively intact as they were handed down generationally. Some ritual abuse survivors report that their cults and families believed in this notion. They believed that they had achieved immortality by inserting their identity into others who would live on after them and would pass on their identities through successive generations. This concept may also be related to the ancestor worshipping beliefs often been observed in a variety of pre-industrial cultures.

Another of the significant developments in the history of Western occultism was seen in the witch persecutions that were rampant from the 14th through 16th centuries. Like the oppression of the Gnostics and other "heretics," this was a particularly vicious movement. Confessions were often, although not always extorted by torture. The victims were often vulnerable, including children and elderly women. Ironically, these crimes against humanity were perpetrated with the approval of the established churches of Europe, both Catholic and Protestant. Given the irrational nature of the accusations and the unreliable methods of obtaining evidence (e.g., torture), some have questioned whether any witchcraft had actually occurred in Europe during that time.

Norman Cohn (1975), Hans Sebald (1995), and Hugh Trevor-Roper (1968) argue that such lore was merely fabricated by medieval churchmen who substantiated their presuppositions by torturing the accused until confessions were forthcoming. Hans Sebald (1995) goes one step further and contends that many of the current allegations of sexual abuse and ritual abuse made by children represent a modern kind of inquisition and witch hunt. On the other hand, Margaret Murray (1921, 1933) states that medieval (and modern) witchcraft represented the continuation of an ancient Western European pagan cult which existed in secrecy since the conquest of Europe by Christianity.[191]

An analytical approach to this debate is offered by Jeffrey Burton Russell (1972), who reduces the question of the actual existence medieval witchcraft into alternative hypotheses:

Within the framework of historical interpretations of European witchcraft, there are at least eight degrees of skepticism (in descending order). (1) Virtually no one in the Middle Ages believed in witchcraft, which was a vicious fraud perpetrated by the Inquisitors and their attendant theologians, who provoked witch scares in order to increase their own power and wealth. (2) Many people (including Inquisitors and theologians) were deluded by the superstitious atmosphere of the Middle Ages into believing that others were witches, but no one believed that he himself was a witch. (3) At least some people were deluded into believing themselves witches. (4) Some of what these witches believed and practiced was real, deriving from old pagan cults, folklore, sorcery, and heresy. (5) Witch beliefs and practices as described by the sources (mainly trial records) did exist to a substantial degree. Witches did worship the Devil; they did believe and practice what was attributed to them, though these beliefs and practices were constantly evolving. (6) A formal witch cult existed virtually unchanged from ancient times (the argument of Margaret Murray and the modern occultists). (7) Weird phenomena, such as flying and shape shifting, are themselves real. (8) The weird phenomena are not only real, but also supernatural, and proof that the Devil is not only real, but also supernatural, and proof that the Devil and his minions live. (pp. 20–21)

Russell suggests that all of the above options are possible, but that the historian has no right to affirm or to deny the last because it deals with supernatural rather than empirical phenomena. However, he argues that the weight of history supports the idea that the truth lies somewhere within the range of options three to five.

It has been noted that there was a resurgence in occultism in the 19th century (Webb, 1974). Helena Blavatsky was one of the first well known occultists of this period. She was born Helena Hahn in 1931 at Ekaterinoslav in the Ukraine. She married at a young age and shortly thereafter left her husband. Subsequently, she lived as an eccentric, eventually becoming a well known spirit medium and co-founder of the Theosophical Society with Henry Olcott. She was also the author of *Isis Unveiled*, *The Secret Doctrine* and *The Key to Theosophy* as well as being the editor of a periodical entitled *Lucifer*.[192] In Blavatsky's *The Secret Doctrine*, she writes, "*Lucifer* is divine and terrestrial light, the 'Holy Ghost' and 'Satan,' at one and the same time" (1888/1988, p. 513). By her own account, Blavatsky's Theosophy was heavily influenced by Gnosticism and the Kaballah (Blavatsky, 1877/1988, 1888/1988).

Another of the prominent personalities of the 19th century allegedly associated with the cult of Lucifer was General Albert Pike, the Grand Commander, Sovereign Pontiff of Scottish Rite Freemasonry in the Southern and Western United States from 1859 to 1891. His purported Luciferian beliefs were stated in Masonic instructions attributed to him, but no original copy exists. The following is from Pike's alleged statement:

> That which we must say to the crowd is — we worship a God, but it is the God that one adores without superstition. To you, Sovereign Grand Inspectors General, we say this, that you may repeat it to the Brethren of the 32nd, 31st, and 30th degrees — The Masonic Religion should be, by all of us initiates to the high degrees, maintained in the purity of the Luciferian Doctrine. If Lucifer were not God would Adonay (the God of the Christians) whose deeds prove his cruelty, perfidy and hatred of man, barbarism and repulsion for science, would Adonay and his priests, calumniate him?
>
> Yes, Lucifer is God, and unfortunately Adonay is also God. For the eternal law is that there is no light without shade, no beauty without ugliness, no white without black, for the absolute can only exist as two gods: darkness being necessary for light to serve as its foil as the pedestal is necessary to the statue and the brake to the locomotive. Thus the doctrine of Satanism is a heresy; and the true and pure philosophical religion is the belief in Lucifer, the equal of Adonay; but Lucifer, God of Light and God of Good is struggling for humanity against Adonay, the God of Darkness and Evil (Short, 1989, p. 94)[193]

The question of Masonic involvement in dark elements of occultism has been a long-standing controversy. Masons sometimes have argued that they are unfairly attacked by narrow-minded, ill-informed individuals. On the other hand, critics continue to accuse them of blatant acts of impropriety and abuse.[194] In her book *Ritual Abuse* Margaret Smith (1993) describes allegations of cult abuse associated with Masonry. In a conversation, Margaret Smith told us that she had been abused in a cult where the members would sometimes express amusement at what they considered to be the stupidity of those who would label their activities as *Satanic*. From their point of view, they were Luciferian. They viewed Satan primarily as a Judeo-Christian myth or metaphor.

Other patients alleging histories of ritualized abuse have sometimes explained the religious views of their Luciferian cults where the deity (who is sometimes labeled Lucifer) is conceptualized not as exclusively good or evil, but as an entity who is capable of both good and evil. Again, these individuals sometimes consider Satan to be a myth or metaphor, but one that must be "experienced" through abusive rituals to create sufficient suffering to achieve "enlightenment." In order to approach the ultimate god of good and evil, one must encounter and engage in both profound evil and good, according to some of these cultists. Some survivors of these cults also report that they were encouraged to attend church and develop a part of their personality that is on "the light side[195]." The concept of a "light" versus a "dark side," which is essential to Gnostic thinking, is frequently expressed in these terms in Gnostic writings as well. It is also curious that the same terminology is commonly used by survivors to describe their "inner," or phenomenological, world. Smith and many survivors with whom we have consulted have described elements of Gnostic thinking in this kind of cultism. Many patients making such allegations have explicitly reported abuse where Masonic regalia, ceremonies, or members were present.

It is not our intention to single out Masonic organizations as being responsible for acts of ritual violence. Although this notion may be true, it is also possible that such perpetrators operate within Freemasonry without the knowledge or consent of the majority of its membership, as they reportedly do within conventional religious and political organizations. It is also possible that some cultists imitate Masonic rituals during their abusive ceremonies. Nevertheless, there are some things about the organization as a whole that are very perplexing. For example, the symbol for the Order of the Eastern Star, the woman's Masonic organization, is an inverted pentagram, a design commonly used to symbolize evil. There are different interpretations of the meaning of this symbol. However, because the star is upside down, some say that it signifies Lucifer described in the book of Isiah (14:12) as "the bright morning star" that fell from heaven. The word *Lucifer* entered the bible text when Jerome translated the bible into Latin around the year 383. *Lucifer* is the Latin word for the morning star.[196] Lucifer, the morning star, is the only celestial body that only appears in the Eastern sky, hence it could also be called the Eastern Star.

It is also clear that Masonry has served to preserve and promote elements of Gnostic thinking, along with other occult traditions such as the Kaballah and the ancient mystery cults. According to Pike, Freemasonry was established by Jacques de Molay, the last Grand Master of the Knights Templar, after which he was burned alive for heresy and sorcery outside Paris (1871/1960, p. 820).[197] Pike wrote that the Knights Templar pretended to be Christians who were loyal to the Church of Rome but, in actuality, their agenda was to keep and transmit the secret knowledge of a sect of middle eastern Gnostics that Pike calls "Johannites" (pp. 815–824).

It has been further alleged that other cult-like organizations have developed in tandem with or under the influence of Freemasonry and Western occultism. Two of the earlier such groups were the Hell Fire Club and the Order of the Illuminati, both reputedly founded by Masons. There actually were several Hell Fire Clubs, but the best known was probably the one founded in England by Sir Francis Dashwood, who also was a member of a neo-Druid brotherhood.[198] Dashwood's particular Hell Fire Club was more accurately called the Friars of St. Francis of Wycombe, and when he later purchased Medmenham (pronounced Med'nem) Abbey, they also became known as the Friars of Medmenham. Curiously, when Sir Francis was renovating the abbey, he had the workmen inscribe, "Do what you will" in Renaissance French over one of the doorways. Over a hundred years later this phrase, expressed in slightly different language, would become the motto for the most well known occult figure of modern times, Aleister Crowley.

The Friars of St. Francis were known to provide their membership with orgies and sometimes performed Black Masses and other similar ceremonial acts. Nevertheless, some authors have interpreted their unorthodox behaviors as not genuinely Satanic, but more as a kind of organized libertinism.[199] English aristocrats and high government officials frequented the club. For example, Sir Francis was himself a personal friend and adviser to King George III and a longtime member of Parliament who later became chancellor of the exchequer. Benjamin Franklin, who was a high-ranking Mason in the American colonies, visited the Hell Fire Club in 1758 while he was in England meeting with representatives the English government on behalf of the American colonies.

The Order of the Illuminati was not the first organization to use the Latin word *Illuminati* ("the enlightened ones") to describe their brotherhood. However, the most well known group using the name Illuminati was the secret society established by Adam Weishaupt in 1776, and first known as the Order of the Perfectibilists. It has been alleged that Weishaupt created the Order of the Illuminati for the purpose of infiltrating Masonic lodges in order to exert political influence over issues of international politics.[200] Evangelist Mike Warnke (1972) wrote about his experience in what he identified as a Satanic cult in which the higher levels of the cult were reportedly Illuminati.[201] Many of my patients have made reference to Illuminati as destructive cultists, either during our therapy sessions or in their journal notes or drawings. Raschke (1990), among others, has described historic accounts of their alleged devil worship. It would be difficult to prove that the Order of the Illuminati continues to exist given that it is supposedly a secret organization. Nevertheless, occult groups that do currently exist sometimes attest to continuing the traditions of the Illuminati.[202] Patients also sometimes report that they were abused using themes and terminology associated with this reputed brotherhood.

According to Vankin (1992), the origins of the Ku Klux Klan can be traced to a group that included Masons and "incorporated Masonic-style initiation rites, symbols and argot words" (p. 281). Bob Larson (1989) states that a prevalent KKK view is that Satan fathered Cain through Eve and from Cain the Jewish people supposedly emerged.[203] The idea that Eve was impregnated by Satan to produce Cain is a Gnostic myth.[204] Furthermore, similar to the KKK, many Gnostic groups were noted for their anti-Semitism, which may have been due, in part, to their belief that the Jewish God of creation was the devil, or at least an evil spiritual entity. Many survivors of ritual abuse allege traumatic experiences associated with what they believe to be KKK activities, and many of these individuals describe the KKK as a cult.

Other Masonic and Gnostic influenced occult organizations emerged in the 19th and 20th centuries, including the Hermetic[205] Order of the Golden Dawn and the Ordo Templi Orientis (O.T.O.). A well known figure associated with both of these organizations was Aleister Crowley. One of the best known biographical works on Aleister Crowley is Symonds and Grant's *The Confessions of Aleister Crowley* (1979). On the cover of this book, he is described as "a saint of the Gnostic church." He was also reputedly a high-ranking Mason and one who called himself the Great Beast, 666, of Revelations. There has been some disagreement regarding whether or not Crowley was a Satanist.[206] One might argue that he was, more precisely, a dualist, a modern Gnostic of the libertine type and a practitioner of ritual magic. It could be easily argued that not all ritual magic is intended to be malevolent. Furthermore, not all black magic is Satanic. For example, in the West African juju cult described by Oke (1989), there is clearly a practice of ritual abuse with altered states of consciousness but no particular belief in Satan. Not all ritual abuse is Satanic, although some Gnostic occult groups probably come close to what many Western people would call *Satanic*. However, in some cases it would be more accurate to label them Luciferian, neo-Gnostic, or dualistic. There may also be cults that incorporate rituals involving or mentioning Satan along with other spiritual entities and concepts but in which Satan is not considered the focus of their beliefs or energies.   With that being said, Crowley's published opinions and acts do show a fascination with dark occultism.

Aleister Crowley devised a sexualized ritual, the Gnostic Mass[207] that became the *central* ceremony for the O.T.O.   He practiced sex magic, that is, sexual rituals intended to cause altered states of consciousness, and he admitted to engaging in ritual human sacrifice.[208] According to Ashe (1974, p. 235), Crowley was noted for "hypnotic powers," which he freely used in sexual seduction.   Ritual abuse survivors often describe similar reactions to their perpetrators, a process that they sometimes call "accessing."   Ashe also observed that Crowley was "like three or four different men" (p. 235).   Crowley reputedly had a history of child abuse.[209]   Crowley himself reported altered states of consciousness in which he confronted other imaginary, dissociative, or spiritual entities.   Did Crowley have a dissociative disorder?   Crowley advocated self-punishment by cutting oneself with a razor blade[210]. Therapists who work with ritual abuse survivors commonly note that self-injury through this kind of cutting is one of the most common characteristics of this disorder.

Crowley joined the Golden Dawn on November 18, 1898.   By the spring of 1900 he had been expelled.   In 1901 there was a public scandal involving the conviction of Theo Horos (also known as Frank Jackson) and his wife, for the rape of a 16-year-old-girl.   The judge concluded that the couple had used Golden Dawn rituals in the sexual exploitation of minors.[211]   According to Kaczynski (1993), other members of the Golden Dawn were practicing sexual rituals in its inner order.

The Golden Dawn demonstrated sufficient credibility in the occult community to attract membership by such a luminary as the Irish poet W. B. Yeats.   However, the organization was plagued with other problems.   The Golden Dawn was created in response to the alleged discovery of mysterious German documents attesting to the organization's ancient, occult heritage transmitted to its British founders. These papers were translated by one of its founding members, Dr. W. W. Westcott, a Mason.   Later it was thought that the documents were probably forged, but forgery was a dubious explanation because such an act was out of character for Dr. Westcott.   In an effort to clarify this question, author Ellic Howe presented samples of Dr. Westcott's writing to a handwriting expert who made the observation that Dr. Westcott probably had MPD because of his markedly divergent writing styles. Gerald Suster, a Golden Dawn advocate (1987, p. 110–171) took issue with the MPD interpretation, noting the very inconsistent handwriting styles of another leading occultist and Golden Dawn Adept Israel Regardie, who had never been diagnosed with MPD nor any other psychiatric disorder. Of course, an alternate interpretation is that both men may have had dissociative disorders caused by their cultic experiences and that the accurate diagnoses are not consistently being made because few mental health professionals know how to appropriately diagnose these disorders.

Karl Kellner and Theodore Reuss, both high-ranking Masons founded the Ordo Templi Orientis. In 1912, the O.T.O. published the following:

> Our Order possesses the KEY which opens up all Masonic and Hermetic secrets, namely, the teaching of sexual magic, and this teaching explains, without exception, all the secrets of Nature, all the symbolism of Freemasonry and all systems of religion.[212]

Frater U∴ D∴ (1991) writes about the practice of sex magic from the occultist's point of view. He observes that altered states of consciousness are sought by the sex magician through erotic rituals to generate what he calls "magical powers" (p. 11). In this process one experiences what he calls "Gnostic trances" (p. 11). This author encourages the ritualistic breaking of sexual taboos emphasizing that "by employing bizarre, unusual practices, we access those altered states of awareness which provide the key to magical power" (p. 17).

In 1912 Crowley was appointed head of the O.T.O. for Great Britain, and in 1922 his authority extended over the entire O.T.O. The O.T.O was first established in North America in 1912, when Charles Stanfield Jones along with twelve associates were chartered as the Agapé Camp in the Vancouver area of British Columbia. It is curious in that one of the local communities, Victoria, was the location of the first case of ritual abuse reported by a mental health professional (Smith & Pazder, 1980). In a book published by the O.T.O., it is reported that this organization has since spread to the "US, England, South America, Germany, Norway, the Balkans, New Zealand and Australia" (Ad Veritatem IX°, 1990, p. 97). According to this O.T.O. publication, the international headquarters are now located in New York City.

Another organization, similar to the O.T.O. with its Masonic structure, philosophy, and origins, is the F.S., Fraturnitas Saturni, or Brotherhood of Saturn. According to Eldred Flowers[213], who writes about them from a sympathetic point of view, they are the "most unabashedly Luciferian organization in the modern Western occult revival" (1990, p. xv). Like the O.T.O., and Masonry in general, the F.S. also places considerable importance on Gnostic terminology and concepts. Flowers makes frequent reference to "Saturn-Gnosis," and specific sexual rituals are described.

Robert and Mary Ann de Grimston in London founded the Church of the Process of the Final Judgment (better known as the Process Church) in the early 1960s. It was there in London that the de Grimstons broke away from their involvement with the local Church of Scientology affiliated with the international organization created and made famous by L. Ron Hubbard.[214] They proposed a theology based on four deities: Christ, Jehovah, Lucifer, and Satan. They essentially created a dualistic matrix in which people could explore the extent to which their own personalities were expressions of the four proposed archetypic gods. The similarity of this point of view and Gnosticism is obvious and was noted by Carl Raschke (1990).

The Process provided role-playing exercises in which the individuals involved expressed or presented "alternate personal identities" (Bainbridge, 1991, p. 304).[215] Some authors suggest that there may have been a connection between the Process Church and the ritualistic homicides perpetrated in the late 1960s by Charles Manson (Raschke, 1990; Terry, 1987). I have consulted with patients who believed that their particular cult used some of the philosophy of the Process Church or that they had been abused in one of its subgroups or affiliates.

Another example of modern occultism is the Neo-Pagan movement, particularly the Craft of Wicca, or what is sometimes referred to as white witchcraft. Some would say that white witchcraft is a contradiction in terms. But like all other new religious movements, it deserves to be evaluated on the basis of its own actual characteristics and not on the preconceived ideas we may have about it.

NOTES

[158] Some authors have emphasized other aspects of Livy's report such as the brutal suppression of the cult by mass executions (see Burkert, 1987).

[159] I have had patients report abuse in cults that engaged in Bacchic revelry, ceremonial magic, and abuse. Many patients with DID report that they have alternate identities that are named for, and patterned after the gods and heroes of the mystery cults.

[160] See Burkert (1987), Da Costa (1964), Howard (1989).

[161] For example, see Cavendish (1967), p. 82; Webb (1989), p. 94.

[162] See Blood (1994), Hill & Goodwin (1989), Katchen (1992), Raschke (1990), Smith (1993).

[163] See Carus (1974).

[164] See Lyons (1988).

[165] See Russell (1984).

[166] See Russell (1972).

[167] See Daraul (1990), Howard (1989).

[168] However, the authenticity of Simon Magus as a Gnostic founder is debated. See Couliano (1990), pp. 59–62; Filoramo (1990), pp. 142–152; Rudolph (1987),

[169] See Pagels (1981).

[170] See Kertzer (1993), pp. 120–121.

[171] However, some later Gnostics (e.g., Bogomils, Cathari) simply argued that the Devil created the material universe.

[172] See *The Hypostasis of the Archons*, in Robinson (1988), pp. 162–163; *On the Origin of the World*, in Robinson (1988), pp. 173–175.

[173] However, some medieval Gnostics were said to have believed that the souls of humans were really the spirits of "fallen angels" who had been ousted from heaven by God. See Couliano (1990), pp. 207–208.

[174] See Pagels (1981), p. 35.

[175] See *The Testimony of Truth*, in Robinson (1988), p. 455.

[176] See *The Gospel of Phillip*, in Robinson (1988), p.159; *The Testimony of Truth,* in Robinson (1988), pp. 450.

[177] See MacGregor (1979), pp. 38–39.

[178] Also see Matthew 13:11 for a similar verse.

[179] See Rudolph (1987), pp. 214.

[180] This is described in Hill & Goodwin (1989) in the mental health literature and Filoramo (1990) and Rudolph (1987) in the literature of the history of Gnosticism.

[181] See Filoramo (1990); Lyons (1988).

[182] Paul Tice (1994) writes about the Bogomils from a sympathetic point of view, yet noting that they were influenced by Messalians who "indulged in sexual excesses" (p. 59). The *Encyclopedia of Witchcraft & Demonology* (1974) explicitly describes the Gnostics as predecessors to Satanists in their philosophy and rituals. (pp. 170, 191–192).

[183] See Mather & Nichols (1993), p. 177; Steffon (1992), p. 205.

[184] See Blavatsky (1877/1988), vol. 1, p. 299; Walker (1983), pp. 553, 818.

[185] Also spelled Caballa, Qabalah, and Kabala, etc.

[186] Although the Kabbalah primarily represents a system of Jewish mysticism, there have also been others, e.g., Christians, who were said to be Kabbalists. It should also be noted that the Kabbalah has heavily influenced much of Western occultism in general.

[187] This name is sometimes spelled Ain Soph. Spellings differ because of the inexact and variable transliterations from Hebrew.

[188] See Couliano (1991).

[189] For further reading regarding the Kabbalah from a scholarly (philosophic and historical) perspective see Idel (1988) and Jacobs (1990). See Fielding (1989) and Fortune (1984) for explanations of the Kabbalah within the context of modern Western occultism.

[190] Nitzsche (1975) has described other variants of homunculi and related internalized "entities" that have appeared in Classical and Medieval Europe including the *genius, daemon*, etc. These entities were often perceived to be spiritual and capable of influencing or actually exerting possession over some people. Magical rituals and ceremonies were sometimes conducted in an effort to placate or negotiate with these perceived entities.

[191] Murray's theory is not generally well regarded in the modern scholarly literature.

[192] See Blavatsky (1877/1988), vol. 2, p. A52.

[193] Also see Robertson (1991), pp. 183–185.

[194] See Knight (1986), Larson (1989a), Shaw & McKenney (1988), Short (1989), Smith (1993).

---

[195] Numerous Christian writings directed against Gnostic practices in the ancient and medieval periods point out that Gnostics sometimes participated in orthodox church activities and "pretended" to be "good Christians" or otherwise appropriately integrated into the Christian community. See Moore (1975). This apparent syncretism parallels Vodoun and Santero sects where the cult members are also encouraged to practice Christianity concurrent with their cultic activities. Regarding Haitian Vodoun, see Gersi (1991, p. 128) and Metraux (1959, p. 323) illustrating the symbiosis between cultic and church activities among these cult practitioners.

[196] Subsequently most modern bibles have taken out the Latin word *Lucifer* and replaced it with terms more synonymous to the original Hebrew.

[197] This position can also be found in Robinson's (1989) *Born in Blood: The lost secrets of Freemasonry*. Although the author is not a Mason, he is clearly sympathetic toward the Masonic point of view.

[198] However, Sir Francis was expelled from the Druid Order in 1743.

[199] Even Warnke (1991) takes this position.

[200] According to Macoy (1989, pp. 170–171), a Masonic writer, the Illuminati were a moral and worthwhile organization who were unfairly maligned.

[201] Some authors have attacked the veracity of Warnke's claims, e.g., Trott & Hertenstein (1992).

[202] See L. Bathurst IX° (1990), p. 153.

[203] See also Stanton (1992), p. 37.

[204] See *The Apocalypse of Adam* in Robinson (1988), p. 280; *The Gospel of Phillip* in Robinson (1988), p. 146; The *Hypostasis of the Archons* in Robinson (1988), p. 165.

[205] As I indicated earlier, Hermeticism is a form of pagan Gnosticism. In fact, among the Christian Gnostic documents recovered at Nag Hammadi, some Hermetic writings were also found.

[206] Some say Crowley was not a Satanist; others say he was. King (1989b, p. 221) discusses this controversy.

[207] See Crowley (1988), pp. 365–384; (1990); (1991), pp. 345–361.

[208] Crowley alleges having performed human ritual sacrifice on the average of approximately 150 times every year between 1912 and 1928 (1991, p. 95n). Some writers doubt the literal truth of this allegation but interpret this claim in the light of ritual magic exercises that Crowley engaged in involving masturbation. Such a ritual would not literally consist in the murder of a living child but from a Gnostic point of view would mean killing *potential* babies. Such behavior would not be sinful to such a Gnostic but in fact is similar to some of the claims made by Epiphanius mentioned earlier. To prevent souls from coming into material existence through conception was, to many Gnostics, a virtuous act.

[209] According to Israel Regardie (1993) who was Crowley's secretary, he was sexually abused as a schoolboy by at least one of his tutors and possibly other boys. Crowley's parents were described as very religious members of the Plymouth Brethren.

[210] See Crowley (1991), pp. 428–429

[211] See Noblitt (1998a); Short (1989), pp. 96–97.

[212] See King (1989a), pp. 96-07.

[213] Linda Blood (1994) writes that Eldred Flowers is second in command in Michael Aquino's Temple of Set.

[214] L. Ron Hubbard was intimately involved in the life of Jack Parsons, an eminent California rocket scientist and onetime head of the OTO in Pasadena, California

[215] See also Bainbridge (1978).

Chapter 12

An Introduction to Wicca

While living in England, I taught university psychology courses in the evening. One of my students, a young man named "Ken," was soft-spoken, bright, articulate, and he wore a gold-colored chain with an inverted five-pointed star around his neck. Once after class, I asked him what the star symbolized. He smiled in his friendly way and said, "I'm a Pagan. I follow the religion of Wicca." I later learned that some Wiccans prefer to use the term *Neopagan* to emphasize that they are part of the new movement to revitalize ancient pagan practices. Because I was unfamiliar with Wicca, Ken explained that it was a nature-worshipping religion: "white witchcraft." It was a form of witchcraft that, according to Ken, advocated "doing no harm."

At the time, I did not realize that it is unusual for Wiccans to wear the inverted pentagram. The pentagram, or five-pointed star, has long been a symbol used by various people who practice ritual magic. When the star is inverted in a Wiccan ritual, it may be used in the ceremonial invocation of a non-Satanic deity that Wiccans call the *horned god* (Crowley, 1989). However, to my knowledge, this symbol has only two other meanings. It may either signify the Order of the Eastern Star, a Masonic women's auxiliary organization, or modern Satanism. Most Wiccans attempt to distance themselves from overtly demonic cults and frequently assert that they are not Satanists in their publications and policy statements.

Some time after returning stateside and entering private practice, I was asked to consult with a patient hospitalized on a medical unit of the nearby community hospital. The patient, diagnosed with multiple sclerosis[216], was referred by a neurologist colleague for psychological evaluation. Her name was Erin, and she was a Wiccan.

My discovery of her religion was accidental. She had not intended to tell anyone at the hospital because she anticipated that some would have prejudicial attitudes toward her if they knew she was a Wiccan. I noticed that Erin had not completed the item designating her religious preference on the hospital intake form, and I simply asked her about her religion. After a moment's hesitation, Erin said that she did not usually discuss her religion with strangers. She paused again and then said she was a Pagan. Once Erin realized that I was not critical of her religious beliefs, alter identities began to emerge and converse with me. Erin was co-conscious with some of her alter personalities, but she was amnestic for the presence of others.

Like most of the other multiple personality disorder patients, Erin's alters eventually described sadistic childhood abuse. None of her alters made allegations of ritual abuse per se, but because I was still relatively unfamiliar with ritual abuse, I did not know how to access the alters that might have memories of such abuse had it had occurred. I later found that people with MPD possess not only a variety of internalized alter identities, but that these alters were also often organized in a series of "layers" or "levels." Generally speaking, the more deeply one explores these levels, the worse the memories. It is as if the layers are arranged to protect the self from its most painful recollections by insinuating many levels of less traumatizing dissociated information in between. Ritual abuse memories, when present, are usually found at the deeper levels of this internal "system." I presumed this patient had experienced no ritual abuse because she never talked about it; but, in retrospect, this possibility really cannot be ruled out because I did not know how to explore it at that time.

I asked about Erin's pagan religion in further detail. She told me that much of it was secret and, for that reason, there were things that she could not disclose. However, an alter personality named "Skye" emerged to talk to me. Skye said that she was a Wiccan high priestess and that she had more authority to discuss the subject than did Erin. She laughed and said that Erin didn't really know many of the secrets any way. Skye also claimed that she had psychic abilities.

Skye explained that in Wicca, there was the belief that "whatever one does, it comes back in threes." For this reason, she said, Wiccans usually do not engage in the practice of black magic. However, she admitted that Wicca could have a dark side. She explained that Wiccan rituals were a celebration of life and encouraged a sense of unity with nature. While describing some of the goddesses and gods of Wicca, she explained that most Wiccans did not have a literal belief in these deities, but that they were viewed as archetypes or symbols of important characteristics that people can find in themselves. She admitted that in Wicca, there were some rituals that were sexual in nature, but she said that children were not allowed to be present at those. Skye imparted more information about Wicca, but it seemed that she was holding back somewhat, perhaps out of respect and concern for the element secrecy that she said was part of her religion. In order to help me understand Wicca, Skye recommended a book called *Earth Magic: A Dianic Book of Shadows,* by Marion Weinstein (1980).

As I delved further into Wicca, I learned that its workings are not entirely secret. Numerous publications about Wicca are accessible to the general readership. Furthermore, many Wiccan rituals have been openly publicized and in some cases are open to anyone who wishes to participate.

I was especially intrigued by the Wiccan concept of magic and the paranormal. Similar views are often described by other patients with dissociative disorders who are not, to my knowledge, Wiccans. It is curious how such beliefs could survive in an age so thoroughly dominated by science.

Erin sometimes described out of body experiences in which she reportedly floated above her body and observed her body from above. She said that she learned to do this when she was a child and did not want to feel the abuse her body was experiencing. I asked Erin whether she believed that she was literally able to float out of her body or whether she thought this was merely an experience she had in her imagination. She laughed and said, "Everything happens in your imagination."

In order to clarify her views, I decided to conduct a little experiment. I requested that Erin turn her head away from me and, when she did, I asked her if she could let her mind float out of her body. She agreed to do this. I wrote a simple word in large letters on the writing tablet that I was holding. I asked Erin if she would watch me from the ceiling of the room and read the word I had written. She reportedly did so, but it is probably no surprise that she was unable to tell me what I had written.

Erin was unimpressed by this experiment. It seemed irrelevant to her whether she could, in fact, see from above. What was significant to her, as she explained, was that she was able to have the experience of leaving her body. Whether or not the experience corresponded to objective reality seemed to be of no consequence to her. Erin's point of view also seemed to be similar to those of other patients as well as authors who have written about Wicca, magic, and the occult.

One could argue that this perspective represents a metaphorical belief in magic. Such a stance does not necessarily reflect a literal conviction in the existence of paranormal events. It may merely represent the belief in magic as a metaphor. In other words, people can have mental images of magical experiences such as floating out of their bodies. Although such fantasies do not necessarily have any correspondence in the material world, they are genuine mental events that may have significance to the individual experiencing them. On the other hand a metaphorical approach to magic need not be totally without practical use in one's efforts to cope with the "real world." Erin told me that she believed that she was able to maintain her sanity through her ability to dissociate away her pain and terror. Through fantasies she had learned to disregard external reality when the need arose.

In her book *Drawing Down the Moon* (1986), Margot Adler writes:

> A few scholars and specialists have studied Neo-Paganism, but the public continues to have an inaccurate picture of it. Misunderstandings begin at the most basic level, with the meanings of words used to describe beliefs and attitudes. Let us consider the word, *magic*. Most people define it as superstition or belief in the supernatural. In contrast, most magicians, Witches and other magical practitioners do not believe that magic has anything to do with the supernatural. (p. 6)

Margot Adler, who is a contemporary leading figure in the Wiccan movement, is also the granddaughter of Alfred Adler and the niece of Alexandra Adler. She describes magic as "techniques that allow communication with hidden portions of the self" (p. 160).

Margot Adler also presents a metaphorical view of gods and goddesses and their corresponding rituals. She seems to be saying that Wiccans do not typically have a literal belief in their deities as much as they view the gods and goddesses as representative of character traits, emotions, and personal strivings. Adler cites a letter she received in which the writer states, "I do not believe in gods as real personalities on any plane, or in any dimension. Yet, I do believe in gods as symbols or personifications of universal principles" (p. 35). According to Adler's explanation, Wiccans seem to eschew dogmas, but they value the psychological experience created in their rituals and gatherings.

Adler uses the term *Neo-Paganism* to distinguish her religion from the pagan beliefs of the ancients, as well as from the current pagan beliefs of other cultures where they have existed uninterruptedly. Wicca has been frequently conceptualized as neo-pagan because it is not clear that Wicca is an ongoing continuation of any particular pagan religion.

The theories regarding Wicca's origins vary in a manner that parallels the disputes about medieval witchcraft already discussed in this book. However, one difference is that Wicca occurs in the present and thus is, to some degree, open to observation. In the case of medieval witchcraft, we must rely on historical documents written by individuals who often had a vested interest in representing witchcraft as an undesirable, if not despicable, practice.

Wicca appears to be a modern religious and social movement that has been shaped by a number of factors. The idea that it is a remnant of an ancient Western nature-worshipping religion cannot be completely ruled out. It is also possible that Wicca is, in part, related to antiquated methods of folk healing frequently seen in many cultures. Certainly there are similarities between Wiccans and the shamans, witch doctors, and other preindustrial healers. Were there such healers in England? Numerous sources, both historic (e.g., Burton, 1927; Scot, 1972) and modern (e.g., Haining, 1975), document the presence of "cunning" men and women[217] in Britain who provided folk healing in much the same manner as the curanderos or shamans in other cultures.[218] However, as has already been noted, there is often a fine line between shamans, sorcerers, and witches. Thus, one might argue that white witchcraft is simply a variant of shamanism.

Although there has been much criticism of Margaret Murray's thesis that a secret, pagan, nature-worshipping religion somehow survived in Western Europe, the truth is we simply do not have enough data to intelligently address this hypothesis. On the other hand, if we observe carefully the modern features of Wicca, we can clearly see that at least some of these characteristics are not derived from an ancient Western nature-worshipping religion. For example, several books on occultism[219] exhibit a picture of a Wiccan marriage, or *handfasting,* officiated by Alec Sanders,[220] one of the leading figures of the Wiccan movement. In the picture are found the words "Tetragrammaton"[221] and "Elohim"[222] between the inner and outer rims of a magical circle. These words are not related to any primitive Western European nature-worshipping religion. Instead they were borrowed from Kaballistic terminology that have sometimes been used in a variety of other magical traditions such as those practiced by the Rosicrucians and Masons. It could be argued that Wicca is an amalgam of different beliefs and traditions and that a variety of factors which have probably affected its development and growth:

1. British folk healers, with their magical traditions of treating illness, have been in existence and have conducted business for hundreds of years (or more) with some

secretiveness due to the periodic persecutions of occultists and heretics. Their beliefs and customs may have influenced Wicca.

2. Other esoteric systems including occult fraternal organizations, individual occultists, and some practitioners whose traditions have been passed down generationally may have contributed to current practice and lore of Wicca.

3. Popular psychology and especially the self-help movement has been a source of encouragement for people finding greater happiness and meaning in life through introspective self-exploration. For some, this has apparently become an alternative track for spiritual growth, as well as a methodology for those wanting escape from the confines of more traditional religions. Some Wiccan rituals resemble group therapy, particularly the encounter groups of the 1960s and 1970s.

4. The feminist movement has made people more aware of the injustices done to women, children, and other unfairly subjugated groups. Wicca eliminates the stereotype of God as a male entity with exclusively male clergy. In Wicca, much emphasis is placed on goddesses and priestesses.

According to Vivianne Crowley, "The origin of Wicca lies not in the distant past but its modern history really begins in 1951 when, with the repeal of the Witchcraft Act, people were free to talk openly about the 'Old Religion' " (1989, p. 20). Whatever the origins of Wicca may be, it appears to be a religious movement growing in numbers and in influence. Margot Adler estimates that there are "at least 50,000 to 100,000 active self-identified Pagans or members of Wicca in the United States" (1986, p. 455). She also discusses what appears to be a growing connection between the Unitarian Universalist Association and the neo-pagan movement. I was invited to speak on the subject of ritual abuse at a local Unitarian church and I found that a large proportion of the church members were reportedly Wiccans. I also noticed literature provided at the information counter in the church vestibule gave announcements and information about Wiccan lectures and other activities.

Wiccans share some other similarities with other forms of Western occultism. Francis King (1970) argues that Gerald Gardner, the official founder of modern Wicca, had assistance from Aleister Crowley in developing the rituals for Wicca.[223] Although they are supposed to be secret, at least some of the ranks, rituals, implements, and traditions of Wicca have been described in various books.

Like Freemasonry, Wicca commonly has three levels, or ranks, and the designations accorded to these ranks vary from coven (group) to coven but often include titles such as priest and priestess, magus (for males), witch queen, high priestess and high priest. Many rituals are conducted within a circle drawn with a nine-foot diameter. Some ceremonial acts are performed naked or as some Wiccans say "skyclad," and some are performed clothed, often in ceremonial robes or other costumes. Wiccans reportedly eschew violent rituals, but symbolic scourging is practiced during some gatherings and sometimes "the Great Rite," ritual sexual intercourse, is performed symbolically or in actuality. Wiccans sometimes call their individual groups *covens*, and these are traditionally supposed to consist of thirteen members but, in actual practice, may vary in size[224].

Individuals who have been ritually abused in violent cults might later be attracted to Wicca in order to carry out some likeness of previous rituals, but without the trauma. I have heard rumors that there are some Wiccans who try to help people escape other, more malignant cults. Although patients of mine have stated that some followers of destructive cults occasionally attend Wiccan gatherings for the purpose of recruiting to their own particular group, I have been unable to either verify or disprove these claims. Nevertheless, I continue to hear similar reports from a variety of different ritual abuse survivors.

Is Wicca a possession cult? Does it promote dissociation? It is not clear that the experience of possession is an essential feature of Wicca. However, individuals who have witnessed Wiccan ceremonies, as well as published accounts of their rituals, seem to indicate that possession states sometimes occur. In the ritual of Drawing Down the Moon, for example, the high priestess is sometimes said to respond with an altered state of consciousness that may include features of possession (Guiley, 1989). Luhrman (1989) also writes about the development of alternate identities in Wiccan rituals through activities that resemble role-playing. However, this author provides no description of participants developing involuntary dissociation of identity (as is common among MPD patients). In *Earth Magic*, Marion Weinstein (1980) explains what she calls the "alternate lives" which coexist within the individual involved in Wicca, perhaps reflecting Jungian views of personality as being normally multifaceted and somewhat dissociated.[225] Or possibly in some cases these alternate lives are the result of genuinely dissociated personalities.

NOTES

[216] It is interesting to note the number of patients diagnosed with both MPD and multiple sclerosis (and other physical diagnoses including chronic fatigue syndrome, lupus, and other disease processes with sometimes non-specific etiology).

[217] Guiley (1989) uses the term *wizard*, which she says is etymologically similar to *wise man* or *woman* to describe these magical folk healers.

[218] The fact that such folk healers have existed in England as they have all over the world is not evidence that they constitute the remnants of an ancient Western European pagan nature-worshipping cult. For example, in Haining's (1975, p. 92) book, *An Illustrated History of Witchcraft*, he provides a photograph of one of the pages of the book of spells and conjurations of the famous English cunning man, James Murrell of Essex (1780–1860). The page shows Hebrew characters, geometric figures, a Seal of Solomon, and two inverted pentagrams, suggesting Kaballistic influence (also possibly a Satanic, Luciferian, or other diabolical magical style) rather than true indigenous paganism.

[219] See *Encyclopedia of Witchcraft & Demonology* (1974, back cover), and Haining (1975, pp. 18–19, 114).

[220] Sanders is considered to be the founder of the Alexandrian covens, one of the major factions within Wicca. His biography by June Johns (1969) reports that his grandmother initiated him into witchcraft as a boy by cutting him with a ritual knife in his genital area.

[221] The word Tetragrammaton refers to the Hebrew four-letter word for God. Because Hebrew does not write out its vowels, the pronunciation cannot be precisely determined from these four letters. The exact pronunciation of the name of God was considered sacred and not to be used by rank-and-file membership. The word *Tetragrammaton* is commonly used in occultism that has derived from Kaballistic sources.

[222] The Hebrew word *Elohim* translates literally to "gods." This term is a curiosity because it is found in the beginning of Genesis, although it was usually translated simply as "God" rather than "gods." However, the Gnostics may have used this fact to illustrate their case that the universe had not been created by the ultimate unknowable god but merely by the demiurge and his assisting Archons (who were often construed to be the angels mentioned in the Bible and noncanonical scriptures). For some Gnostics these Archons, along with the Demiurge (often considered an Archon, himself) may have been the Elohim.

[223] However, it is only fair to note that some authors have expressed skepticism, or at least uncertainty, about the claims of Aleister Crowley's involvement in the origins of Wicca (e.g., Adler, 1986).

[224] The term *coven* derives from the word *convent.* It is curious that there are so many alleged parallels between occultism and monasticism (e.g., the Knights Templar, the Friars of Medmenham, etc.). The number 13 may be significant because there are 13 lunar cycles in a year, or in other cases, among cults that aim to mock Christianity the number 13 may represent Jesus and his 12 apostles. Curiously, the Friars of Medmenham (i.e., the Hell Fire Club) also utilized rituals where members dressed as monks and the women who participated in their orgies presented as nuns. Also, the inner circle of the Hell Fire Club consisted of 13 members.

[225] Jungian views, along with the concept of "subpersonalities," were discussed earlier, in Chapter 8

Chapter 13

Satanism?

The term *Satanism* appears frequently in this book. Exactly what is Satanism? Like other concepts associated with obscurity or secrecy, it is difficult to define in a precise, scientific manner. Satanism may represent an organized belief system or religion such as the Church of Satan. It may be seen merely as a vague and dramatized concept of extreme rebellion against Western norms and conventions such as the so-called "Satanism" flaunted by some rock musicians. It may be a mythological vestige of medieval religious thinking that still lingers in modern times. It may also be a deviant practice used to intimidate and control others through ritual abuse.

If Satanism is associated with ritual abuse, one can also say with certainty that not all ritual abuse is Satanic.[226] Many of these abusive occurrences have been present in societies or under conditions where Satan is not a recognized spiritual or demonic entity.[227] In earlier times, it was not uncommon for Western scholars and travelers to sometimes ascribe the influence of Satan to primitive religious practices, which to them appeared to be idolatrous or violent. Even now, one occasionally hears the notion that if something is not Christian, it is the result of Satan's power or seductiveness.

How can we distinguish Satanism from other pagan religions, and Satanic ritual abuse from similar malevolent practices by non-Satanic individuals and groups?[228] Many problems emerge in any attempt to answer this question, but perhaps the most formidable is the reported secrecy associated with such organizations. This is not to say that all variants of Satanism are secretive.

The Church of Satan, founded on April 30 (Walpurgisnacht), 1966, in San Francisco, California, openly operated as a religion. Its founder, Anton LeVey, repeatedly asserted that the Church of Satan does not engage in any illegal activity such as ritual murder or sexual abuse of children. Instead, this relatively recently created religion publicly has espoused a position of hedonism and materialism along with the rejection of Christianity. Its publicly stated philosophy is so mild mannered that author Francis King (1989b) commented that "there is nothing particularly Satanic about this" (p. 221).

The Church of Satan has been described from an anthropological perspective by Edward J. Moody (1974) who, by his own accounts, was a member of the Church of Satan in San Francisco for two and a half years. Moody notes that one common denominator of the membership of this organization (also known as the Church of the Trapezoid) is that the members appeared to be socially deviant in some way, although Moody asserts that the Church of the Trapezoid appears to be an effective means of resocialization for these individuals — at least within this group. Thus, Moody argues that the Church of Satan may assist these people in developing a more functional and adaptive mode of living and concludes that "Perhaps it is for this reason that marginal religions such as the Church of the Trapezoid should be encouraged" (Moody, 1974, p. 382).

Whether the Church of Satan is a healthy outlet for "socially deviant" individuals is questionable. Arthur Lyons reports that during a "lecture on cannibalism, a severed human leg was brought from East San Francisco Bay Hospital by a physician-member, basted in Triple Sec, and served to the less queasy in the group" (1988, p. 107). Cult crime expert Carl Raschke cites cultist Michael Aquino, who claims that this "was actually leg of mutton roasted with exotic herbs" (1990, p. 240). Nevertheless, Blanche Barton, a biographer of LaVey, writes that this was "a cooked thigh of a young white woman" (Barton, 1990, p. 78).

A former member of the Church of Satan, Lieutenant Colonel Michael Aquino, established his own cultic brotherhood, the Temple of Set. Although this organization also professes to be law-abiding, author Linda Blood (1994) states that Michael Aquino was under investigation in response to child abuse allegations associated with the Presidio, an army post in California.

> By December 1988, *San Jose Mercury News* staff writer Linda Goldston was able to report that Lieutenant Colonel Michael Aquino had been formally "titled" under the uniform code of military justice. According to CID spokesperson Mary Melanson, this step signified that the authorities "feel there is sufficient evidence to believe that a crime has been

committed. The closest thing in civilian terms would be a grand jury indictment." (Blood, 1994, p. 180)

However, "Ultimately no charges arose out of these investigations, and Aquino said that he and his wife had never molested any child 'anywhere, anytime.' " (Blood, 1994, p. 182). According to Blood, the Judge Advocate General's team chose not to force a court-martial so that the children would not have to undergo testifying and being cross-examined. Instead "an Army Reserve continuation board recommended discontinuing Aquino's military service, ands he was subsequently processed out of the army" (Blood, 1994, p. 185).

Where did Satanism begin? In an indirect form, the predecessors of Satanism may be found in archaic religions in which gods were worshipped, not because of their inherent goodness, but because of their perceived power. For example, the ancient Greek and Roman gods were such an amoral assemblage of deities. Few showed many admirable character traits. These gods were often depicted with all the foibles and veniality of mere mortals. Many of the cults devoted to such gods and goddesses allegedly involved traumatizing rituals (e.g., the mystery cults). On the other hand, some religions specifically worshipped and supplicated overtly evil deities.

However, in some cases appearances may be deceiving. For example, the Yezidi sect of Turkey, Syria, Armenia, and Iran, worship Ahriman (who, in the Zoroastrian religion, is roughly the equivalent of Satan). However, the Yezidi believe that Ahriman is no longer evil, having asked for and having received God's forgiveness. They consider it an outrage to equate their Ahriman with the Satan of Christianity, and Islam.[229]

In other cases, what appears to be the worship of an "evil deity" may simply represent the worship of a spiritual entity who no longer enjoys favored status. There are examples in history in which a culture's demons were really past divinities, no longer revered, and sometimes given new and less attractive roles. Such revolutions among the gods sometimes resulted from conquests, whereupon the new gods of the conquerors take the place previously held by the gods of the conquered.

In other instances, evil may be revered or worshipped outright. In cultures in which Christianity is prevalent one might assume that the worship of evil would entail some devotion to Lucifer or Satan, the primary names given to the Euro-American spiritual representation of evil. To many traditional Christians, Satan and Lucifer are equivalent but different names for the same demon. However, many theologians make the distinction that Lucifer is the name of Satan before his fall.

Within some occult traditions there is even a clearer discrimination between Satan and Lucifer. As already mentioned, within certain cults Lucifer is sometimes portrayed as a Promethean figure, the "bringer of light." In the tradition of some Gnostics, Lucifer is represented as the rebellious spirit opposed to Christianity and the god of creation who is instead portrayed as the one responsible for introducing evil by creating a material world. Thus, Luciferianism reverses the Judeo-Christian-Islamic concept of a good creator and an evil demon. Satan is occasionally presented in such relatively benign terms[230] but, more often, Satan is described as the personification of pure evil. Such a Satanic theology would attribute goodness to the Judeo-Christian God, but Satanists worship Satan because he is perceived to be more powerful or because the cultist might view himself or herself as being beyond redemption by a benign deity. In this system of thinking, goodness itself is characterized as a weak, ineffective, and futile goal. Spence describes a similar dichotomy in views of Satanism and Luciferianism although he defines his terms slightly differently:

> Modern groups practicing Satanism are small and obscure, and unorganized as they are, details concerning them are conspicuous by their absence. Plentiful details, however, are forthcoming concerning the cults of Lucifer, but much discrimination is required in dealing with these, the bulk of the literature on the subject being manifestly imaginative and willfully misleading. The members of the church of Lucifer are of two groups, those who regard the deity they adore as the evil principle, thus approximating to the standpoint of the Satanists, and those who look upon him as the true god in opposition to Adonai or Jehovah, whom they regard as an evil deity who has with fiendish ingenuity miscreated the world of man to the detriment of humanity. (1993, p. 123)

The wearing of dark, hooded robes is a commonly reported feature of these cults, but survivors describe a variety of different costumes and ritual acts. One patient arrived at my office with a ceremonial cowl.[231] When she brought it to me, neither she nor I knew what it was. Without identifying the patient to whom the item belonged, I asked other survivors if they recognized the article of clothing, and I was told that it was a cowl, a form of ceremonial headdress. The survivors indicated it was authentic, pointing to details of its construction that I had not even noticed. The patient who brought it to me reported that she had awakened from a trance in her own house. The cowl was on her head, but she did not know how or why it had gotten there. Some survivors describe the wearing of a miter by high-ranking members of their cult. The miter is a somewhat cone-shaped ceremonial hat worn by Catholic bishops and abbots. Some of the artwork from earlier times depicting the trial and execution of "heretics" by the Inquisition shows them dressed in miters and robes.

Sexual abuse, torture,[232] and murder are often alleged to be important components of Satanic cult rituals. However, some of the survivors claim that rituals involving the torture or murder of a person can be simulated. In these cases, the simulation is conducted in a sufficiently realistic manner that many of the participants will believe that they witnessed the deliberate ceremonial killing of a person. In the Fran's Day Care criminal case, a child testified that he was told to close his eyes and that his perpetrator was cutting on his arm to perform surgery to replace his bone with the bone of Satan. However, the child revealed to the court that he unobtrusively peeked and saw that the "surgery" had not actually happened.

An adult patient described an abusive act she once observed in which a naked woman was tied to a chair in front of a table where a bloody razor blade was prominently displayed. The woman was then blindfolded, and the perpetrator took a straight pin and slowly ran it across the victim's body, causing slight scratches. According to my patient, the victim's reaction showed her terror — she believed she was being sliced with the razor blade, and consequently, she appeared to go in and out of numerous dissociated mental states.

Acts of ritual murder also are reportedly simulated for the purpose of terrorizing those present into silence and creating further states of dissociation. "Actual human sacrifice of children and adults may also be performed, but only on special occasions. Mock killings are performed more often and are designed to look as believable as real killings" (Smith, 1993, p. 130). Barb Jackson (1993), another survivor, describes her observations of an abusive cult in which abusive rituals actually occurred but also were sometimes simulated. Both reportedly had the capacity for being overwhelmingly traumatizing.[233]

Hearing countless reports of ritual abuse by patients and others, an obvious question arises: why would anyone want to *do* these things? The stories seemed to lack any redeeming features whatsoever. What would motivate people to carry out such practices? When asked, the patients sometimes have an answer to such questions. The most commonly given explanation is that such rituals provide an intoxicating sense of power to those who are in the role of perpetrating the abuse. Such a practitioner experiences the sense of power over life and death, either simulated or in actuality. During such abusive acts one exerts great control over the minds of the abused and dominion over the creation of what might appear to be new souls or, as one patient explained, "the souls of dead people," which can then "inhabit" the body of someone present at the ceremony. In actuality, these "souls" are more likely to be alternate or dissociated personalities created via traumatizing rituals.

Nevertheless, in such a role, the cultist not only "plays god," but for the purposes of those present, actually becomes the god (e.g., through a state of possession) and is recognized, respected, and worshipped as the god by the followers. On other occasions the cultist simply enjoys being in the powerful role of a god.[234] The following was written by one of my patients about such an interaction. According to the patient, an abusive male repetitively claimed he was God before sexually abusing her:

> Was taken into a room and thrown down on a bed. The man was very big and blonde. Muscular. Over 6 ft. tall. Very angular features. Had been "led" to the room by others. "He" told them to leave me alone with him. Said he was going to teach me a lesson. We talked back to him. He got right in my face and said he was God. He repeated it over and over. He kept saying he was God. "God. God. God." When we first were taken in to the room, we were scared. After he kept saying God, we were very compliant [*sic*].[235]

Another ritually abused patient sometimes switched to altered states, describing in terror her experience of being tortured by "gods." But the gods she described were not metaphysical abstractions; they were merely people who had taken on the role or persona of gods in rituals she had been forced to attend. My patient called one of these "gods" Satan.[236]

The pursuit of power[237] may appear particularly attractive to those who have been coerced into conditions of extreme powerlessness, a feature of being in the victim role in such a cult. Apparently all, or almost all, members of Satanic cults reportedly are, at one time or another, in the victim roles of these abusive rituals. However, as one's rank increases in the cult, the extent of victimization decreases; thus as the cult member rises in power, he or she is increasingly placed in the role of a perpetrator of painful ceremonies and procedures.[238] Power can be desirable for its defensive as well as offensive potential. Getting power decreases the harm experienced by the individual. Sometimes the power of "the dark side" may be sought because the individual has lost any hope of protection from "good" people or a good deity. As one patient explained while in the state of a child alter, "God can't protect you. Satan can."

Several patients describe rituals in which Christian ceremonies are parodied and the victim of the abuse is told to pray to God for help. No help is forthcoming because the participants deliberately orchestrate the situation so that no aid can appear under such conditions. In some circumstances, no relief is offered until the victim makes a sincere plea to Satan or until the victim is transformed by the torture into another identity (through dissociation), one who is a devoted follower of Satan.

The power that exists in Satanic (and Luciferian) cults is reportedly reflected in an organized hierarchy with incremental ranks.[239] These positions may vary somewhat from one group to another, but one such hierarchy consists of: page, knight, priest (or priestess), prince (or princess), high priest (or high priestess), king (or queen), savior, and god (sometimes goddess, but goddess is not always the feminine equivalent of god and vice versa). As one increases in rank, one is taught more about the programming cues or "triggers" used in ceremonies with the other followers of the cult. Some of these triggers are relatively generic and thus can be used with a relatively large number of people. The example given earlier in this book is the repeated use of the word *deep* or *deeper*. When this word is used repeatedly, even unobtrusively, (e.g., in ordinary conversation) many survivors of Satanic and Luciferian cults will enter into a trance or show some other signs of change in mental state or other physical response such as an eyeblink or altered gaze.

Those who increase in rank are not only taught a variety of triggering stimuli that they can use in controlling others (via such programming methods), but they are also reportedly deprogrammed so that their responses to these lower-level generic cues are less powerful. Thus, survivors who are higher ranking in the Satanic (and similar) cults are "trained" with more highly specific and idiosyncratic programming cues so that the majority of other members will not readily have control over them. Such control remains with the elite, who are higher in rank and skill.

The origins of Satanism are certainly as obscure as any other occult belief system. One can never be precisely certain when such practices started. Nevertheless, some of the historical accounts of Satanism in Europe may clarify some of the evolution of thinking about Satanism. The history of Satanism may be traced to a variety of possible sources: (1) European witchcraft, sorcery, and shamanism, (2) Gnostic-derived religions (e.g., the Cathari)[240] which viewed the established Church as an oppressive adversary, (3) the general traditions of Western occultism (which are often seen as encompassing a "dark" or "left-handed path") and (4) what Francis King calls "the bad theology of a minority of Roman Catholic priests" (1989b, p. 219).

Centuries ago, after the military defeat of the Christian crusaders in Palestine, many Europeans may have began to doubt that God was really on their side. Others may have begun to doubt that God's power was great enough to protect them. Countless natural disasters and an oppressive social order further challenged the beliefs and hopes of medieval European Christians. According to John Robinson (1989), the devastating bubonic plague epidemic of the 1300s called the Black Death may have seriously shattered the faith of many who survived this horrible event. Some may have "believed an appeal to Satan was the only alternative, now that they had been abandoned by God" (p. 5).[241]

Some of the practices of the Church may have indirectly provided opportunities for the further abuse of people. In addition to the previously mentioned Inquisition and inhumane persecution of those accused of heresy and witchcraft, arose the notion that flagellation (whipping or scourging) was an acceptable way of doing penance or making atonement for sins. In some cases the practice of flagellation clearly became excessive, and the Church eventually prohibited certain kinds of extreme self-mortification.[242] However, even today, the Penitentes, or Brothers of Our Father, Jesus, a Catholic sect in New Mexico and northern Colorado, continues to engage in relatively severe forms of physical punishment. The Penitentes reportedly engage in various forms of "discipline"[243] which, on rare occasions, have left the penitent permanently injured or dead. According to Darley (1968), there are eyewitness accounts of actual crucifixions of people conducted by this sect in secrecy, although the Penitentes deny this accusation.[244]

The pervasive superstitions in medieval Europe were probably also a factor in the evolution of dark occultism. During that era, even the Church appeared to be steeped in superstition.[245] Many had a magical conception of Christianity and a belief that religious ceremonies could be used to create benign or malevolent outcomes. Rituals for worship services evolved for procuring the death of a living person — the Death Mass — and the Amatory Mass, used ostensibly for obtaining sex or love. There were also a number of defrocked priests and "wandering"[246] priests and bishops who performed such magical masses for a fee, although the 7th-century Council of Toledo banned the practice of the Death Mass.

The Black Mass may have evolved from such magical masses along with the alleged blasphemous and reversed masses attributed to various Gnostic and Gnostic-inspired sects. In *The Golden Bough*, Sir James Frazer (1963) describes the Mass of St. Sécaire, which allegedly has been conducted in Gascony, France, for the intended purpose of causing harm to another individual. This ritual involves sacrilegious acts and a reversal in the wording of the Catholic ceremony of the mass.[247]

In the 15th-century, French baron and onetime marshal of France, Gilles de Rais, was found to have engaged in numerous murderous and sadistic acts, some of which were alleged to be associated with bizarre rituals in which he was assisted by Francesco Prelatti, a Florentine priest and occultist. Gilles de Rais was noted to be a man whose character and personality seemed to be extremely variable at different times. Sometimes noted for his kindness, he was distinguished for his bravery in his military assistance of Joan of Arc. However, there was a great deal of consistent testimony provided by witnesses as well as material evidence pointing to his guilt.[248]

According to Francis King, Satanism was sufficiently prevalent in 16th- and 17th-century France that its presence was noted by the police:

> It is difficult to know how widespread such Satanist activities were among the nonmonastic clergy of the Middle Ages, but they seem to have become common in the 16th and 17th centuries. Exactly how common, no one knows, but if the rest of Catholic Europe was anything like the ecclestiastical underworld of Paris at that time, then they were very common indeed. For in France Satanism had attained the status of big business, its practitioners forming a kind of occult Mafia, a noisome octopus with tentacles which reached into almost every segment of Parisian society and which was uncovered by Nicolas de la Reynie, the Police Commissioner of Paris. (1989b, pp. 219—220)

Louis de Vanens, a self-avowed Satanist, was arrested in November of 1678 for forgery. A year later, a fortune-teller, Catherine Deshayes (using the name La Voisin), was arrested for poisoning. At her home were found not only poisons but also ingredients for occult rituals. La Voisin admitted having sold poisons to young wives who intended to murder their elderly husbands. She also confessed to conducting numerous abortions and organizing magical masses intended to cause death or amorous conquests. She allegedly had clandestine dealings with several priests, one of the more notorious being Abbé Guibourg.

If these police investigations are to be trusted, then we should also note that material evidence was reportedly found, including the remains of infants, which had allegedly been sacrificed during these Black Masses. Apparently many prominent individuals and members of the aristocracy were implicated, but when it was discovered that the Madame de Montespan, a mistress to King Louis XIV, was involved, the king silenced all who knew the details of the case and ordered that the records were to be destroyed.[249]

Later, in 1839, Pierre Vintras, a foreman of a French cardboard box factory, professed that he was a reincarnation of the prophet Elijah and that he had come to prepare the way for the second coming of Jesus. Believing that he had received a letter from Michael the Archangel, Vintras founded a sect called the Work of Mercy which later was identified as the Church of Carmel. This group was condemned in 1848 by Pope Gregory XVI. Vintras performed strange Masses in which bizarre events reportedly occurred, including the spectacle of chalices magically overflowing with blood and blood appearing on communion wafers. Vintras claimed that his Masses were intended to counteract the evil forces generated by Satanists who, he said, were performing Black Masses during that time. However, the famous occultist Eliphas Levi reportedly observed these events and noted that the communion wafer used for these Masses was triangular and reddish and that Vintras wore an inverted cross on his vestments which, to him, were indicative of Satanic influences.[250]

When Vintras died, the leadership of his sect passed to Abbé Boullan, a defrocked priest who had already achieved some notoriety when he and a nun by the name of Adèle Chevalier established a group called the Society for the Reparation of Souls in which rituals involving sex magic and ritual murder were reported. Francis king writes, "According to a document which survives in the Vatican archives, on 8 January 1860, Boullan and his mistress celebrated a Black Mass which incorporated the ritual sacrifice of their own bastard child" (1991, pp. 116–117). He goes on to say that:

> Documents survive which provide evidence that Boullan and his disciples engaged, or imagined that they engaged, in sexual activities not only with angels and other heavenly beings but with the spirits of the mighty dead — Cleopatra and Alexander the Great, for example. The techniques used to achieve these ghostly copulations were largely masturbatory, the man or woman concerned was simply fantasizing that he or she was having sexual intercourse with a disembodied being. On occasion a human partner, also a member of the Church of Carmel, was involved. In this case each would imagine the other to be an angel. Boullan also seems to have approved of bestiality, sexual relationships between animals and human beings on the grounds that it speeded up the spiritual evolution of the animals concerned. There is no hard evidence that he acted on this theory, but some of his followers may have done

so. Such teachings as those described above were only given to
those in the inner circle of Boullan's so-called Church. In public
he posed as a man of great, if eccentric piety. (1991, p.117)

Apparently Boullan had friendly encounters with J.K. Huysmans, who
authored the novel *Là Bas*, depicting what many consider to be realistic
descriptions of the Black Mass.[251] Huysmans, by his own admission,
attended such a ritual.

In 1895, a Luciferian chapel was found in the Borghese Palace in
Rome. The magnificent Palazzo Borghese had been leased to other
residents by the Borghese family. Later, during an unexpected
examination of the property by representatives of the family, they found
a room with the words "Templum Palladicum"[252] inscribed upon it with a
large tapestry of Lucifer, an altar, and other occult paraphernalia.[253]

In modern America, Satanic symbols and themes are visible and
popular features of music, literature, and movies. Increasing numbers of
reported survivors are coming forward to claim they are victims of such
cults. Are these reports merely rumors or fantasies, or are people being
harmed by ritual abuse? Unless we seriously investigate these reports,
we will never know for certain.

NOTES

[226] Survivor Margaret Smith (1993, pp. 78–79) also makes this point.

[227] However, some Christians might maintain that Satan is the primary representation of
evil in the world regardless of whether other cultures recognize him as such or not.

[228] In *The History of the Devil and the Idea of Evil*, first published in 1900, Paul Carus
(1974) provides a secular and scholarly account of demonology in a variety of cultures,
mostly European, many of which are pagan.

[229] See Guest (1987).

[230] For example, by Anton LaVey.

[231] A cowl is a more tight-fitting hood-like article of apparel. The one brought to me was
made of fabric that was somewhat stretchable and when it was worn it looked something
like a ski mask with one opening exposing the wearer's two eyes.

[232] See Golston (1992).

[233] Dr. Harry Wright, a Philadelphia dentist, described witnessing what appeared to be the
ritual sacrifice of a child in a jungle village in Brazil. Horrified he planned to leave the
village the next day but found the girl in question was unharmed. He implies that this
was accomplished by slight of hand (1957).

[234] Symonds, a biographer of Aleister Crowley, and one of the editors of Crowley's
autobiography, *The Confessions of Aleister Crowley*, notes Crowley's conception of
himself as a god (Symonds, 1979, p. 21).

[235] Notice that the patient often uses the plural term "we" in making reference to herself.
This is one of the frequently observed features of multiple personality disorder.

[236] In some cases, perhaps many cases, the "gods" described by ritual abuse survivors
may reflect not so much Satanism as other varieties of occultism, e.g., as described in
Chapter 10.

[237]Although some claim that there is actually a psychic or spiritual power to be achieved in such cults I have never observed any evidence of that. Instead the power that can be obtained is (1) the license to inflict harm on others during such ritual activities and (2) the opportunity to learn programming skills to influence or control others by using programming cues (often outside the context of the ritual activities).

[238] E.g., see McShane (1993), p. 207.

[239] Certain very high-ranking positions are held exclusively by certain individuals. However, in the tradition of some Gnostics (see Pagels, 1981) a variety of individuals may have some rotating role of relative importance (e.g., priestess or high priestess).

[240] Some authors have argued that the Cathari (whose name means "pure ones") could never have engaged in the horrible rituals identical or similar to Satanists. However, the process of dissociation works best when there are markedly different (e.g., religious) views present in the same individual. I have previously explained that some Vodoun cults specifically require that their members also be Roman Catholics. Additionally, one might argue that one (misguided) method of achieving the strict kind of purity followed by the "perfect" of the Cathari, which included absolute celibacy, would be to occasionally dissociate as some other "person" or "spirit" who could act out the unacceptable sexual and aggressive urges of the "perfect one," who would later be amnestic for the transgressions committed by his or her alters. Additionally, the "perfect one," in part satiated and, to some degree, traumatized, became adverse to further sexual and aggressive stimulation or gratification. Girard (1972) has argued that the violent rituals sometimes found in religions and cults were devised to provide a way of controlling and redirecting socially deviant behaviors. Also from a point of view more sympathetic to the Cathari, Guirdham (1977) argues that not all Cathari were expected to live a pure life. The priestly *parfait* were expected to live an ascetic life but the *croyants*, or rank and file believers had no such obligations.

[241] According to Michelet (1992), some medieval folk were driven toward Satanism and witchcraft out of a sense of desperation. Such extreme feelings were in responses to the deprivations and horrors of medieval life, including the evils inherent in the feudal system.

[242] Shortly after the bubonic plague's began, an organized movement of flagellants spread throughout Europe.

[243] It may be interesting to note that the word *discipline* derives from the word *disciple*.

[244] See also Chavez (1974) and Weigle (1976).

[245] See Flint (1991), Thomas (1971).

[246] I.e., not assigned to a particular parish and thus not under any close supervision.

[247] See Frazer (1963, pp. 61–62).

[248] See Hyatte (1984).

[249] These historical events have been interpreted from several different perspectives. See King (1989b, 1991), Lyons (1988), Mossiker (1969), Robbins (1981), Russell (1988, 1991), Stevens (1991), Summers (1992).

[250] The inverted cross so often equated with Satanism may have actually been a Gnostic symbol. The Gnostics viewed the cross with contempt, as a Roman Catholic symbol of the material instrument used to create the illusion that the spiritual Jesus had been killed.

[251] For a recent English translation see J.K. Huysmans (1986). *Là Bas* (Lower depths), London: Daedalus.

[252] The word *Palladian* has several meanings. In architecture it refers to a style developed from the work of Andrea Palladio, a celebrated architect of the 16th century who began his career as a skilled mason. In occultism, the term has referred to the Palladium, which in Greco-Roman mythology and religion was "the scepter of Priam, in

the likeness of a male sex organ" (Graves, 1955, p. 266). According to Walker (1983), this instrument was used in a ritual to "marry" the Vestal Virgins to the phallic god of the Palladium in Rome. The expression, *Palladian,* also refers to an allegedly Luciferian-Masonic sect in Charleston, South Carolina which was described by Leo Taxil and later denied by him (See Howard, 1989; King, 1991; Waite, 1970, Webb, 1974). It is also unclear whether the alleged Palladian cult in Charleston is related to the Order of Palladium, also called the Sovereign-Council of Wisdom established in Paris on May 20, 1737, and described by Ragou (see Spence, 1993, p. 314) or the Order of the Palladium, which according to Macoy (1989) first appeared in Douay, France.

[253] See Summers (1992), pp. 152–153.

Chapter 14

The Politics of Psychotherapy

By 1990, my practice increasingly attracted individuals with DID and people who were, by their own accounts, survivors of ritual abuse. As this occurred, I also found myself with a steadily increasing caseload of marginally functioning patients with little or no funding for their psychological treatment. As previously indicated, this patient population includes a large proportion of individuals who are unemployed or underemployed because of the severity of their psychiatric symptoms.

As a consequence of their periodic risk of self-harm and occasional danger of harm to others, these patients sometimes require close supervision and hospitalization. However, in many cases they are discharged prematurely when their funds are exhausted or their managed care provider determines that they must be discharged, regardless of their capacity for maintaining a minimal level of functioning. Help in the public sector is inconsistent and unreliable. The county and state facilities are unprepared to cope with and effectively treat these individuals, and commitment typically results only in sedating and warehousing these patients, not in treating their disabling symptoms.

I was concerned that although some of my patients periodically required the protective environment of a hospital setting, they often did not have the financial or emotional resources to be in a hospital. Inpatient psychiatric treatment is expensive and can deplete even generous insurance policies in a very short time. Additionally, hospitalization is extremely stressful. Not only is it disruptive to one's day-to-day routine; the hospital politics often interfere with the patient's care by introducing conflicts in philosophies within the treatment team. It is not uncommon for patients to report that other members of the treatment team express disbelief in the diagnosis of DID and ritual abuse and tell patients that their recollections are merely fantasy. Ritual abuse survivors often report that their perpetrators said similar things to them when they were children (e.g., "you just had a bad dream") in order to prevent them from describing their abuse to others or otherwise "telling the secrets." Psychiatrists unfamiliar with the psychopharmacology of DID sometimes prescribe medications or other procedures that are contraindicated and counterproductive.

Unfortunately, there are often no alternatives to hospitalization when these patients feel overtly self-destructive. Some of the hospitals provide day treatment or partial hospitalization, but such programs typically do not have effective measures in place to insure patient safety at the end of each day when the patient leaves the facility. The argument of the hospital administrations is that if a patient cannot ensure his or her own safety outside the partial program, then he or she should be in an inpatient facility. Additionally, the expense of partial hospitalization, physician fees, psychotherapy, and other related charges is still outside the reach of many of these patients. Many insurance policies and managed health care programs not only impose limitations on the dollars spent on psychiatric services, including hospitalization; they often limit the length of treatment.

Because of this apparent need, an experimental day treatment program was developed within my office, and as far as I know, was the first such non hospital-affiliated day treatment program specifically for dissociative patients in the United States. In order to participate in this program, patients were required to have a "safe" living situation established. This was possible for some of the patients who had existing relationships with spouses or other persons who were familiar with their capacity for self-harm and who were, as far as we are able to ascertain, symptom free or no danger to the patient. For patients who did not have any such relationship already established, we encouraged a roommate, or "buddy," system whereby compatible individuals shared the expenses and responsibilities of their food and shelter while providing one another with appropriate emotional support, nurturance, and occasional monitoring for their safety. This situation worked out well for several of the patients, providing them with reduced living expenses, often in a safer environment than they previously had, and with the benefit of another person available to support and ground them and to assist in insuring their safety from periodic real or perceived external threats. By having patients reside with other "safe" individuals when they were not in the day treatment program, it was possible to reduce or even avoid hospitalization for many of these patients when they otherwise felt self-destructive.

Over time, the original concept was expanded to provide patients with services comparable to what they could receive in private psychiatric facilities, including the availability of mental health technicians, groups, and art therapy. My staff assisted patients in coordinating their efforts with the state rehabilitation commission and other city, county, state, and federal agencies and programs designed to facilitate the patient's reintegration into society, job training, and placement and receipt of appropriate social services. At the same time, it was possible to minimize the expense to the patients and the financial burden to their insurance by eliminating many of the standard costs of hospital-affiliated programs such as nursing staff and daily fees for the attending psychiatrist.

It was during the time of our day program's development that several area psychiatric facilities were aggressively marketing their services to me. Some of the hospitals gave me an opportunity to provide group therapy and other services within their psychiatric units. At the time, I believed I was recruited to deliver these services because of my experience caring for patients who were typically very problematic to the hospital staff and who created conflict on the unit. However, I eventually realized that my participation was often solicited for purely business reasons — because I specialized in treating high risk patients who, despite my best efforts, had no alternative to hospitalization when they became self-destructive, suicidal, and even homicidal.

This fact was brought home to me when on at least one occasion the groups I provided to a particular hospital were discontinued because I was unwilling to refer my patients exclusively to that particular facility. Referring patients exclusively to a hospital in exchange for financial remuneration is unethical. Referrals should always be made with the only consideration being the patient's welfare and best interest. This questionable policy continues to be the modus operandus of some psychiatric hospitals, which pay stipends and provide other benefits to psychiatrists and therapists in exchange for what is essentially referral brokering.

Despite the fact that there are several psychiatric hospitals and psychiatric programs available locally, it has become increasingly difficult to find appropriate placement for my patients. Many of these patients have inadequate insurance benefits to support long-term treatment that, in freestanding psychiatric hospitals, could cost over a thousand dollars a day, exclusive of the fees of the attending physician, individual therapist, medications, and other special needs. Some hospitals are not interested in treating those patients who are violent or uncooperative. Some of the hospitals are ill equipped to deal with patients who are at substantial risk for self-harm or who frequently attempt to elope from the hospital before appropriate discharge. Few hospital staff and fewer psychiatrists have either experience or a willingness to develop the necessary skills to prepare them for the treatment of these difficult patients.

In spite of the fact that this was not a particularly profitable patient population, there were, at one time, at least three different hospital programs in the Dallas area purported to specialize in dissociative disorders. Gary Lefkof, M.D. founded the first, at the Cedars Hospital in De Soto, Texas. In 1992, Dr. Lefkof moved his program to Brookhaven Psychiatric Pavilion, a facility more conveniently located in the heart of North Dallas. However, when the scandal involving the Psychiatric Institute of America (PIA) and its parent company, National Medical Enterprises (NME) erupted, Brookhaven, a franchise of that company, failed and folded.

The second and third programs were established almost simultaneously at Charter Hospital of Dallas and Bedford Meadows Hospital near Fort Worth. For the dedication of the Bedford Meadows program, Bennett Braun, M.D. and Trudy Chase, author of *When Rabbit Howls*, were featured speakers. The program at Bedford Meadows was originally developed by Jerry Mungadze, Ph.D., a counselor who developed a program with a Christian orientation for the treatment of DID. When Bedford Meadows also fell victim to the PIA fallout, Dr. Mungadze moved his program to the Cedars Hospital.

I was most intimately familiar with the program offered by Charter Hospital of Dallas, having created the original inservice training and groups for patients with dissociative disorders. The nursing staff seemed not only willing to work with these patient's special needs; they appeared enthusiastic as well. I was often responsible for as many as six or seven inpatient admissions at any given time. None of the physicians on staff had much previous experience treating dissociative patients, and many of the psychiatrists were not interested in dealing with these patients.

In 1991, Charter invited me to chair a national symposium on multiple personality disorder to coincide with the opening of their unit for the treatment of patients with DID. I recommended Colin Ross and Chris Sizemore, "Eve" of *The Three Faces of Eve*, to speak at the symposium. I also suggested to the administration of Charter that clinicians representing other facilities and programs be invited to participate, but the hospital administration would not accept that recommendation. It has always been my belief that if the therapeutic community is to be successful in working with these patients, we must set aside our competitiveness and egos in order to share our knowledge and experience. The conference appeared to be successful, establishing Charter as a viable facility for the treatment of dissociative disorders and providing for Colin Ross's recruitment to the staff of Charter.

In the 1980s in Dallas, and, I presume, in other metropolitan areas around the country, mental health professional services flourished. As I mentioned earlier, there were several psychiatric programs in the area, both in freestanding psychiatric facilities and units incorporated in medical-surgical hospitals. Hospitals programs marketed themselves aggressively both locally and nationally. In 1991, allegations of improper referral procedures utilized by some of the hospitals appeared in the media. Some of these procedures included paying "bounties" to referral sources, including juvenile court personnel, schoolteachers, and counselors, and private referral agencies. Hospitals frequently encouraged patients to apply to various state funded victims assistance programs in order to subsidize lengthy hospital stays. Patients were often hospitalized for unnecessarily long periods of time, and frequently they were subjected to inappropriate and excessive treatment modalities such as involuntary restraints. Often, patients were hospitalized until their funds were exhausted; at which time they were discharged without the capacity to obtain appropriate continuing care.

As a consequence of these questionable practices and subsequent investigations by state and federal authorities, a number of hospital corporations withdrew from providing mental health facilities. National Medical Enterprises, the parent company of Psychiatric Institutes of America (PIA), dissolved PIA and closed all of its facilities in the immediate area, including Brookhaven Psychiatric Pavilion and Bedford Meadows. Hospital Corporation of America (HCA) also ceased to provide psychiatric services locally in a freestanding facility. Although I was not aware of it at the time, Charter, like many others, was apparently paying fees to at least one outside agency for psychiatric referrals, an impropriety for which it was eventually required to pay a large cash settlement negotiated by the state attorney general's office. There continue to be local, state, and federal investigations into the questionable business and treatment practices of these and other hospitals and hospital corporations.

The consequences of these improprieties have had far-reaching effects on the mental health community, including both patients and clinicians. In response to complaints of unnecessarily long hospitalizations, third-party payers, including indemnity insurers, Preferred Provider Organizations (PPOs), Medicare, and CHAMPUS, have substantially reduced their funding for inpatient psychiatric services. Unfortunately, they have also, for the most part, placed severe constraints on outpatient services, making appropriate treatment, particularly for chronically high-risk patients, difficult or impossible to obtain. The surviving psychiatric hospitals and programs, in an effort to police themselves, are also restricting inpatient stays and are reducing the availability of treatment modalities such as voluntary restraints for those occasions where such procedures would be therapeutically helpful and appropriate.

In 1996, President Clinton signed the Mental Health Parity act into law. This law provides for insurers to cover mental health related services at the same rate as medical services. This law essentially restrains insurers from imposing separate, lower limits on mental health coverage, higher co-payments for services, and other inequitable differences imposed on psychiatric patients. Unfortunately, insurers have discovered loopholes in this law and continue to limit the availability of mental health services to those who require them. Evidently, even Medicare disregards the law by imposing different standards of payment for psychiatric services. For medical expenses, Medicare determines the reasonable, customary and usual fee for the service rendered in the geographical area where the service occurs. It then pays 80% of that fee, leaving the 20% balance to be paid by the patient or secondary insurer. However, for psychiatric services, Medicare pays only 50% of the usual, reasonable and customary fee, with the resultant 50% the responsibility of the patient or secondary insurer. Also, Medicare provides for only 180 days of hospitalization in free-standing psychiatric facilities per lifetime of the Medicare beneficiary, whereas hospitalization for medical problems is virtually unlimited. Medicare and managed care both require that medical necessity for services be demonstrated in order to justify payment for those services. However, claims reviewers are seldom qualified to make such a determination. When even many psychiatrists and mental health specialists are undereducated in the area of dissociative disorders and the sequelae of childhood trauma, how can we expect nurses and physicians with no special training or experience in this area to discern medical necessity for specific services?

At the heart of the limitations on payment and availability of services is the apparent discrimination against the chronically and pervasively mentally ill. Despite the passage of the Americans with Disabilities Act, individuals suffering from mental illness are routinely discriminated against. They have fewer resources available. They are funded at lower levels that deny them the frequency and intensity of treatment they require for improvement.   It is more difficult to obtain disability status for the mentally ill through the Social Security Administration because of the subjective nature of psychiatric evaluation.   Many individuals are initially denied disability and must appeal the decisions, sometimes more than once, to secure approval.   Because of their frequently fragile emotional state, these individuals may not have the resources to pursue the process. Many individuals give up the struggle, suicide, or wind up homeless and on the street.   Some even end up in the criminal justice system.

In addition to their search for treatment and eventual recovery, many of these patients are experiencing a struggle for survival. Public programs, at least in Texas, are poorly equipped to deal with the magnitude of problems that these patients often present. Such programs often lack either the funding or training to adequately deal with these patients.   Public services are so overwhelmed in Texas that there are frequent announcements of freezes on mental health services.[254] It is not an uncommon event when patients who are so disturbed that police must be called to subdue and transport them to a public inpatient facility are discharged within hours.   Clinicians willing to treat these patients are encountering serious financial burdens as a consequence of the patients' inability to pay for necessary services. I personally know of psychiatrists and other mental health professionals who have been forced into bankruptcy by the combination of hospital failures and poor funding for needed mental health services.

As a result of these conflicts, an atmosphere of mistrust and divisiveness has emerged that has precluded effective communication and collegiality within the professional community. At a time when we should be working together to solve the enormous problems confronting us, many of us are isolated from one another and divided in our resolve.[255]   The ordinary concerns of the mental health professionals are compounded by those treating the effects of cult and ritual abuse. A sense of paranoia has sometimes been directed toward those providing treatment services to these survivors. Rumors run rampant, and the standing joke is that if you haven't been accused of being involved in a cult yourself, you're probably not an effective therapist.

Once I was disturbed to hear such a rumor about myself. According to the story, I was alleged to be the high priest in a Satanic coven. I addressed this issue in a daily group therapy session with my patients because it has always been my policy to openly confront rumors. Attempting to add a touch of levity to what was actually an embarrassing and professionally harmful situation, I announced to the group, "You know, I'm really sort of offended that with all that I know about programming, I'm accused of being *only* a high priest.[256]" A patient alleged to have been highly ranked within her cult put me in my place with, "You don't know *enough* to be a high priest," and the group erupted in laughter.

I was particularly disappointed to learn that this rumor had originated with a well known mental health professional practicing in an area psychiatric hospital. When dealing with a patient population that engenders considerable controversy, the support of one's peers is particularly important. Collegiality is becoming an increasingly scarce commodity, and I have heard many mental health providers say that they have felt both personally and professionally isolated.

In communicating my concerns with other therapists working with these patients, I found that many other therapists are encountering a pattern of increasing hostility directed toward them. We concluded that the organizations currently in place to provide support, continuing education, and collegiality among mental health professionals were insufficient. In fact, as I conversed with individuals representing different professional disciplines, many reported a sense of abandonment by colleagues and their professions. Police officers recounted experiences of both subtle and overt ridicule by peers and supervisors. District attorneys pursuing prosecutions against perpetrators of ritual abuse, and attorneys involved in the civil and criminal legal cases involving ritual abuse were confused as to how to convey factual information to judges and juries.

This dilemma is part of the reason for establishing an organization to promote communication, cooperation, and collegiality among professionals, survivors, and the lay public regarding the issue of cult and ritual abuse. The International Council on Cultism and Ritual Trauma (formerly the Society for the Investigation, Treatment and Prevention of Ritual and Cult Abuse) was established in March of 1993. It was formed to serve as a multidisciplinary association to address the concerns of clinicians, attorneys, law enforcement agents, social welfare representatives, clergy, media representatives, educators, survivors, and the public. Its goals are to facilitate the collection and distribution of data relevant to the diagnosis and treatment of ritual abuse; to establish investigatory, diagnostic, and treatment protocols; to provide continuing education; to foster communication among various organizations confronting problems related to cult and ritual abuse; and to provide support to survivors and their advocates. It is the mission of the ICCRT to study the issue of ritual abuse from a scientific perspective in order to reduce the hysteria, paranoia, and sensationalism frequently associated with this subject.

NOTES

[254] Texas Mental Health and Mental Retardation (MHMR) currently estimates there are in excess of 40,000 people awaiting services through their facilities statewide.

[255] In spite of the divisiveness in the community of mental health professionals there seems to be much agreement among those who work with dissociative disorders that ritual abuse is a genuine rather than imaginary problem (see Perry, 1992).

[256] The term "high priest" is not necessarily indicative of a high rank in many cultic organizations.

Chapter 15

The Media

The media have played an important role in the unfolding story of ritual abuse. Unfortunately, the media have tended to focus on the sensational or they have portrayed ritual abuse claims as absurd or even ridiculous. Such journalistic ventures fail to promote what is needed — a fair and impartial, but serious investigation of this subject. Nevertheless, my first experience with the national media exceeded my expectations for journalistic fairness.

At that time I was invited to be a guest on the Geraldo Rivera talk show for a program depicting the complications of family life when one of the parents is diagnosed as having DID. It occurred to me that if these patients were merely faking their symptoms, such dissimulation would probably be recognized by someone, such as a family member, who observed them daily. It was interesting to note that of the families present on the program, all believed and supported the family member diagnosed with DID. This particular program portrayed patients as believed, loved and respected by their family members, in spite of the significant disruption of the family that periodically results from the disorder.

From time to time we see television, newspaper, and magazine accounts of dissociation and ritual abuse. In some cases, we ourselves have been interviewed to provide background for some of these journalistic enterprises. Thus, we have had the opportunity to witness, sometimes as participant-observers, the inner workings of the media. What we have seen is often disturbing, particularly when we find the journalist to be deliberately suppressing and distorting information in order to create a sensational story that appears to have been concocted prior to completing the research.

This appears to have been the strategy for a cover story by Gary Cartwright in the regional magazine *Texas Monthly*. In describing the Fran's Day Care sexual abuse case, Cartwright concluded that the obtained convictions were the result of hysterical reactions by the community and the mental health professions. In late February 1994, I was contacted by a man who identified himself as David Mormon, a fact checker employed by Cartwright. He interviewed me over the telephone for more than an hour. He read those portions of the article that referred to me for comment and correction. When the article appeared in print two months later, I was surprised that most of the information I had provided, either in response to his questions or volunteered by me, had been left out of the article. Additionally, others who recounted their solicitation for input in the article, including the parents of the young victims, report that their information was misrepresented or disregarded in the published article. I wrote a letter to the editor of *Texas Monthly* to address my concerns that the case and my role in it had been misrepresented. My letter was not published.

We witnessed another example of biased and distorted journalism after representatives of ABC's *Prime Time Live* attended a training seminar offered through my office on the subject of ritual abuse. The production staff of *Prime Time Live* videotaped many hours for their segment reporting on the ritual abuse controversy. They taped an hour-and-a-half informal group with several patients, my six-hour seminar, and a two-hour interview between correspondent Jay Shadler and myself. Additionally, producer Steve Reiner and Jay Shadler spent several hours with a patient, "Vanessa," who also shared a videotape incorporating separate interview sessions between Vanessa and myself. Editing makes it possible to rearrange the sequencing of recorded events so that a very different meaning of an interviewee's statements is conveyed. Thus, because the segments were cut and arranged in a predetermined sequence, it gave a false impression that I made suggestions to a hypnotized patient that thirteen people, or a coven, may have come to her door, and thus, she may have attended a cult meeting. However, this interpretation of the televised material is patently false. In fact, the patient and I were discussing the number of her alternate identities that had a particular function. (i.e., the job of going to the door) *not* cultists. *Making Monsters,* by Ofshe and Waters (1994), cites these misquotes of me taken from this *Prime Time Live* program. Ofshe and Waters then use this misinformation to argue that therapists are brainwashing their patients into believing that they were sexually abused in Satanic cults.

Furthermore, neither Ofshe and Waters nor *Prime Time Live* mentioned the fact that the patient in question was aware of sexual abuse by her father and others before consulting any therapist or that her claims were validated by her sister who had endured similar experiences. No false memories could have been implanted by a therapist because the memories existed prior to seeing a mental health professional. Both *Prime Time Live* and *Making Monsters* erroneously implied that this patient considered herself a survivor of Satanic ritual abuse. In fact when I saw her she described ritual abuse but made no statements about Satanic ritual abuse.[257]

In addition to a general misrepresentation of professionals who treat survivors, the ABC newsmagazine contained a number of more specific fallacies. One example was the assertion that a seven-year FBI study revealed no evidence of organized cult or ritual activity in the United States. In reality there is no such study. The day following the ABC program, my office contacted the FBI and requested a copy of the alleged study. The bureau responded in writing indicating that no such study existed. Rather, the document featured on the program and to which the correspondent referred is entitled *Investigator's Guide to Allegations of "Ritual" Child Abuse* and contains no data nor research methodology whatsoever. This monograph by Special Agent Ken Lanning (1992) is merely a guide for those who may investigate this phenomenon, as the title indicates, and not a study. The author is a well known skeptic regarding cult and ritual abuse allegations who has consulted on a number of cases but to our knowledge has not personally investigated the majority of these cases, some of which have produced convictions.[258]

During my conversations with the *Prime Time Live* staff, Reiner and Shadler, I referenced several criminal and civil cases in which allegations of cult and ritual abuse were prominent, including instances in which convictions had been obtained. I went into specific detail regarding the case of Fran's Day Care because of my involvement as an expert witness. My office informed Reiner of the outcome of the Fran's Day Care case prior to the airing of the segment on *Prime Time Live*. However, the producer of the program chose to omit this information and to misrepresent or misinterpret the FBI study.

Prime Time Live also demonstrated faulty logic and a biased perspective in their discussion regarding the case of Gloria Grady. Grady, a Dallas area resident, had sought professional counseling because of a severe eating disorder. During the course of her therapy with several local therapists, Grady began to reveal a history of ritual abuse perpetrated against her by her father, a Baptist minister. Grady and her plight was the subject of two articles that appeared in *D Magazine*. The perspective of both articles was that Grady and her parents were the victims of unethical therapists who deliberately and maliciously implanted Gloria Grady with false memories of abuse. However, Gloria Grady stands by her story and maintains that she is a victim of abuse at the hands of her parents, from whom she has been estranged since recalling that abuse.

Three other patients who were in therapy during the same period as Grady and who also reported having recollections of ritual abuse perpetrated by their parents, recanted their stories and subsequently sued their therapists. One of these women settled her case out of court over the objections of the therapists. However, their malpractice insurance carriers believed a settlement to be less costly than a trial and ordered their legal team to resolve the matter out of court. A condition of settlement was that the patient not discuss the case, not reveal the therapist's names, nor the location where they practice. Most of these conditions appear to have been violated over time. The second case went to trial and although the jury awarded a verdict in the patient's favor, the judge attributed 60 percent of the responsibility to the therapist and 40 percent responsibility to the patient.[259] Both of these women have appeared on several talk shows, usually accompanied by professionals representing the False Memory Syndrome Foundation philosophy. One of the women is already promoting her soon to be published book. The third case was also settled. Although one of the therapists involved was absolved of any wrongdoing by his licensing board, his malpractice carrier canceled his coverage, an act that normally limits a therapist's ability to practice. The disruption to his practice by the notoriety of the cases, his lost hospital privileges, and his diminished patient load resulted in his bankruptcy.

In the course of the *Prime Time Live* segment, Shadler appeared to be implying that Grady sued her parents and that her parents prevailed. The only court action involving Grady and her parents of which we are aware is Grady's request that her parents be restrained from attempting to communicate with her. The judge apparently denied her request because Grady could not demonstrate to the court's satisfaction that her parents' pursuit of her constituted harassment.

A curiosity about the ABC program was a peculiar comment made by Jay Shadler in reference to Reverend and Mrs. Grady. Shadler asserted that neither Reverend nor Mrs. Grady could be guilty of their daughter's allegations because "she is a Sunday school teacher," and he is "a minister." This comment was particularly inappropriate because, in fact, Jay Shadler has no direct knowledge of Reverend or Mrs. Grady's guilt or innocence. Yet, Shadler made this observation while litigation related to this matter was ongoing and could have been affected by his unwarranted pronouncement. This statement also shows considerable naiveté on Shadler's part if he believes that innocent people may correctly be identified by their appearance or professions. In fact, in recent times, media have publicized numerous cases of clergy who are involved in criminal and immoral activities.[260] In her research on survivors of ritual abuse, Margaret Smith (1993) reports that clergymen are frequently identified as perpetrators of ritual abuse. Guilty people typically do not wear scarlet letters or other external or overt signs of their guilt.

Although *Prime Time Live* did not televise the material we provided regarding the outcomes of several cases, another television program did document some legal findings relevant to allegations of ritual abuse. The *American Justice* series, aired on the Arts and Entertainment channel, produced a program entitled "Satan, Rituals and Abuse" documenting the Fran's Day Care and the Country Day Walk cases, both of which were resolved by successful prosecutions. Additionally, and perhaps more significantly, both cases featured confessions by one of the defendants.

A controversial documentary addressing the ritual abuse controversy was aired on the *Frontline* series on the Public Broadcasting System (PBS). Produced by Ofra Bickel, this documentary proported to examine a witchhunt of innocent parents by therapists perpetuating the myth of ritual abuse among fragile psychiatric patients. Once again, the content of this program had a clear bias. Ms. Bickel used the program as a forum to promote sympathy with the False Memory Syndrome Foundation. The program's bias was so obvious as to generate the following letter from William Freyd, brother of FMSF founders Peter and Pamela Freyd:

> Peter Freyd is my brother. Pamela Freyd is both my stepsister and sister-in-law. Jennifer and Gwendolyn [Freyd] are my nieces. There is no doubt in my mind that there was severe abuse in the home of Peter and Pam, while they were raising their daughters. Peter said (on your show, "Divided Memories") that his humor was ribald. Those of us who had to endure it, remember it as abusive at best and viciously sadistic at worst. The False Memory Syndrome Foundation is a fraud designed to deny a reality that Peter and Pam have spent most of their lives trying to escape. There is no such thing as False Memory Syndrome. It is not, by any normal standards a Foundation. Neither Pam nor Peter has any significant mental health expertise. That the False Memory Syndrome Foundation has been able to excite so much media attention has been a great surprise to those of us who would like to admire and respect the objectivity and motives of people in the media. Neither Peter's mother (who was also mine), nor his daughters,

nor I have wanted anything to do with Peter and Pam for periods of time ranging up to more than two decades. We do not understand why you would "buy" such an obviously flawed story. But buy it you did, based on the severely biased presentation you made of the memory issue that Peter and Pam created to deny their own difficult reality. (Freyd, 1995, p.38)

The program focused on the treatment approach of psychologist Judith Peterson, Ph.D., and on several of her former patients who recanted their previous assertions of ritual abuse. These individuals filed complaints against Dr. Peterson's license and filed civil suits against her. Although the complaints against her license were dismissed, Dr. Peterson's malpractice insurer settled all lawsuits before the plaintiffs were deposed. As a consequence of the publicity generated by the documentary and the complaints and civil suits, the federal government took the extraordinary measure of filing criminal charges against Dr. Peterson. Prosecutors alleged that she defrauded the patient's insurance companies by charging for services to treat a mental disorder she had herself created and for billing for those fraudulent services through the federal postal system. After many months and hundreds of thousands of dollars in legal costs, the criminal charges against Dr. Peterson were dismissed. For the first time, the prosecution's witnesses, plaintiffs in the civil suits against Dr. Peterson, were cross-examined and their testimonies subjected to the scrutiny of the court. Therapy records, family histories, and additional information predating Dr. Peterson's intervention demonstrated that the patients' symptoms existed long before they entered treatment. It is likely that if Dr. Peterson's malpractice insurer had funded a more aggressive defense, the results of the lawsuits would have been much different.

Why do the media appear to be invested in distorting facts in order to present one particular point of view? We continue to be puzzled by ABC's and PBS's decisions to slant the perspective of their programs. Why was it important to represent individuals who could have been perpetrators as victims?[261] For whatever reason, ABC and PBS are not alone in their prejudicial stance regarding ritual abuse.

The *Jane Whitney Show* contacted my office asking if any of the patients would be willing to appear on her nationally syndicated talk show. The producer specifically asked for patients who were originally from the East Coast, perhaps hoping that a free round trip would entice them to accept her invitation. None of my patients expressed any interest in appearing, and when the program aired, I was relieved that none of my patients participated. Two patients and a therapist were pitted against individuals representing the False Memory Syndrome Foundation. We considered it inappropriate for this program to have invited patients to reveal such personal information about themselves, and then be subjected to an unexpected attack by professionals who never examined the patients but who were willing to criticize their allegations on national television.

The *Leeza Gibbons Show* invited me to Los Angeles to explain the psychological damage caused by ritual abuse. They requested that I ask a survivor to accompany me and I invited "Mary"[262] a ritual abuse survivor who was fully recovered and anxious to spread a message of hope to other ritual abuse victims. I spent several hours on the telephone speaking with the producer of the program and I was assured that "Mary" and I would be provided a respectful forum in which to address ritual abuse and its consequences. Instead, we were introduced midway through the program which had been devoted to the story of a young woman who alleged that she had been victimized by mental health professionals who implanted false memories of abuse in her mind. An apologist for the False Memory Syndrome Foundation, Paul Johnson, accompanied her and her mother and sister, with whom she had recently reunited. Periodically, captions would scroll across the bottom of the television screen backstage citing the alarming but inaccurate statistics accumulated by the FMSF stating that there were thousands of families destroyed by "false memories." Our attempts to speak to the issues were drowned out by Ms. Gibbons and her other guests. Comments that I had made to explain my position were cut out of the tape that finally appeared on television.

Maury Povich invited children who had made allegations of ritual abuse while enrolled at the McMartin Preschool in Manhattan Beach, California, to appear on his program along with their parents. One of the points made in the program was that excavations had been conducted that had revealed the presence of the underground tunnels the children had reported to authorities as the site of some of their abuse. Povich also invited Paul and Shirley Eberle, authors of *The Abuse of Innocence* (1993), to appear on the same program. The Eberle's' book argues that the children were not ritually abused at the McMartin School, but that they had been victimized by their therapists and "the system," which the Eberles' accuse of encouraging children to make false allegations. Two of the mothers of the abused children present for the program, Marymae Cioffi and Jackie MacGauley, became particularly frustrated when Povich refused to allow them to present information regarding the Eberle's' history and dubious qualifications to address child abuse. The Eberle's were publishers of sexually explicit periodicals, including *Finger,* a Los Angeles tabloid containing pornographic photographs, drawings and stories about children. When Povich refused to allow this material to be presented, Cioffi and MacGauley left the stage and distributed examples of the Eberle's' work to the studio audience.[263]

The McMartin case is also the subject of the cable movie, *Indictment*, produced for Home Box Office. Several children's advocacy groups expressed concern that the film's focus appeared to be slanted in favor of the accused perpetrators. The newsletter for the organization Believe the Children contained an impassioned plea to its readers to relinquish their subscriptions to Home Box Office (HBO) in protest of this film's airing. An article featured in that newsletter entitled "Sex Abuse, Lies and Videotape" (1995) describes the genesis of the program and voices its concerns that the true victims of the McMartin case, the children, might be damaged by the perspective of the film's author, Abby Mann. According to the article, Mann and his wife, Myra, became advocates of the operators and staff of the McMartin preschool during the course of their trial. Because of the Mann's involvement in the case and their relationship to the accused perpetrators, the article expressed the concern that the film might reflect an unbalanced portrait of accused and accusers such that roles might be reversed in the eyes of the viewing public. This has, in fact, proven a correct assumption. Reviews of the cable movie featured in magazines such as *Time* (Bellafante, 1995) and *TV Guide* (McDougal, 1995) on the film's depiction of an overzealous prosecuting attorney, a mentally unbalanced parent of a child victim, and a punitive therapist all lend themselves to the perpetuation of the idea that the true victims are the alleged perpetrators. Ironically, this film also casts the media in an unfavorable light implying that the media's over-the-top reporting of the event led to a veritable witch-hunt.

Television is not been the only medium providing a slanted, biased, or otherwise incomplete or inaccurate depiction of material relevant to this social problem. Several regional and national magazines have published articles that, with few exceptions, portray ritual abuse as a fantasy and a fraud, those exceptions appearing in *Vanity Fair* (Bennetts, 1993). and *MS Magazine* (Rose, 1993). The first publication provides a discussion with both sides of the controversy represented. The second accurately represents the experience of a ritual abuse survivor from her point of view. On the other hand, the lurid articles that appeared in *Mirabella* (Harrison, 1993). and in two consecutive issues of *The New Yorker* (Wright, 1993a, 1993b) served to further depict an extreme and sensational point of view. In the *New Yorker* article in particular, the author failed to accurately represent the claims of survivors and he omitted the substantiating evidence for their reports. This was particularly disheartening to us because we had spoken at some length to the author, Larry Wright, while he was researching ritual abuse for his article. Later, I learned that other individuals well acquainted with ritual abuse issues had also cooperated with him in an effort to assist him in producing a factual article that fairly represented the issues. Instead, Wright elected to focus on a particular case where he argued that the evaluation of an alleged perpetrator[264] might have been corrupted by poor interviewing technique. Wright portrayed this scenario as typical of cases involving ritual abuse claims. In 1994, Wright's articles were expanded to book length and published as *Remembering Satan* (1994).

Although the national media have often taken an unduly critical attitude toward ritual abuse allegations, some ritual abuse cases go virtually ignored. This is what happened during an ongoing police investigation involving allegations of widespread child abuse, ritual abuse, police and governmental corruption, kidnapping, murder, and cannibalism, in a small East Texas community. In 1992, fifteen children in Gilmer, Texas, were removed from their extended families of origin and placed in protective, therapeutic foster care after investigations by Child Protective Services revealed their sadistic sexual abuse and victimization by parents, grandparents, aunts, uncles, and others. A special prosecutor was appointed to bring the alleged perpetrators to justice. Scott Lyford, a Galveston attorney, and his investigative team were able to accumulate sufficient evidence to gain indictments and convictions against the eight defendants.

As the children became increasingly secure in their foster care environment and in their therapeutic relationship with a mental health professional, they began to reveal details of their victimization that included elements of ritualistic abuse such as being forced to ingest blood, urine and feces, deviant sex practices, and other behaviors indicative of ritual activities. One of the abused children disclosed special knowledge regarding the disappearance of an area teenager, Kelly Wilson. This child implicated his sexual abuse perpetrators and an area police officer in the abduction, rape, torture, and murder of Wilson, a 17 year old Gilmer resident who disappeared on January 5, 1992.

When confronted with the child's testimony, two of the accused adults confessed to the offenses and one of the adults directed the investigative team to a property owned by the paternal grandparents of the children where the adult alleged some ritual activities had taken place, including the murder of Kelly Wilson. The two adults subsequently recanted their confessions, and later confessed again. One of the adults plea-bargained to a lesser offense for which she has since been convicted but not sentenced. Both adults submitted to polygraph evaluations whose results supported their confessions.

After the disclosures of ritual abuse, the allegations regarding the murder of Kelly Wilson, and the implications by some of the victims and some of the perpetrators that others, including a Gilmer police officer were involved in the crimes, the Texas Attorney General's office replaced the special prosecutor and his investigative team. Assistant Attorney General Shane Phelps reportedly directed the grand jury to "no bill" the defendants. However, the grand jury apparently ignored this direction and instead dismissed the indictment without prejudice allowing the state to reconsider the case at a future date.

The Special Prosecutor, his investigative team, and the CPS caseworkers continued advocating on behalf of the fifteen children. They alleged that the attorney general's office has lost evidence, misinterpreted their investigation, not proceeded with its own investigation, interfered with the children's psychotherapy, and removed the children from their therapeutic foster care without concern for the well-being of the children. These individuals further alleged that the state of Texas, via the attorney general's office, retraumatized the children by forcibly removing them from their foster mother and by engaging in punitive and damaging strategies in order to command the children's cooperation. The State Attorney General at that time, Dan Morales, continued to be unresponsive to residents of Gilmer and others who expressed concern for the welfare of these child victims. The request for a complete and thorough public disclosure regarding the circumstances of the children's victimization was also ignored.

The special prosecutor, his investigative team, and the CPS caseworkers have been sued by some of the accused child abuse perpetrators for malicious prosecution and other alleged improprieties. The state of Texas denied these individuals the option of state funded independent legal counsel, despite evidence of a conflict of interest between the attorney general's office and these individuals. The children's foster mother's ability to visit with and nurture these children has reportedly been made contingent upon her assistance in soliciting the children's cooperation with their current psychotherapeutic team. There was an implication that her failure to assist might result in the children's return to their abusive families of origin.[265]

According to Bruce Perry, MD,[266] the psychiatrist who headed the children's treatment team, there were serious errors in judgment on the part of the attorney general's office that resulted in the retraumatization of these severely abused children. Dr. Perry was specifically referring to the abrupt and violent manner in which the children were removed from their therapeutic foster mother's custody and placed in a facility in Waco, Texas. In a bizarre twist, on November 16, 1994, the Gilmer Police

Department confirmed that on Halloween night, October 31, 1994, at least six boxes containing police records and evidence involving the Kelly Wilson case accumulated by the special prosecutor and his investigative team mysteriously disappeared from police headquarters.[267]

Despite the length of time this case was under investigation and the huge number of victims and accused perpetrators, and the extraordinary nature of the allegations, there was little media coverage of the Gilmer events. The lack of balanced local coverage is easy to explain, but difficult to comprehend. The editor of the local newspaper, *The Gilmer Mirror*, was also on the Upshur County grand jury that heard the allegations. During her tenure on the grand jury, the editor published articles critical of the idea that ritual abuse occurs which appears to demonstrate a serious conflict of interest. In the meantime, *Dallas Morning News*, reporter Victoria Loe wrote articles about the Gilmer case that would be more accurately described as editorials than journalistic reports. Several of the principals in the case including the investigative team, family members of the children who recounted their own victimization, and members of the Justice for Kelly Wilson Committee spoke at length and in great detail with Loe regarding specific incidents wherein the case had been contaminated through interference by the Texas Attorney General's office, the Gilmer police, and others. Loe never included this information in her articles. Loe was rewarded by being named a best reporter in 1994 by *The Dallas Morning News*. The *Dallas Morning News* has not, to our knowledge, published anything about the missing police files from Gilmer.[268]

In the Gilmer case, the media had complete access to the facts of the case and yet elected to ignore the story out of hand or to portray events in context with their preconceived notions of what constitutes abuse and who can be an abuser. However, the media is often denied access to information about crime that may include ritual abuse elements.

Media problems were also evident in the reporting of the 1990 murder of Mark Kilroy and others in Matamoros, Mexico. Although this was a horrendous crime that did attract international media attention, the details involving the mutilation of the victims and actual testimony by the perpetrators were withheld from the media. The media de-emphasized the ritual aspects of the crime and interpreted the murders as being more drug than cult-related. Co-author Pamela Perskin viewed the recorded confessions of some of the accused perpetrators and their exhumation of the murder victim's bodies videotaped by the Mexican federales. These videotapes made clear that these were ritual murders intended to grant magical powers to the perpetrators. Although the accomplices to the murder of Kilroy confessed to additional sacrificial murders and indicated willingness to lead police to more burial sites, the Mexican police refused to investigate further. We have found other occasions where the police or other government officials have misrepresented details of particular crimes to the media in order to obscure facts that allude to the crimes having a ritual aspect.

During the course of a training session for the Texas Council of Occult Crimes Investigators, police officers representing a variety of agencies discussed cases involving what they believed to be ritual crime. However, upon direction from their supervisors, they concealed the ritual elements when discussing the cases with media. One case, for example, involved a young female murder victim discovered roadside along a major highway in San Antonio, Texas. The media reports were limited to identifying the victim as a prostitute and suggesting her murder was drug related. However, the autopsy film reveals that the victim had been horribly mutilated. The young woman had several tattoos with bizarre designs, some with cult connotations, adorning her body. Her eyes had been gouged out. She had been stabbed multiple times and her uterus had been torn from her body.

Why the police chose not to disclose the specifics of this case or similar ones is unknown. Police officers speculate many possibilities including that police are suppressed by city, state, and county governments who fear a public relations backlash. Others postulate more sinister motivations. We believe that more openness and candor is needed in the area of reporting regarding ritual abuse both from law enforcement and the media. Accurate information about ritual abuse, like any other kind of criminal violence, should be available so that the problem can be more effectively addressed by an informed public.

What is clearly needed is balanced and fair reporting of events, equal access to the media by proponents of disparate views, and open communication between law enforcement and the media. As this book approaches republication, it is clear that this goal is as yet unmet. A cursory review of current journalistic presentations of such topics as psychogenic amnesia, sexual abuse and ritual abuse reveals an over-representation of publications and programming which reflect an anti-therapist, anti-victim perspective. As a consequence of sensationalized accounts of the cult and ritual abuse controversy, many survivors report feelings of hopelessness and despair. For many survivors, the message to keep the silence is reinforced by repeatedly biased and sometimes inaccurate or untruthful renderings of their stories. Frequent media portrayals of mental health professionals as villains, and accused perpetrators as victims, leave survivors fearful that no justice will be forthcoming. Ideally, the media should provide a conduit of undiluted, undistorted information between the source and the consumer. Perhaps a better educated and more discriminating public will demand more of its media resources.

NOTES

[257] "Vanessa" sought legal counsel in an attempt to sue ABC for misrepresentation and slander. She was unable to afford the attorney's fees and unable to interest an attorney in accepting her case on a contingency basis. The attorneys all agreed she had a valid case, but were concerned that because of ABC's wealth, it could prolong the case resulting in a huge financial investment that might not be justified by the case's outcome. Nevertheless, "Vanessa" pursued the case , without legal counsel, and ABC did make a financial settlement.

[258] In *Lessons in Evil, Lessons from the Light*, Ken Lanning is described as obstructive and unhelpful in the investigation of this particular patient's allegations of abuse (Feldman, 1993, pp. 297–298).

[259] The court did not find the therapist implanted false memories of abuse in the patient's mind. However, the therapist was ascribed a portion of responsibility in the case because he kept insufficient patient records to demonstrate the appropriateness of his therapy strategy. This exemplifies a common ethical dilemma among therapists who frequently must choose between documenting allegations by patients which may be self-incriminating and could cause considerable hardship to the patient in the event of their release via subpoena in legal proceedings such as divorce or custody hearings, or by keeping more cryptic, less informative notes which protect the patient's confidentiality but which may leave the therapist at risk.

[260] The case of Father William Porter, convicted of sexually molesting many children over the course of his career, comes immediately to mind. Other instances include scandals involving Father Rudy Kos, and Reverands Jimmy Bakker, and Jimmy Swaggart.

[261] Given that it is impossible to know whether the accused were innocent or guilty do we not have a moral obligation to refrain from making assertions one way or the other?

[262] See Chapter 4.

[263] We visited with Marymae Cioffi in Los Angeles and she provided us with copies of the Eberle's work. Until actually seeing these publications we were somewhat skeptical of this story. It is still incredible to us that a national television talk show host would allow child pornographers to critique a case of ritual abuse while suppressing the history of the authors' previous work in child pornography. The Eberle's book is cited as one of various "sources by reliable authors and researchers" by Hans Sebald (1995, p. 245) after a warning that "a lot of utter nonsense and distorted information has been published on the topic" (p. 245) in Sebald's book, *Witch-Children: From Salem Witch-Hunts to Modern Courtrooms.*

[264] Now convicted perpetrator.

[265] Most of the children were indeed ultimately returned to their families of origin.

[266] Dr. Perry's name may be familiar to those who have read Maury Terry's book, *The Ultimate Evil.* He is the husband of ritual murder victim Arliss Perry. Not only did Dr. Perry supervise the care of the Gilmer children, he also headed the treatment team charged with the care of the child survivors of the Branch Davidian compound.

[267] According to a report in *The Gilmer Mirror*, the disappearance was originally reported by the newspaper on November 9, 1995, but was not confirmed by the Gilmer police department until November 16, 1995.

[268] It is interesting to note that the *Dallas Morning News* is the only daily newspaper in Dallas and is owned by the same parent company that owns Channel 8, the local ABC television affiliate.

Chapter 16

Will "The System" Protect Them?

When "Jane" first arrived in my office, she had just been discharged from a lengthy hospitalization on a dedicated dissociative disorders unit. She feared that because of her history of uncontrollable, violent acting-out, I would be unwilling to treat her. Indeed, she had been refused treatment by several local and national hospital programs and therapists. She was barely surviving financially and living in bleak poverty. She was, literally and figuratively speaking, at the end of her rope.

It has not been my habit to refuse treatment to a patient simply because other therapists choose not to work with that individual. I believe that our society must recognize that there are people who go begging for psychiatric help and that we do them and ourselves a disservice when we arbitrarily turn them away. In Jane's case, her therapy became a trial by fire. She had violent abreactions that created havoc in my office. It was not uncommon for me to have to engage the entire staff in restraining her from harming herself or one of us.

On one occasion, Jane eloped from the office and made her way to the parking lot of the building. One of my mental health technicians followed Jane and attempted to calm her, but Jane grabbed an empty bottle from the curb and, holding it by the neck, in one deft movement she smashed it against the side of the building and held her weapon against the body of the tech. As the technician continued to try to reason with her, Jane abruptly turned the bottle against herself and cut her own arm. Fortunately for all of us, neither Jane nor staff was seriously injured. When Jane's destructiveness escalated in this manner, the only available option to us was to recommend hospitalization and hope that we could find a hospital that would take her.

However, when I referred Jane for hospitalization, things were not much better. Once, she broke a wooden chair against the wall of a room where we were engaged in a therapy session and threatened me with the jagged leg, which she wielded like a spear. It became increasingly difficult to find hospital programs willing to accept her. Jane was unresponsive to the prescribed medications, and hospitals were often unwilling to accept the responsibility of restraining her, even when she herself requested restraints.

Eventually in the course of our therapy sessions, Jane revealed that she had been highly placed in several cults,[269] which had included Satanic, African-derived, Native-American, Masonic, and quasi-Masonic rituals. She had, reportedly, been a "programmer". Through a process of trial and error, I was able to isolate a number of alleged cult cues, or "triggers" to which her system responded with de-escalation of her violent behaviors. Once Jane was able to exert control over her behaviors such that she was able to minimize her self-destructive acting-out, she began to make significant progress in therapy. At those times when she felt unstable and dangerous, she entered the hospital, although her hospitalizations became increasingly briefer and more infrequent. In fact, to date she has not been in a psychiatric hospital in over seven years and has shown no violence in my office for an even longer period of time. Jane has been employed for the last several years, something she had not previously been able to do. She has also returned to college and is making excellent grades.

Prior to my meeting her, Jane moved to Texas secretly and lived anonymously under a pseudonym. She believed that she was at risk for being abducted by her "organization" and that if apprehended by them, she would be forced to return or she would be killed. It was impossible to objectively judge the veracity of her claims or the extent to which her concerns represented genuine threats to her safety. However, on several occasions, Jane reported having been "accessed" by someone with an interest in hurting her or returning her to the cult.

One day, my office received an emergency call from Jane's roommate requesting an immediate appointment for Jane. The secretary instructed the roommate to bring Jane in right away so that we could somehow work her into the schedule. Upon arrival, the roommate explained that Jane had come to her workplace complaining that her back was hurting. Jane's roommate took her to the women's restroom in order to inspect Jane's back. When she lifted Jane's shirt, the roommate said that she saw a sheet of paper stapled to the skin of Jane's back. The roommate then removed the paper and the staples from Jane's back.

Jane was unable to account for the time between dropping her roommate at work and the time she returned to her roommate's workplace.

As a male psychologist, it would not have been appropriate for me to examine Jane's back to see whether it indeed been punctured; however, some female members of my staff did so and reported that it appeared as though staples had been embedded in Jane's skin. What the staff members described was a fairly orderly, symmetrical placement of puncture wounds consistent in size with staple marks located in the center of Jane's back, between her shoulder blades. Jane is a woman who was in her mid-thirties at that time who did not appear to have the agility to staple a piece of paper to her back in the manner in which it appeared to have been done. The paper that had purportedly been stapled to Jane's back showed evidence of having been attached by staples to skin because it was bloodstained in a manner consistent with the description by Jane and her roommate. Two words were written in a childish scrawl across the paper — "Doctor Noblitt."

As I questioned Jane regarding the meaning of the note and her recollection for the events, she dissociated as a child alter. In this state, she explained that Jane had been abducted, assaulted, abused and threatened. According to the child alter, she had been directed to write a note saying, "Doctor Noblitt: Back Off." The child alter agreed to write my name on the note but refused to write the message to me as it was dictated by her perpetrators. Eventually, the incomplete note was stapled to her back. Jane was in an acutely traumatized state and I believed that she needed hospitalization.

I was able to convince a local hospital to admit her. Before going into the hospital, Jane thought that she was being followed and she feared for her life. Although I could not ascertain whether she was really under the threat of external perpetrators, I had no doubt that she believed she was, and given the incident of the stapled note, I was prepared to accept her allegations, at least hypothetically.

Jane made good progress in her therapy. She elected to discharge from full hospitalization to partial hospitalization. Typically, Jane drove her roommate to work, then came to the partial hospital program. At the end of the day, she picked her roommate up on the way home.

One day, I was approached by one of the nurses of the inpatient unit. She asked me if I happened to have Jane's patient chart, and I responded that I did not. The nurse admitted that the chart was missing, and no one could account for it. The hospital staff suggested that somehow Jane had pilfered her own chart. This notion seemed completely absurd to me. Hospital charts were kept in a locked nurses' station, on a locked unit separate from the unit where Jane was attending the partial hospitalization program. Jane did not have access to the unit, let alone the nurses' station. I believe the speculations leveled against Jane were conjectured by hospital staff in order to defer responsibility for the missing records.

A few days later, I was on the dissociative disorders unit seeing patients when I received an emergency page from the office of the partial hospitalization program. I made my way downstairs to find Jane curled up in a fetal position on a sofa in the hospital's day treatment program unit. As soon as she saw me, Jane jumped to her feet and, under the influence of a child alter, and before any of us could react, she lifted her shirt and revealed her naked back to me. Positioned directly between her shoulder blades was a burn, a brand, in the design of either a number "6" or "9" (depending upon one's vantagepoint).

Jane's child alter complained of significant gynecological pain and of having been sexually assaulted. I requested that the hospital examine Jane and provide any treatment that might be needed. The hospital staff declined stating that if she had indeed been sexually assaulted, Jane would have to be evaluated in one of the county medical facilities where special forensic examination procedures were in place to accumulate evidence. Jane was subsequently transported to a neighboring county hospital in the area where she alleged her assault to have taken place.

The emergency room staff at the county hospital conducted a gynecological examination that revealed that papers had been forcibly inserted into Jane's vagina and rectum. Upon examination, it was determined that these papers were a part of her missing hospital chart. Coincidentally with Jane's examination, the cover and remainder of her hospital chart were left on the desk of a sheriff's deputy in still another city. According to the deputy's report, the chart was hand delivered and left on his desk by persons unknown.

When a facsimile copy of the emergency room physician's report arrived at the psychiatric hospital where Jane was again an inpatient, it was totally illegible. Faint words were visible on the margins of the paper, but the middle section of the page was entirely blank. Upon retransmission, the results were still unreadable. The county hospital staff agreed to mail another copy of their report. When it did not arrive within a reasonable period of time, staff called and was informed that Jane's chart at the county hospital was missing. Days later, the chart was located.

Although the police appeared to take the attack on my patient seriously and attempted to investigate the incident, their efforts to prosecute the perpetrators were obstructed by uncooperative hospital staff from both the psychiatric hospital and the county hospital. I can only hypothesize that their concern for their liability and the reputations of their hospitals took precedence over the safety and recovery of their patient.

In the course of my work with individuals who allege ritual abuse, I have been asked to testify, sometimes as an expert witness, sometimes in my capacity as a therapist, in both civil and criminal cases.[270] In 1992, I was contacted by the district attorney's office of Travis County, where Austin, the state capital, is located. The Assistant District Attorney, Judy Shipway, asked if I would be willing to consult with her office regarding allegations of ritual abuse made by children who reported that they had been abused in a day care setting. I did not personally evaluate the children who had made the outcry, but I did examine all the data in the possession of the district attorney's office relating to the children's complaints, the setting in which the abuse allegedly occurred, information about the alleged perpetrators, and clinical data regarding the children's history, ongoing psychotherapy and current functioning.

Upon an initial partial review of the information, I advised Shipway to focus her prosecution on the sexual abuse aspects of the case. In my opinion, the sexual abuse allegations were clear and easier for the jury to comprehend, and there was less likelihood for generating a sensational case that could confuse the important legal questions.[271] In reviewing the materials, I had no doubt that the alleged perpetrators were guilty of sexual *and* ritual abuse. I did not want to see the state risk its opportunity for convictions by forcing the prosecutors to explain a concept as foreign as ritual abuse to the court. I was concerned that the issue at the core of the children's allegations, their sadistic, criminal abuse, might get lost amidst intellectual, philosophical, and religious arguments denying the existence of the ritualistic nature of the sexual assaults. I agreed to be available as an expert witness in the event that the subject of ritual abuse was raised for any reason.

As the case unfolded in court, it was not the prosecution who introduced the subject of ritual abuse, but the defense. The first of the alleged perpetrators to be tried were husband and wife, Dan and Fran Keller, the owners and operators of Fran's Day Care. The attorneys defending the Kellers used the children's reports of blood sacrifice, drinking blood, even murder, to cast aspersions on their reliability as informants. The case against the Kellers floundered when the court forced one of the accusing children, a youngster barely five years old, to testify in open court in the presence her alleged perpetrators. At that time, the child not only recanted her allegations but denied that she had ever been subjected to any kind of abuse. She also denied ever having attended the day care facility.

Judy Shipway asked me to testify in order to explain to the jury how ritual abuse occurs and how it could account for the child's reaction in court. Not only was I called upon to explain ritual abuse; it was also necessary for me to refute the arguments of the defense's primary resource in supporting its contention that the children's allegations were untrue and were provoked by adults, including parents, therapists, and others.

The defense attorney introduced a book entitled *Sex Abuse Hysteria: Salem Witch Trials Revisited,* by Richard A. Gardner (1991). Gardner's thesis is that allegations of child sexual abuse are the fabrications of adults who vicariously live out their sexual fantasies through children. According to Gardner, many adults, including those who act in advocacy roles for abused children, are latent pedophiles who obtain sexual gratification through the sexual experiences, real or imagined, of children. As ridiculous as this argument may sound, it has been the foundation of many legal arguments in defense of alleged perpetrators of child sexual abuse.

The district attorney's office had wisely directed that the families involved should not communicate with each other about the children's allegations in order to reduce the possibility of the complainants being influenced by one another. The prosecutors were responding to the precedent of the McMartin case, in which the defendants' legal counsel argued that the children in this ritual abuse case had been influenced by numerous sources. Although I know of no scientific evidence that would prove such an assumption,[272] it has been argued that children's memories are often unstable and easily influenced by others. However, not all researchers agree with this hypothesis and, for the most part, see children as typically reliable and truthful respondents.

Regarding the case of Fran's Day Care, the jury reached a guilty verdict and Dan and Fran Keller were each sentenced to 48 years in prison. Although I was pleased that the children were believed and the Kellers were held responsible for their actions, I was disappointed at the outcome.

Prior to the sentencing, I sent a message to Shipway's office recommending that the convicted couple be evaluated for DID themselves. The reason for this recommendation is that ritual abuse is commonly transgenerational. Perpetrators may have such abuse histories in their own backgrounds. If they are to be rehabilitated, it is essential to know whether their perpetration was a result of their own experience resulting in their own dissociation of identity. Furthermore, they may have been entitled to use the insanity defense if they were sufficiently dissociated when the offenses occurred. I received no response. A third defendant in the Fran's Day Care case confessed to sexual abuse of a child and was sentenced to a ten-year probated sentence. The two other alleged perpetrators were deputy constables in the Travis County Sheriff's Department. They have never been brought to trial.

As an interesting footnote to my participation in the Fran's Day Care trial, I received a call from an individual who identified himself as a television news reporter from Channel 7 in Austin. He called because he had observed one of the defendants, Mr. Keller, to engage in a brief series of bizarre hand movements that included what looked like American sign language. Some of these hand signs happened to have been captured on videotape. He asked if I would be willing to look at his film and comment on it for his television station. I agreed and the next day received a copy of the videotape of the mysterious hand signals. The following day, a reporter and camera crew from a local television station arrived at my office.

On camera, I explained how cult triggers are alleged to work and hypothesized that Dan Keller may have been signaling to someone in the court, possibly victims, jury members, or others. I retained a copy of the videotape from Austin showing Dan Keller's signaling. The consensus among patients and other therapists who have seen this film is that it is most probably a case of utilizing such signaling techniques.[273] Patients report that unobtrusive signals are used in the court venue in civil and criminal cases. They are reportedly sometimes utilized in the jury selection process to stack the deck in cases that affect the interests of other cult members. There may be occasions when the presence of merely one or two friendly jurors may affect the outcome of a trial. Such signals are also allegedly used to intimidate susceptible witnesses, attorneys, and others. Obviously, not everyone would be influenced by such techniques — only people who had been subjected to traumatizing programming.

I encountered what may be a less subtle form of this signaling approximately a year previous to the Keller case when I appeared as an expert witness on behalf of a mother and her children involved in a custody dispute with the children's father. The children had alleged that their father had sexually and ritually abused them. The mother, herself allegedly a survivor of lifelong abuse, first in her family of origin and later via her ex-husband, had a history of psychiatric treatment, including hospitalizations. Her children, however, maintained that their mother had never been their perpetrator, and they all wished to be in her sole custody.

One morning I sat in the courtroom behind the mother's attorney, awaiting the commencement of the day's proceedings. The door to the jury room opened and, to my surprise, and to the horror of the mother, the entire jury entered wearing red shirts. After an uncomfortable silence, the judge made a weak joke about there being no conspiracy. I asked the mother's attorney if he had ever seen such a display by a jury in his lengthy career in law, and he said that he had not.[274] Other ritually abused patients have told me that they had been sent messages that were conveyed through the color red, which was usually intended, they said, to disrupt the survivor and cause the survivor to obsess or act on thoughts of cutting oneself (i.e., producing blood). Although the father denied having ritually abused his children, he did admit that he had pointed a loaded gun at one of his children on one occasion. Nevertheless, the father was awarded full custody of the children. This story did eventually end happily for mother and children. The children's father voluntarily released the children to the custody of their mother over the course of the next few years due to the mother's and children's continuing efforts to be reunited.

Custody cases are notoriously difficult venues in which to deal with ritual abuse allegations. There are invariably counter-claims by the accused that the plaintiff has created or encouraged false allegations to punish or control. In every custody case in which I have been involved, the defense has relied on various texts by Gardner, Underwager and Wakefield and other apologists for the False Memory Syndrome Foundation's doctrine. Furthermore, in almost every instance, the mother is at an extreme financial disadvantage and often cannot afford to hire an aggressive lawyer or expensive, well-known experts. In addition, because the court systems are still overwhelmingly male dominated and bastions of the "good old boy" network, protective mothers are frequently put on the defensive and unfairly characterized as having ulterior motives when their children make allegations of sexual or ritual abuse. In fact, when mothers have come to me asserting that their children have made an outcry against their fathers, it has been necessary to first explore the possibility that such notions were deliberately insinuated in the children by their mother or others in order to prepare for this often used defense argument.

One such woman called me from another city. She identified herself as the divorced mother of two little girls. She described situations involving the children that had concerned her enough that she was seeking mental health consultation for her daughters. The mother described precocious and bizarre sexual acting out by her three and five-year-old daughters. The mother, a schoolteacher, attempted to deal with the situations in a gentle, nonjudgmental way. However, despite her attempts to discourage the children from acting out individually and with others, they were not deterred.

As the children's behaviors became increasingly out of control, the mother sought advice from a therapist in her local area. The therapist told the mother that the children demonstrated emotional and behavioral evidence of sexual molestation. Devastated, the mother turned to Child Protective Services (CPS) for additional assistance. A CPS caseworker informed the mother that based on her experience, she believed the children had been ritually abused. The caseworker referred the mother to a police officer who verified that based on the children's bizarre actions, he too believed that they had been ritually abused.

The mother sought a consultation with me in order to obtain a second opinion regarding the children's possible ritual abuse, and specifically, the identity of the children's perpetrator(s). Over the course of several weeks the children began to divulge information indicating that their father had abused them. Their mother reacted with shock and dismay to these revelations. Further, I was obligated to notify Child Protective Services.

The mother requested that the court amend the visitation agreement so that the father was permitted only supervised visitation with their children. Among the children's complaints against their father had been his abuse of them utilizing an aerosol soap dispenser. According to the girl's reports, their father had inserted the tip of the dispenser into their rectums and their vaginas. When the father arrived at the court-ordered supervised visits, he brought the children gifts of the same soap dispensers. The children were unusually compliant during his visits and became highly agitated at home with their mother.

In spite of the favorable impression the mother made on me, the father made an even more favorable one upon the court.[275] In a conversation with my assistant following my court appearance, the mother's own attorney exclaimed, "Maybe he [the father] might have done something he shouldn't have done with the little girls, but I don't think he *hurt* them. When he was on the witness stand, he was crying. He loves his children." Such naiveté is commonly found in cases of sexual and ritual abuse where the alleged perpetrator presents as a sincere and caring individual who proclaims his or her innocence over the protestations of accusers. In some cases, the perpetrator may even pass a lie detector test.[276] In some instances, the perpetrator has dissociated the memories of the abuse and sincerely feels innocent.

I was referred an inpatient consultation some years ago. The patient, a young mother married to her second husband, was hospitalized when she suffered severe decompensation in response to her children's allegations of sexual abuse by her husband, the biological father of the two younger children and stepfather of the older children. I was asked to evaluate the patient and found her to be highly dissociative. In a dissociated state, the patient described a history of sexual and ritual abuse perpetrated against her by her family and others during her childhood, by her first husband, and by her current husband.

I reported my findings to the psychiatrist in charge of the children's case, and he requested that I also evaluate the children and the father for ritual abuse histories while they were all hospitalized at the same facility. Before I was able to interview the children their Child Protective Services caseworker overruled the physician's orders and removed the children to a distant psychiatric facility where they remained until their insurance benefits were exhausted.

I spent quite a bit of time with the father. Curiously, the father admitted to some of the abuse of which he was accused. However, he denied certain of the allegations with great apparent sincerity. This aroused my curiosity. Why would he admit some of his guilt, but not all? In fact, he pled guilty to the charges against him and is currently in prison. I believe that this individual was amnestic for some of the episodes of abuse.[277] This is not to suggest that he should not be held accountable or that his children should not be protected from him. But I believe that this constitutes another indicator of significant psychological disturbance that is poorly addressed in a prison. I suggested to the father that he might be able to obtain psychological assistance if he were to plead insanity, something that he could justifiably claim if he was in a dissociated state when the crimes occurred. The patient discussed this option with his attorney, who advised against it. According to the attorney, such a plea would inevitably result in his being imprisoned (via forced psychiatric hospitalization) for even longer than his expected prison sentence.

Many persons who believe that they have been ritually abused also often think that they have been guilty of some acts of perpetration themselves. This is because a commonly reported feature of ritual abuse is that the individual is forced into situations in which he or she either actually perpetrates a criminal act or a simulation is set up whereby the individual, often after being drugged and tortured, believes himself or herself to have engaged in some horrible act.[278] Such forced "perpetration" allegedly occurs to cause the individual to acknowledge and fear the cult's ability to implicate them in real or simulated criminal acts. The outcome of such a scenario is to cause the person to feel that escape from the cult is futile and that any efforts to resist or fight the will of the cult leader will be severely punished.

The agencies with the responsibility of providing support and advocacy for victims have often instead become serious obstacles to their safety and recovery. My personal experiences with Child Protective Services have been very unusual, yet I am not alone in my observations regarding their problems in managing these cases. Many other professionals with whom I have consulted have also had frustrating experiences with this agency. Because we cannot, as a profession, rely on this agency to carry out its mission to protect children, it is a complicating factor in trying to obtain appropriate services for children we suspect are abused.

On one occasion, Child Protective Services referred a family for evaluation. The family consisted of father, mother, and three children ranging in age from seven to eleven years. Child Protective Services were consulted when school authorities noted that the middle son was absent from school an inordinate amount of time. On investigation, CPS learned that the child was being evaluated by a number of different medical specialists; however, none of the physicians were able to diagnosis any particular physical problem.   The CPS caseworker determined that the child was the victim of the mother's symptomatology of Munchausen's syndrome by proxy and had all three children removed from the home and placed in three different foster care facilities.

Munchausen's syndrome is a psychiatric diagnosis that refers to a condition wherein an individual seeks and obtains medical treatment for nonexistent maladies.   Munchausen's syndrome by proxy consists of obtaining unnecessary treatment for someone else, typically a child. This is a rather obscure disorder, and I was curious how the CPS caseworker could have made this diagnosis on so little corroborating evidence.[279]

As I evaluated the parents and children, I discerned a pattern of abuse emanating from the father, not the mother. The children and their parents all acknowledged the father's emotional distance and aloofness from the children. The mother revealed that her husband exerted unusual control over her and their children. He was, by his own admission, a "control freak." They all agreed that the father had behaved violently and unpredictably from time to time and related an incident where the father fired a gun loaded with Teflon-coated bullets, "cop killers," in the house. The mother herself presented as a warm and affectionate woman who had suffered a serious head injury in childhood that had resulted in some minor neuropsychological deficits.   Because her son was undersized, she had taken him to a physician and, when that physician remarked that he could find no apparent problem but that a specialist might be better able to assess the problem.   Thinking she was appropriately following his advice, the mother consulted with specialists.

I was unable to find any evidence that the mother was attempting to use the child's "poor health" as a means of satisfying her own needs. In fact, she consulted others and relied on their advice because she did not have confidence in her own judgment. The children all reported a close and loving relationship with their mother and a distant and unpredictable one with their father. The oldest son described physically abusive confrontations with his father. He reported that his father had come into his bedroom, awakened him, and beaten him without provocation. The youngster's siblings and mother corroborated these claims, which were denied by the father.

When I made my initial report to CPS, I indicated that the mother was an appropriate custodial parent, but that the father was unstable and posed a threat to the safety of the family. I recommended that the children be returned to the mother, that the father reside elsewhere, and that the family engage in individual and family therapy to work toward resolving the core problems that had resulted in their dysfunctional family relationships. In response, CPS inundated my office with copies of journal articles documenting various cases of Munchausen's syndrome by proxy. Although I repeatedly explained that nothing in my evaluation or observation of this family or its members supported that diagnosis, the CPS caseworker and her supervisor persisted.

Eventually, CPS relented and followed my recommendations. However, it was made clear to me that I would receive no further referrals from that agency in the future. The children, once returned to their mother's custody, thrived in the absence of their father. The mother learned to trust her instincts and live independently of the father. The father did not seem much interested in resolving his psychological problems or reuniting with his family. The parents ultimately divorced, and the mother retained sole custody. Although the father was granted usual visitation rights, he has not exercised them in the years since the divorce.

On another occasion, I was contacted by Child Protective Services in a distant city. They were requesting an evaluation of a six-year-old girl whom they suspected of having multiple personality disorder. The child arrived at my office accompanied by her foster mother and a CPS caseworker. I initially met with the two adults without the girl present to explain that when I examine a patient for DID, I also evaluate for the presence of ritual abuse. I explained that I do not utilize hypnosis in my evaluation; rather I unobtrusively incorporate what I am told are cult "triggers" into the clinical interview process and then observe the patient's response. The CPS caseworker appeared very interested and asked numerous questions.   When she was satisfied, the child was brought into the office.

With the caseworker and foster mother present, the interview with the child commenced.   It a short while, the child responded to the unobtrusive triggers by falling into a trance state during which alternate identities emerged.   Surprisingly, these triggers apparently affected the caseworker, who entered into such a deep trance that her head lolled on her shoulders as she reclined limply against a sofa with her mouth opened and her eyes rolled up.   The foster mother looked puzzled, wondering what had happened.   Because the caseworker was not my patient, I did not attempt to question or interview her.   At the end of the session, I used the procedure for bringing the child out of the trance, and the caseworker simultaneously responded to the same technique.

The caseworker reacted with surprise when she awoke and exclaimed that I must have hypnotized her even though I had previously explained to her that I would use no hypnosis in this interview.   The caseworker was evidently rattled by the experience.   The foster mother, having observed the effects of the interview on both the girl and the caseworker, seemed very perplexed regarding what she had witnessed.

In the course of another case in which a mother and her adolescent daughter were both under my care for treatment of DID and ritual abuse, the CPS caseworker visited the mother at her place of work.   The caseworker reportedly asked the mother about the nature of our therapy sessions.   The mother, "Ann," explained that she often entered into a trance state during our sessions and could not account for much of what transpired.   The caseworker reportedly told the mother that I might be sexually abusing both mother and daughter while they were in a trance state.   Furthermore, the caseworker stated that the mother should keep a journal, and recommended that it be divided into five parts delineated by colors with the following designations: "red is for blood, black is for death, green is for peace, blue is for running away, and white is for silence."

The next morning, Ann arrived in my office in a highly agitated state.   She reported that after hearing what the caseworker had said to her, she felt an overwhelming compulsion to either cut herself ("red is for blood") or to engage in a cult ritual.   She reported that she had done the latter, in a private ceremony where no people were harmed, but where she had allegedly sacrificed her pet cat and eaten its heart and burned its body.

She explained that although what the caseworker had told her was upsetting, she knew that no improper behavior had occurred in our sessions and she was amazed that her CPS caseworker would make such an inappropriate suggestion. Nevertheless, the caseworker had instilled new fears in the patient's daughter. Prior to Ann's appointment, the caseworker had again appeared at her workplace wearing a blue dress. Ann reported an almost irresistible urge to run away and abandon her child, her work, and her therapy.

Ann's allegations about her caseworker necessitated a meeting of all the concerned parties. If Ann had misunderstood what her caseworker had said to her, then this misperception needed to be corrected. If Ann's perception was accurate, then her caseworker was evidently behaving unprofessionally and interfering with Ann's care as well as her safety. I requested a meeting between Ann, the caseworker, the caseworker's supervisor, myself and another staff member.

As Ann and I addressed our concerns in the meeting, the supervisor had an opportunity to observe the highly inappropriate behavior of the caseworker. The caseworker spent the entire meeting looking at a pad in her lap and scribbling on it at a furious rate. She never looked me in the eye, never looked up from her pad, and never entered the conversation, even to respond to direct questions. The supervisor appeared confused and agreed to investigate further. Later, my office was informed that the caseworker had been reprimanded and removed from Ann's case. However, a short while later, the caseworker was reassigned to Ann.

In 1995, I was requested by the Department of Social Services in another state to evaluate siblings who had been placed in an adoptive home when the parental rights of their biological parents had been terminated on the basis of extreme neglect. These children presented with symptoms that included involuntary, intrusive flashbacks, nightmares and night terrors, involuntary trance states, dissociation, sexualized acting-out, self-mutilation, violence toward others, and reports of auditory hallucinations. I spent several days interviewing and observing the children, their adoptive parents, and treatment team, examining the living environment, and reviewing records of the children's histories. I concluded that the children met the criteria for dissociative disorders. I also found that the children's symptoms and reports were consistent with histories of ritual abuse.

I submitted a 21-page report of my findings including numerous recommendations for treatment of the children and support of the adoptive parents. Five years later, most of the recommendations have not been implemented. The children have not received adequate treatment, the adoptive parents are overwhelmed. Rather than provide necessary services, DHS and the Medicaid managed care contractors responsible for funding the childrens' care commissioned additional evaluations by other mental health specialists. To date, the evaluations have been in agreement with my findings and recommendations, yet compliance with those recommendations has not been forthcoming. I pointed out to all concerned that failure to address the childrens' treatment needs would likely result in the childrens' psychological and behavioral deterioration and increase liability for the state[280] and the Medicaid contractors. I believe that in this case, DHS was looking for an alternative explanation for the source of the children's psychological, behavioral and emotional problems because the children's biological mother had been a minor at the time she conceived and delivered each of the children and had been under the scrutiny of DHS throughout her own childhood. DHS faced potential liability because of its failure to protect the mother and subsequently her children. In addition, there is evidence that the children had been physically and sexually abused in at least one of their foster families prior to placement with their adoptive family, again while supposedly under the scrutiny of the state. The Medicaid contractor may have supported these ongoing evaluations hoping that eventually someone would provide an interpretation of the children's conditions that would be less expensive to manage and effectively treat.

There are other examples of inappropriate or potentially dangerous behavior by Child Protective Services. A year before the Branch Davidians made national news in Waco, their compound, Mount Carmel, was visited by Child Protective Services. Reports by former cult members and survivors indicated a pattern of physical and sexual abuses against the children in the compound. Reportedly, a CPS caseworker visited the compound and interviewed some of the children. She determined that abuse was occurring and requested that her agency remove the children from the compound. The caseworker's supervisor declined to follow the caseworker's recommendation.

Child Protective Services acts as an arm of the justice system, making recommendations regarding the disposition of allegations of child abuse and advising the court as to appropriate custodial arrangements for minor children. Yet many caseworkers appear to be distinctly unqualified to discern some forms of child abuse and do not seem able to recognize perpetrators, even when the perpetrators identify themselves.

"Theresa" came to me with a history of ritual abuse allegedly perpetrated by her parents. Theresa's three children had been removed to the custody of Child Protective Services that became involved with this family when the children were reportedly abducted from their home by a family acquaintance. While the children were in CPS custody, an investigation into Theresa's background revealed her to be a practicing Wiccan. Caseworkers from CPS expressed disapproval of her lifestyle.

The children described a history of abuse emanating not from Theresa, but from their stepfather. The children reported that when Theresa discovered the abuse was occurring, she separated from her spouse in order to protect her children. The children begged to return to their mother. However, because she participated in a nontraditional religion, CPS recommended that the children be removed from her care. The three children were placed in three separate foster homes.

For months, Theresa was denied visitation, despite her agreement to divorce her husband, renounce her religious affiliation, and embrace a traditional Christian orientation, maintain a proper home, and arrange alternate living arrangements. Theresa made excellent progress. She complied with every demand made by CPS and the courts. She attended parenting classes and therapy, determined to be reunited with her children. She was granted supervised visitation and never failed to take every opportunity to be with her children. Although monthly reports from my office kept CPS and the court appraised of Theresa's progress and recommended the children's return to her custody, new obstacles continually appeared in her path.

The most disturbing problem for Theresa was that while she was being denied the opportunity to visit with her own children, her parents, whom she had named as her own childhood abusers and from whom she had been estranged for years, were given unlimited access to Theresa's children. It was the view of CPS and the courts that because the parents embraced more overtly traditional and acceptable standards of behavior, they were more appropriate influences in the lives of the children. Although the reports my office generated repeatedly advised CPS that Theresa maintained that her parents were abusive, neither the court nor CPS responded with any precautions regarding the children's exposure to their grandparents. Theresa's children were finally returned to her custody about three years after they had been removed.

Examples of miscarried justice appear to be common in divorce proceedings when allegations of sexual or ritual abuse are made. Whether the allegations are made at the time of the divorce or in subsequent custody hearings, the protective parent (usually, but not always the mother) risks losing custody and sometimes even visitation when she supports her child's outcries of abuse. A scenario that we have seen repeated time and time again is exemplified by what happened to "Emma."

Emma was an elementary school teacher in a small town who had divorced her husband the year before after enduring years of his alcoholism, that resulted in his disappearance from the home for extended periods, extramarital affairs, and the loss of his job. "John" was the son of a wealthy and prominent family in the community and following his separation from Emma, he returned to his parent's home. At the custody hearing, John, was granted liberal visitation consisting of every Tuesday and Thursday, every other weekend, and a portion of holidays and summer vacations.

Emma's two preschool-age daughters began acting out in sexually inappropriate ways following overnight visitation with their father. They began having nightmares and night terrors. They began wetting their beds and fearing sleep. They aggressively masturbated in the home and in public and engaged other children in sexually oriented play. They expressed unwillingness to attend visitation with their father; yet after visitation, they expressed anger and violent rage at their mother, hitting her and talking about killing her. At first, Emma believed that the girls were expressing normal feelings of confusion and anger following the emotional upheaval of the divorce. Emma took the girls to a counselor to help them sort through their conflicted feelings.

In the counselor's office, the children were allowed to go into a playroom, where the counselor observed the children's activities. She noted that the children were engaged in very aggressive, sexually driven play with the dolls in the playroom. The girls removed all the Barbie dolls from the shelf and undressed them. They manipulated the dolls into sexual positions emulating oral sex postures. They made stabbing motions with pencils and crayons in the vaginal and anal areas of the dolls. The girls repeated this type of play with the family of dolls in a dollhouse. They selected the "daddy" doll and the "children" dolls for their play.

When the counselor joined the girls, she asked what they were playing. They responded that they were playing with their daddy. The children began to speak about what was clearly sexual abuse. The counselor immediately called Child Protective Services and referred a shocked Emma to a physician to perform physical evaluations on the girls. The physician discovered signs of vaginal and anal penetration exemplified by scarring. Furthermore, these three and four-year-old sisters had a venereal disease.

Emma called her lawyer and asked him to make immediate application to restrict her ex-husband's visitation with the girls. The lawyer argued with her, saying that he thought she was being "spiteful and vindictive." He said that if she persisted in her plan to alter the visitation agreement, he could no longer represent her. Emma contacted every lawyer in her small community, and each one declined to represent her against her ex-husband. Emma had to seek legal representation from an attorney from a neighboring city.

As the children continued in therapy, they made outcries of specific sexual and ritual abuses perpetrated by their father, their paternal grandparents, their aunts and uncles, and others whom they could not specifically identify by name. Child Protective Services reported that they could find no evidence that the children had been abused by their father; the CPS caseworker instead focused on Emma's fiancé and members of her family, none of whom had been named by the children or had any history of inappropriate or illegal activity.

The court ordered psychological evaluations of Emma and John. The court-appointed psychologist testified that John demonstrated no significant psychological problems. However, his interpretation of Emma's test results indicated that she has "high-strung, hysterical, and controlling," characteristics which neither the children's therapist, her colleagues at work, nor her social acquaintances had ever observed.[281] The court-ordered psychologist also examined the children and reported to the court that she believed that the children were being used by the mother as a weapon against her ex-husband. According to the psychologist, the children were not victims of ritual abuse, but of ritual abuse hysteria emanating from their mother and the children's therapy team.[282] Emma's quest to alter the visitation agreement failed. In rendering his decision, the judge warned Emma that if she attempted to appeal his findings, he would terminate her parental rights and assign custody of the girls to John.

This outcome is not unusual. In case after case, protective mothers have lost custody, visitation, and even their parental rights. One of the most famous cases involved Elizabeth Morgan, M.D.[283] When Dr. Morgan's daughter, made outcries that her father, also a health care provider, was sexually molesting her during court-ordered visitation, Dr. Morgan attempted to modify the visitation agreement. After she had exhausted all her legal options, Dr. Morgan arranged for her daughter to go into hiding with her maternal grandparents. Dr. Morgan spent two years in jail for contempt of court for refusing to reveal Hilary's location until she was released by congressional order. Since then, she has been living outside the United States as an exile in order to prevent Hilary's continued abuse by her father and by the system of justice that failed to protect her.

How is our justice system to address the issue of ritual abuse in a manner both fair and just and where vulnerable people who have been victimized are protected? Our interactions with our justice system have thus far been discouraging. The punitive attitude sometimes seen in the criminal justice system may actually discourage arriving at an effective solution based on remediation. The more we can encourage perpetrators (or individuals who believe that they have participated in criminal activities) to divulge their secrets, the closer we may come to finding the answers to fundamental questions of how and why these criminal activities persist. It is incumbent on our society to refrain from engaging in another modern version of witch-finding hysteria. Instead, we need a compassionate but dedicated search for solutions and for healing of all parties involved.

NOTES

[269] For some of these groups she preferred the term "organization" rather than "cult."

[270] In Chapter 15, the Fran's Day Care case was introduced.

[271] At that time, Texas did not have a law in the penal code criminalizing ritual abuse. A law was introduced into the penal code by the Texas legislature a short while later, only to be remover by Texas Attorney General Dan Morales on the basis that the terms were vague and poorly defined, thereby making the law unenforceable. However, other states have enacted laws criminalizing ritual abuse, including: California Penal Code Section 667.83 (1995), Idaho Code Vol. 4, Crimes Section 18-1506A, Illinois Revised Statute 5/12-33, Louisiana Revised Statute Section 14:107-1, Montana Code Annotated Section 27-2-217 and 45-5-627.

[272] Although analog studies have investigated isolated effects of influence on children's statements, there have been insufficient investigations of the influence of children when the following factors are involved: actual psychological treatment circumstances, allegations of ritual abuse (or other equally bizarre claims), and the effects of suggestion on implicit memories.

[273] As mentioned earlier, I had been invited to speak at the First Annual Christian Conference on MPD and SRA. I presented on the subject of ethical and forensic concerns regarding the evaluation and treatment of ritual abuse. During my presentation I played a videotape of a patient explaining how some cults are able to confound jury trials by signaling both during the jury selection process (in order to stack the deck) and during the trial itself. I also played a videotape of the signaling that appeared to be occurring during the Keller trial.

[274] Another author who has described personal experiences involving irregularities in the judicial process regarding allegations of ritual abuse is former State Senator John De Camp (1992) of Nebraska.

[275] A few months following the hearing, the judge who heard the visitation amendment accepted a partnership in the firm of the counsel representing the father in this case.

[276] In many cases this is true because they are dissociated themselves.

[277] Because of confidentiality concerns, I am unable to present additional evidence regarding this man's dissociation for at least part of the crimes for which he was convicted.

[278] See Smith (1993).

[279] Technically speaking, the CPS caseworker was not a licensed professional who legally had the authority to make a psychiatric diagnosis. Unfortunately, such individuals involved in a child protective agency will sometimes take on more authority than they are qualified by training and experience to assume. Often other mental health professionals will simply go along with such situations because of their desire to cultivate referrals from the agency.

[280] There is a precedent for the state's liability. In North Carolina, the state was sued because it did not provide adequate treatment to a psychologically disturbed youngster.

Named for the child involved, the Willie M. program was commissioned by the state to pay for necessary treatment, even if the child must go outside the state for help.

[281] See Laurence & Weinhouse (1994, pp. 264–292) for a discussion of the gender bias in women's mental health which may account for the disparity in the court ordered psychologist's interpretation of Emma's psychological test scores and the observations of other mental health professionals working with the family.

[282] Almost a year after this case, the court-ordered psychologist was arrested when in the course of another of her court-appointed evaluations, she reportedly admonished a child for making allegations against her father. There was evidence to suggest that the child was indeed being victimized and the therapist was in violation of her duty to protect the child and inform authorities of the child's complaint. The therapist lost her license to practice as a consequence.

[283] The national organization, Alliance for the Rights of Children (ARCH) was formerly called Friends of Elizabeth Morgan.

Chapter 17

Cult and Ritual Trauma Disorder

"Jean" entered an inpatient chemical dependency unit in New Mexico where she successfully became "clean and sober." She had a long history of drug and alcohol abuse and finally decided to do something about her addictions. However, while in the process, she began to have flashbacks about Satanic ritual abuse perpetrated by her father, an Episcopal priest. Jean was subsequently diagnosed with multiple personality disorder, and she sought treatment. After researching her options, she selected the inpatient dissociative disorders program under the direction of Gary Lefkof, M.D., which at the time was housed at The Cedars Hospital in De Soto, a suburb of Dallas, Texas.

Jean made considerable gains during her hospitalization, and when she was ready to be discharged, she was referred to me for outpatient care. Her inpatient therapist told me that Jean was very highly placed in her cult. When I met her, she said she had no direct knowledge of her role in what she said was her father's cult. Sometimes when we spoke she dissociated and, while in alternate identity states, Jean would speak to me about her role as a high-ranking individual and a "programmer."

I wanted to test her claims but initially had no idea how to do it. As we developed rapport, I asked Jean's alters to tell me more. What was meant when she said that she was a "programmer?" There was much resistance to this question. She became secretive and sometimes hostile as she dissociated as different alternates. She made it clear that the information was secret and that only a few of her alternates had enough knowledge about it to answer my question. She told me that she definitely could not impart this purportedly secret information to me. However, over time she would dissociate and in some alter states she would begin to provide (often fragmentary) answers to my earlier questions. For example, she described techniques that could be used to access other alters in her system of inner identities. She described an experience frequently reported by other patients with DID in which she perceived herself as lacking the experience of a whole and unified self. Instead she experienced herself as an aggregate of separate and disconnected identities. Some of the identities would not participate in therapy without the use of particular accessing methods.

These methods generally worked with Jean in accessing other dissociated states, including a variety of alternate identities. However, I questioned the possibility that these cues and signals worked with Jean simply because she had suggested that they would work that way. It was conceivable that she could have simply invented them in her own imagination. In order to test her claims that these were cult-created methods of access, I introduced some of these same cues into sessions with other patients who also described histories consistent with having been ritually abused. This was done unobtrusively so as to avoid producing results simply by suggestion.

Many of the patients, but not all, responded in a predictable manner to these cues. Many would go into deep trance states, some of which resembled coma states in which the patient was entirely unresponsive to the external environment until brought back to consciousness by the correct technique or until the patient slept until waking naturally. In other cases, alternate identities emerged and sometimes corrected the manner in which the accessing techniques were used. In many cases a militant protector alter would emerge for the purpose of lambasting me verbally or even with threats of physical violence because I had intruded on the patients' supposedly secret phenomenological worlds. Curiously after such episodes, and when the usual host identity returned, these patients were often amnestic for the events that had transpired. When given the opportunity to observe what had happened on videotape, many of these patients expressed amazement.

I later learned that many alleged cult survivors believe that some programming is general or generic and is used in the cult training of a variety of individuals — even in different cults and in different locales. Another frequently reported belief is that some cult programming is not generic but is very specific to a particular cult, a particular programmer, or a particular person being programmed.

On one occasion, Jean was speaking and casually mentioned to me, "You know, since all multiples have been ritually abused. . . ." I stopped her, "What do you mean *all* multiples have been ritually abused?" At that time, and even now, the prevailing theory is that dissociation of identity is caused by severe and prolonged childhood abuse, not necessarily ritual abuse alone. Jean looked at me, smiled, and said, "When I was in the Cedars, 80 percent of the patients were talking about ritual abuse. The others just haven't gotten to those memories yet." At first this idea seemed preposterous. I had many patients with DID who had never said anything about ritual abuse. But as time went by, I had some other cult survivors say the same thing. Curiously, the ones who believed this notion were by their own self-report, high in rank and allegedly trained as programmers.

These alleged programmers also talked about having been involuntarily involved in what they called "the organization." They appeared to be describing a variety of "organizations," some of which they identified with right-wing or other radical political philosophies such as the Christian Identity movement, the Aryan Brotherhood, and Neo-Nazi groups.[284] Some of them described histories of exposure to Satanic or Luciferian cults in childhood and later involvement in other "organizations," some of which sounded very similar to David Koresh's Branch Davidian sect and other apocalyptic and militia-like groups.

Although I had not specifically worked with any survivors of Koresh's religious cult, I was interviewed by several radio stations during the crisis involving the Branch Davidians because of my previous work with other cult survivors. During that time, I became aware of an excerpt from a 1987 interview of David Koresh which aired on March 2, 1993, on a syndicated television program, "A Current Affair" (broadcast locally on the Fox network).

The television interviewer asked Koresh if he was involved in a Satanic cult, if he was a "warlock," and if it was true he had an upside-down cross imprinted on the skin of his chest. Koresh replied that he was not a member of a Satanic cult and was not a "warlock." He admitted to having an inverted cross-shaped scar on his chest and offered the following explanation. According to Koresh, he had purchased a cross at a five and dime store. While playing with the cross by passing it over a candle flame, he accidentally dropped the cross on his bare chest, resulting in a burn scar in the shape of an inverted cross.[285] Of course, an alternative explanation is that Koresh had some earlier involvement in a demonic cult and had been branded with this mark. Cult survivors commonly report such experiences (and they frequently show scars they say were caused by cutting, burning, or branding.) However, in many cases, cult survivors have bogus explanations for their scarification, or they simply report that they do not recall any details about the injury that produced the scar.

With the deadly confrontation[286] between the Branch Davidians and the ATF personnel and later the FBI, the world became more aware of the potential explosiveness associated with some modern cults. In 1978, 913 deaths were attributed to the People's Temple, after cult leader Jim Jones ordered his followers to drink punch which was poisoned with cyanide (Kilduff & Javers, 1978, Wooden, 1981). In October of 1994, deaths in Canada and Switzerland were attributed to the mass suicide and/or homicide of members of the Order of the Solar Temple (Serrill, 1994). And in March of 1995, a Japanese cult was responsible for releasing poisonous gas in the subway system resulting in deaths and injuries.[287]

With the advent of religious cults, some writers complained that an anti-cult movement had arisen that was prejudicial toward new religious movements.[288] Some anti-cult zealots themselves may have violated the law in cases in which they allegedly have forcibly abducted cult members for involuntary "deprogramming."[289] It is obviously wrong, and presumably illegal, to physically force a person into or out of a cult without some due process of law. However, it may not always be clear whether any given cultist is participating as a result of a freely made choice. Some ex-cultists allege that they were kept in the cult by threats of harm to themselves or their families.

The word *cult* is a curious one and appears to be in a state of transition regarding its usage. Many dictionaries first define *cult* simply as a religion or religious practice. In history and anthropology we know that the term *cult* is often used in reference to the devotion to a particular god or spirit, often in the context of a polytheistic religion. However, in modern usage the word *cult* is increasingly being used to refer to groups that subjugate the rights and endanger the well-being of the individual for the benefit of a few members of the group through the use of coercive persuasion or other methods of mind control.[290] Some people use the expression *destructive cults* to specify that the cult in question is not merely a religion or a sect within a polytheistic spiritual system, but that additional malignant characteristics are involved.

The concept of mind control is an important feature of many destructive cults. But where does one draw the line between abusive mind control and normal persuasion? A distinction may be made where *normal persuasion* is defined as the use of logic or reason in an atmosphere often governed by compromise, negotiation, and mutual respect for the needs of the various parties involved. *Coercive persuasion* may be construed as the use of harm, threats of harm, or manipulation in order to motivate a person to do the bidding of another. *Coercive persuasion with traumagenic dissociation* may be used to describe situations where there is not only harm, threats of harm, or manipulation, but that these methods have been carried out to an extent that the targeted victim has developed inner dissociated identities or other dissociated mental states that may then be further manipulated (e.g., through the use of triggering cues), often without the victim's conscious awareness. Groups that use methods based on coercive persuasion with dissociation or *trauma-induced dissociation with programming* should always be classified as destructive cults in the sense that they are clearly using abusive mind control techniques.

Given the variety of destructive cults, it may be helpful to have a system of categorizing them into more specific subgroups.[291] For this purpose, we have formulated a system for organizing the various possible destructive cults into categories. These categories are not meant to be mutually exclusive, and some destructive cults may have characteristics of more than one of them. The system that we are currently using is as follows:

> 1. Destructive religious cults are associated with a particular religious practice, belief or system of rituals and may be further subdivided as follows:
>
> a.   Destructive apocalyptic cults promote fear and paranoia along with unfounded predictions that the world is about to end. Destructive apocalyptic cults may be distinguished from apocalyptic religions in that the former utilizes abuse, exploitation and mind control methods. Examples would include the Branch Davidians, Order of the Solar Temple and Aum Supreme Truth.
>
> b.   Destructive pre-industrial cults meet the criteria for destructive cults and also embody the traditions of pre-industrial cultures (e.g., African and New World Vodoun and Santeria sects). Although some such religions may be considered destructive cults, one should not automatically assume that all are. Again the criteria of abuse, exploitation, and mind control are essential to defining a cult as destructive.
>
> c.   Destructive demonic cults meet the criteria for destructive cults and also promote the worship or reverence toward a malevolent deity, spirit or principle (e.g., Satanism, Luciferianism) or those cults that use others' fears of demons to manipulate or control them.
>
> 2. Fraternal organizations that meet the criteria for destructive cults. These groups are often secret and may

also espouse particular philosophic, religious, or sociopolitical ideals (e.g., the Bizango of Haiti, the Egbo, or Leopard Society of West Africa, and various subgroups within Masonry and other quasi-Masonic groups may meet these criteria).

3. Destructive sociopolitical cults would include the Ku Klux Klan, Aryan Brotherhood, and Neo-Nazi groups. We would include the Christian Identity movement here even though technically it is a religion. However, it is not clear that the religious aspects of the Christian Identity movement are as cultish as are their racist values and politics.[292]

4. Organized crime groups that function as destructive cults exist for the primary purpose of supporting criminal activities where there is a need for utilizing mind control procedures because of the nature of the crime (e.g., child prostitution and pornography may require such mind control procedures if the perpetrators are to produce children who appear to be enthusiastic about the sexual activity that would normally be aversive to them). Even though coercion is presumably commonly used in criminal groups we don't think it would be appropriate to categorize all crime organizations as cults. However, when there is evidence of trauma-induced dissociation and programming, we would classify such a group as a destructive cult.

5. Government and intelligence-related destructive cults refer to the alleged organized use of cult mind control procedures surreptitiously conducted by individuals within government agencies (e.g., CIA) to further their purposes of intelligence gathering and the facilitation of other secret operations.[293] Unfortunately, the United States government has allowed itself to become enmeshed in a complex organization of secret information and procedures that would allow unethical or illegal activities to occur without the knowledge of the general public (e.g., the Iran-Contra affair, the Watergate break-in, the use of United States citizens as guinea pigs for radiation research, etc.). Furthermore, because of the existence of what is called Sensitive Compartmented Information[294] within the various national security and intelligence agencies, it is possible to have secret information and operations to

which other individuals with Top Secret security clearances have neither access nor the capacity to scrutinize. Essentially the intelligence community is "dissociated" because of the way in which information has been "compartmented." Given this network of government enforced secrecy it may be difficult or impossible to fully or accurately assess many of the complaints of abuse made by survivors. Nevertheless, these reports should be seriously investigated.

6. Experimental destructive cults are groups that conduct coercive mind control research, typically without the victim's consent. An example would be the work of Donald E. Cameron, M.D., a past president of the American Psychiatric Association. Donald Cameron conducted experimental mind control research on unsuspecting psychiatric patients in Canada that was funded by the CIA.[295]

For these purposes we have defined cult abuse simply as any abuse perpetrated by a cult (using the previously stated definition of *cult*). *Cult abuse* is thus similar, but not identical, to *ritual abuse,* which we define as any deliberate abuse carried out in a ceremonial or circumscribed manner for the purpose creating or manipulating already-created dissociated states of mind. The differences between these two definitions are that cult abuse does not necessarily cause dissociation, and ritual abuse is not necessarily always carried out in a cult. Combined, the term *Cult and ritual trauma disorder* is proposed as a diagnostic category to be included in a future revision of the Diagnostic and Statistical Manual of Psychiatric Disorders.[296] Such a diagnosis would promote scientific and professional attention to this often neglected problem and would aid in providing clarity for forensic evaluations.

Ritual abuse, like other forms of victimization of people, has been slow in gaining recognition. As in child abuse,[297] the abuse of women,[298] and political torture,[299] our culture has been historically reluctant to confront such problems directly or in a timely manner. We all have a duty to respond to in a rational way to reports of human suffering. That is not to say that all such reports should be judged, *a priori,* to be true. Nevertheless, all such allegations should be given a fair hearing. Those of us who are social scientists should be willing to consider all the evidence and all possible interpretations of the phenomena in question.

The process of making a psychiatric diagnosis follows a similar procedure. The clinician observes the client's verbal report, history, and presenting behaviors and considers all the possible diagnoses in an attempt to determine which one best defines the client's problems. On March 17, 1993, I wrote to the Work Group to Revise the DSM requesting that they consider an additional diagnosis that would account for ritual abuse to include in the American Psychiatric Association's *Diagnostic and Statistical Manual-IV (DSM-IV)*.[300] In my letter, I cited empirical research on the subject. I received a polite letter in response indicating that such a category would not be included because of a lack of empirical evidence. In my letter, I pointed out that both *DSM III* and *DSM III-R* have acknowledged "dissociated states that may occur in people who have been subjected to periods of prolonged and intense coercive persuasion (i.e., brainwashing, thought reform, or indoctrination, while the captive of terrorists or cultists)" (e.g., *DSM III-R*, p. 277). The diagnoses of atypical dissociative disorder and dissociative disorder not otherwise specified found in *DSM III* and *DSM III-R*, respectively, include the above statements about captivity by "cultists." So did the draft of the *DSM-IV*. However, when the final *DSM-IV* (American Psychiatric Association, 1994) was published, not only was there not a category for ritual abuse, but even the term "cultists" had been deleted.

One curious addition to *DSM-IV* is what is referred to as *dissociative trance disorders*, a new diagnostic term that is inclusive of what were previously known in psychiatric textbooks as exotic disorders (e.g., *amok, bebainan, latah, pibloktok, ataque de nervios,* and possession). These are disorders which, for the most part, are seen in pre-industrial cultures, but they have not been listed in the diagnostic manual until this year. The diagnostic manual also makes the association between these disorders and *possession trance*.

Possession trance is a term that has been distinguished from possession state in the literature of anthropology. However, *DSM-IV* (p. 490) appears to confuse the two categories designating them both as "possession trance," but on pages 727 through 729, describes both "trance and possession symptoms" (p. 728). Furthermore, *DSM-IV* states that individuals with dissociative identity disorder "can be distinguished from those with trance and possession symptoms by the fact that those with trance and possession symptoms typically describe external spirits or entities that have entered their bodies and taken over" (p. 728). This distinction is not practical, nor is it consistent with the reports of patients with DID who also report the experience of developing alternate identities modeled after external people. Therapists sometimes call these *introjects* or *introject alter personalities*. Also, it is commonly known that patients with DID sometimes experience alter identities that they perceive as spirits or demons. Scholars such as James Friesen (1991) and M. Scott Peck (1983) argue that in some cases of dissociation, actual demonic possession may be involved. Others, myself included, see this as an entirely naturalistic phenomenon resulting from the trauma that is a component of ritual abuse.

Either way, the reports of patients and the descriptions of anthropologists do not seem consistent with the *DSM-IV*'s explanation of possession trance and its relationship to DID. The *American Psychiatric Association Diagnostic and Statistical Manual*, *IV*, contains 315 separate listed categories (not counting some subcategories) of psychiatric diagnoses. Yet, not one of these addresses ritual abuse. As previously mentioned, such exotic "possession trance" disorders as *amok, bebainan, latah, pibloktok, ataque de nervios* and possession are listed, but there is not a word about the phenomenon of ritual abuse.

Given that (1) a large percentage of mental health professionals perceive ritual abuse to be a genuine problem experienced by some patients, (2) these patients exhibit many common characteristics, and (3) there is external corroboration for at least some of the patient's allegations, a relevant diagnostic category should be formulated. But there are other reasons to justify a diagnostic category for ritual abuse. It should be noted that although the phenomenon of ritual abuse shares features and characteristics with other established diagnoses, no single DSM category, nor any combination of DSM labels, completely accounts for it. In order to provide reliable clinical diagnoses and advance clear research outcomes, objective diagnostic criteria are needed.

Some skeptics claim that the current allegations of ritual abuse are mere fabrications of therapists' and patients' fantasies, or that they are simply delusional material or are part of manipulative or attention-seeking interactions. If this is the case, then clear diagnostic criteria will aid in determining the extent to which ritual abuse claims are in fact genuine phenomena versus features of factitiousness, or delusions, or other problems. Such distinctions are not only important for appropriate clinical diagnosis and treatment but also to lend further clarity to the growing number of legal cases in which mental health professionals are asked to provide forensic evaluations. The lack of clear, empirically validated criteria for distinguishing genuine ritual abuse from other diagnoses could result in courts failing to remove children from abusive environments or in innocent defendants going to prison in misdirected criminal cases.

NOTES

[284] See Flynn & Gerhardt, 1989.

[285] It surprised me that this incident did not appear to be reported in any of the major written works on David Koresh that I have reviewed.

[286] See Bailey & Darden (1993), Beck (1993a, 1993b), Breault & King (1993), Kantrowitz (1993), Lacayo (1993), Linedecker (1993).

[287] Regarding the Aum Shinrikyo or Aum Supreme Truth cult, see van Biema, 1995.

[288] See Bromley & Shupe (1981), Shupe & Bromley (1985).

[289] To avoid confusion, I rarely use the term *deprogramming* in reference to the forcible efforts to remove individuals from cults. The term exit counseling is in my opinion, a more appropriate term for professional efforts to assist an individual in leaving a cult. I reserve the term *deprogramming* to mean the process whereby control over dissociated mental states is returned to the dissociated person. Forcible indoctrination by a "deprogrammer" is simply another form of programming

[290] Tucker (1989), partly in jest, defines *cult* as "someone else's religious group that does not agree with mine" (p. 15).

[291] A number of encyclopedia-like reference works have appeared on the subject of cults. See Larson (1989a, 1989c), Marrs (1990), Martin (1980), Mather & Nichols (1993), McDowell & Stewart (1992).

[292] See Flynn & Gerhardt (1989)

[293] This category may surprise some readers, but I have heard such reports from dissociative patients and from other therapists who work with this patient population. There is also a body of literature that addresses this alleged problem. *The Manchurian Candidate* (Condon, 1988) is one such fictional account. In the area of nonfiction can be found *Operation Mind Control* (Bowart, 1994), *The CIA and the Cult of Intelligence* (Marchetti & Marks, 1974), and *The Search for the "Manchurian Candidate": The CIA and Mind Control* (Marks, 1979), which present information about the CIA's interest in mind control techniques and its allegedly dubious methods of exploring this topic. Also note past State Senator John De Camp's (1992) report of a government cover-up of a case in which he was involved as an attorney involving allegations of ritual abuse. In her book *Lessons in Evil, Lessons from the Light*, Gail Feldman reports how an investigation of her client's allegations of ritual abuse appeared to be obstructed by the FBI.

[294] See Bowart's (1994) Operation Mind Control, Thomas's (1989) Journey into Madness: The True Story of Secret CIA Mind Control and Medical Abuse, and Weinstein's (1990) Psychiatry and the CIA: Victims of Mind Control.

[295] See Breiner (1990), deMause (1994), Masson (1992), Miller (1986).

[296] See Ehrenreich & English (1973), Eisler (1987), Greer (1971).

[297] See Stover & Nightingale (1985), Seáz (1992).

[298] See Noblitt (1993b).

[299] Modern, historical, and anthropological examples of the circumscribed use of trauma in creating and controlling dissociated mental states (programming) is reviewed by Noblitt (1993a) and elsewhere in this book.

Chapter 18

Nihilists and Revisionists

Patients who allege that they were ritually abused commonly say that their perpetrators threatened them with additional harm if they ever disclosed their abuses. Further, these patients often say that they were told that if they ever did disclose, no one would believe them. Such reports also create a dilemma for the treating therapist. On the one hand the therapist often has a duty to be an advocate for the patient (e.g., fiduciary responsibility), but on the other hand the therapist cannot assume that every thing the patient says is entirely true and accurate. However, the therapist should not assume that everything that the patient says is untrue simply because the therapist is unfamiliar with the kind of allegations that the patient is making or simply because there is a bizarre quality to the allegations.

In 1992 I was invited to participate in a panel discussion on the topic of "Breaking the Cycle of Child Abuse — Working Together for Change" at the Third Annual Texas Dissociative Disorders Conference. The topic I was there to discuss was ritual abuse. Before beginning my presentation, I asked the audience of some eighty to ninety professionals in the fields of psychology, counseling, and social work, to respond with a show of hands to several questions. I asked the audience how many of those present thought that at least some of the allegations that patients have made about being ritually abused were true. About 90 percent of the audience raised their hands in the affirmative. I then polled the group inquiring who believed that none of the patients' allegations about being ritually abused was true. No hands were raised. I asked how many were not sure. Only one woman raised her hand. Frankly, I was surprised to see the overwhelming acceptance for the veracity of at least some of the stories about ritual abuse.   Had this been a conference specifically addressing ritual abuse, the results might not have been so surprising. However, this conference dealt with dissociative disorders, and ritual abuse was only an adjunctive topic of discussion.[301]

George Greaves argues that four groups have emerged in response to patients allegations of ritual abuse: "(1) *nihilists*, (2) *apologists*, (3) *heuristics*, and (4) *methodologists*" (1992, p. 46).   Greaves explains the nihilist position as follows:

> *Nihilists* seem to see their function as explaining how the presentations made by SCSs [Satanic Cult Survivors] *cannot* be true.   They believe that because they can concoct alternative explanations of the data, the data *are not* true.   They hold themselves to no other empirical criterion of truth, but they, nevertheless, rigorously demand such of others.   Many of them fly the flag of scientific skepticism, but their skepticism — and their data gathering — are often unscientific in method.   Rather than proving their hypotheses scientifically, they strike the pose of claiming that their hypotheses are factually correct until someone empirically proves them wrong.   Among the nihilists I would include George Ganaway (1989, 1990), Richard Noll (1990), Arthur Lyons (1988), Robert Hicks (1990a, 1990b), and Kenneth Lanning (1989).   Ganaway and Noll hold that SCS reports are the results of various kinds of psychodynamic distortions and/or artifacts induced in SCS subjects by clumsy or unwitting interviewers.   Lyons, Hicks, and Lanning argue the *reductio ad absurdum* fallacy that if the reports were true, there would be physical evidence to back them up which they claim, there is not. (1992, p. 46)

There are other logical fallacies apparent in the literature produced by those who argue that ritual abuse is merely an imaginary phenomenon. For example, Sherrill Mulhern states:

> The current revival of popular belief in the existence of an international conspiratorial satanic blood cult has been promoted primarily by public declarations of alleged cult survivors, whose testimonies have been accredited by authoritative mental health professionals.   These eye-witnesses can be divided into two groups: (1) adult mental patients, who claim to have been raised in transgenerational cults that "brainwashed" them through ritual torture, and (2) very young children, who allegedly have been subjected to ritual torture by cult recruiters while in day care. Both groups are said to have dissociated their memories of these

horrifying experiences, recovering them only recently in psychotherapy. (1991b, p. 145)

Mulhern's argument is an example of what some call building a straw man. Rather than correctly identifying the case she wishes to argue against, Mulhern selects a specific variant, e.g., the allegation of an "international conspiratorial satanic blood cult," and presents this as being representative of the entire case.[302] She then attacks this straw man of her own construction. Finally, she incorrectly states that the witnesses for these allegations fall into the above two categories and, in both categories, the witnesses dissociate their experiences and only recover them in psychotherapy.

A more blatant example of this kind of misuse of logic can be seen in a chapter entitled "Occult Survivors: The Making of a Myth," by Philip Jenkins and Daniel Maier-Katkin (1991). The authors criticize the claims of survivor Michelle Smith, who related her history of abuse in *Michelle Remembers* (Smith & Pazder, 1980). Jenkins and Maier-Katkin argue that no Satanic cults existed in the Vancouver area when Smith was a child:

> Before 1965, however, the religious fringe was more sparsely populated. The closest approximations to "devil worship" were strictly confined to geographic areas far removed from the locations of Michelle and Jenny — above all, to California. The Agape Lodge in 1930s Hollywood had been associated with wealthy decadence; by the 1940s, Jack Parsons transformed it into the Crowleyite Church of Thelema, based in Pasadena. At least in rumor, this group was active in orgies and sacrifice, but the tiny cult was moribund in the mid-1950s. (1991, p.138)

This "tiny cult" that the authors are making reference to is the Ordo Templi Orientis, long affiliated with Aleister Crowley. According to a publication of the O.T.O., they are neither moribund nor tiny but have an international organization. Furthermore, their first local affiliate in North America was not in California, but in the Vancouver area.[303]

It is not our intent to imply that the O.T.O. was responsible for Michelle Smith's abuse. We merely wish to show that the assumptions of Jenkins and Maier-Katkin are untenable. The fact that one cannot find evidence of a secretive group in a particular area does not mean the group does not exist.

Jenkins and Maier-Katkin further state that "30 or more deaths" have been associated with an allegedly African American "Church of Sacrifice" in Louisiana, and that Native Americans are known to have a history of witchcraft practices. However, they err when they claim that "none of the current survivors appears to be referring to these alleged ethnic traditions" (p. 142). Earlier chapters in this book have specifically described such patient allegations. It appears that Jenkins and Maier-Katkin are simply unfamiliar with the literature of ritual abuse and the accounts made by these survivors.[304]

If one wishes to criticize the arguments supporting the existence of ritual abuse, then one must first accurately identify them. These arguments may be summarized as follows:

1. There is ample historical and anthropological evidence that ritual abuse has occurred in a variety of cultures throughout history. Among those groups where traumatizing rituals have reportedly been used, there have also been some accounts of dissociation, amnesia, and alterations of the individual's identity.

2. In modern times, reports of ritual abuse have been made by people who claim to be survivors of such abuse both in North America and in other geographic locations. Many of these survivors show dissociative symptoms, and many state that they have recovered their memories of abuse in therapy. However, it is important to note that these survivors do not universally report or show overt signs of dissociation; nor have they all recovered their memories in therapy.

3. Some perpetrators of ritual abuse and other criminal activity associated with cults are self-confessed.

4. Other witnesses to cult criminal activity have come forward including a police officer who reportedly infiltrated a Satanic cult and an attorney who states that she was abducted by members of a cult at gun point while she was attempting to prosecute a case in which there were allegations of ritual abuse. These witnesses tell their stories on a videotaped documentary, *Children at Risk: Ritual Abuse in America* (1992). I have also spoken with two other individuals who were not psychiatric patients and who reported, in one case, witnessing abusive cult rituals and, in both cases, being threatened by an avowed cult member or members. Both of these informants requested that I not cite them nor refer to them by name because of the threats against them.

5. There have been convictions in criminal cases in response to allegations of ritual abuse. These convictions, by law, are based on certainty "beyond a reasonable doubt."

6. Civil cases won against individuals accused of ritual abuse. By law, these verdicts are based on a "preponderance of evidence."

7. Cases of ritual murder (e.g., at Matamoros) are a matter of public record.

8. The abusive acts of some cults (e.g., the People's Temple of Guyana, Branch Davidians, Order of the Solar Temple, Aum Supreme Truth) are publicly known.

9. The great majority of therapists who work with patients reporting ritual abuse tend to believe that the allegations of ritual abuse are true (as per studies by Bottoms, Shaver & Goodman, 1991, and Perry, 1992).

10. In a series of workshops and in group and individual professional supervision conducted by Noblitt, the facilitator has publicly demonstrated that many of these survivors respond to preprogrammed cues with switching to alternate identities and trance responses. The patients were not trained to respond to these cues in therapy, and videotapes of patients who have never before seen Noblitt show them responding to these cues (that are alleged by some patients to be used in cult programming).

Given that there is corroborative evidence for some cases of ritual abuse (e.g., Faller, 1994) we have to question why certain people are motivated to publicly deny the existence of this phenomenon while they refrain from accurately citing the evidence.

Consider this ethical dilemma. A little girl states that she is being ritually abused. The perpetrator draws upon the arguments published by these *nihilists* to support his or her innocence. In some cases, a perpetrator could be aided by those attempting to discredit the reality of ritual abuse. A truly victimized child might be further traumatized and silenced by the failure of others to believe her story because the perpetrator, defended by the ritual abuse critics, is more readily believed. This is not to say that the field of ritual abuse should not be open to critical scrutiny. However, scrutiny should be fair minded and show a willingness to examine all the data.

Christine Comstock makes an interesting observation:

> Now that the possibility of ritualistic abuse affecting great
> numbers of people has arisen, I believe it is a good time to
> question our personal and organizational response. If the stories
> we hear about ritualistic abuse are true, it seems imperative that
> we accept some responsibility to do what we can to stop this
> devastation. It may be that our nonresponse could be considered
> to be on the same order as the nonresponse of the German
> citizens during the Third Reich. (1991, p. 7)

Like the early reports of Nazi atrocities, allegations of ritual abuse
have tended to be ignored. Most of us do not want to think about such
unpleasant things. When his fellow Nazis confronted Hitler concerned
that the world community would not tolerate his treatment of the Jews,
he is reputed to have responded that he was not worried. Why would
there be serious objection to his actions when decades earlier the Turks
successfully perpetrated genocide against the Armenians? "Who still
talks nowadays of the extermination of the Armenians?"[305] According to
Simpson, "the Turkish government even today continues to refuse to
acknowledge *Ittahadist* responsibility for the Armenian massacres, and
has instead in recent years financed a large and sophisticated publicity
campaign aimed at rewriting the history of the war years" (1993, p. 37).
It is also well known that there are organizations that deny the reality of
the Nazi Holocaust even in modern times. Such people are sometimes
called *historical revisionists.*

In 1993, an organization was founded that makes revisionist
interpretations about the modern phenomenon of child abuse — the False
Memory Syndrome Foundation (FMSF). The name is something of a
curiosity in that the organization appears to have no interest in the
numerous ways that memory can be false. Instead, the FMSF is invested
in proving that most of the recent epidemic of reported sexual and ritual
abuse are the fanciful product of overzealous or incompetent therapists.

The FMS Foundation disseminates data that are derived from biased
and unscientific sources and from these data draws unwarranted
conclusions. The information published by the FMS Foundation is
composed of testimonies by individuals who claim that their alleged
victims have falsely accused them of criminal activity. These
testimonies have been used to "prove" that the allegations of wrongdoing
are due to false memories. This is obviously an absurd and illogical
conclusion. The only thing that the False Memory Syndrome Foundation
does document is that there are a number of people who state that they
have been called perpetrators and that these alleged perpetrators deny the
reported claims. However, such discrepancies could be due to a variety
of reasons other than "false memories" on the part of the alleged victim.

Perpetrators can also presumably have false memories.[306] Another prospect to consider is that one or both of the discrepant parties may be lying or may have misperceived an event or experience. However, to our knowledge the False Memory Syndrome Foundation does not address these possibilities.

Another cause for concern regarding the False Memory Syndrome Foundation is the fact that although it has a professional advisory board, it has no publicized board of directors. It is disturbing to note that a tax-exempt organization that placed its earnings for the fiscal year 1992 of $365,000 (FMS Foundation Newsletter, vol. 2, no. 7) is not accountable to a publicized governing board of directors. For an organization that represents itself as devoted to science and scholarship, this is especially irregular. Typically such organizations are democratically run with elected officers and a board of directors to share in decision-making and to provide peer review regarding the ethical considerations for their organization. In addition, the FMSF leadership frequently misrepresents the size of its membership, how it collects data, and promotes its goals. Researcher Stephanie Dallam discovered marked inconsistencies in the data published by the FMSF regarding the size of its membership and the manner in which data is collected and interpreted. The FMSF cites these cases as evidence that there is an epidemic of "false memory syndrome." The FMSF claims that their "data" show that there is an epidemic of "false memory syndrome." According to Stephanie Dallam, RN:

> In 1994, a spokesperson revealed that the FMSF does not investigate the accuracy of the reports it receives and thus the group has no "documented" cases of FMS in its files. However, that same year, the FMSF's newsletter reported 11,000 "documented cases". (1997, p. 29)

Dallam (1997, 1998) researched the "data" collected by the FMSF and found it to be inaccurate and often misrepresented in publications. Dallam demonstrated how the FMSF has reported cases of telephone inquiries as "documented cases" resulting in the release of inflated numbers of false memory claims in their own publications and to media representatives. Thus, Dallam demonstrated that FMSF claims are without an empirical basis despite being widely promoted in the media.

The FMSF has redefined for us the identities of the real perpetrators: therapists and others who put "false" ideas in the minds of fragile psychiatric patients who come to erroneously believe that they were abused in childhood. Although we know of no single case in which it has been proven that any therapist implanted such false memories, the

FMSF argues that this practice is widespread. Given the absence of substantiating evidence, the claims of the FMSF are inflammatory and may have prompted frivolous legal action against therapists who are merely trying to practice in an ethical and appropriate manner. There are times when a therapist's job includes listening to patient's reports and recollections of childhood abuse. It has become easier for those accurately identified as perpetrators to successfully sue therapists because of the propaganda generated by the FMS Foundation. It is also likely that some therapists will refuse to work with patients who make such allegations out of fear for their own liability. As one of my colleagues once commented, "In America you can sue anybody for anything."

However, there may be other harmful consequences of the FMS Foundation's propaganda efforts. When a victim's outcry is not believed, the victim may be exposed to further injury when protective action is not implemented. Furthermore, perpetrators who believe that they have an influential organization on their side may feel safer in engaging in further abuse. Given the serious consequences of sexual or ritual abuse cases, we question the appropriateness of inventing jargon that has the appearance of being scientific while being unsupported by empirical evidence. Such terminology could be construed as false and misleading and thus, unprofessional and unethical.

Currently, FMS is not generally accepted as a valid scientific concept within the mental health community and some professionals view it merely as an unfounded attempt to create a legal defense for perpetrators (Lowenstein, 1992) and to support unjustified and frivolous civil actions against psychotherapists who work with sexually abused clients.[307] According to Richard J. Lowenstein, M.D., former president of the International Society for the Study of Dissociation:

> although writings by FMS board members tout the foundation's "scientific" approach, I know of no clinical research or tradition of clinical description that empirically validates or supports that such a clinical condition exists as such. FMS is a syndrome without signs and symptoms (the defining characteristics of a syndrome). The FMS Foundation's written materials are selective, biased, and incomplete in their fragmentary reviews of selected articles and books in the childhood trauma literature. The FMS Foundation literature is replete with fragmentary anecdotes describing unscrupulous behavior by therapists that causes patients to believe they have been sexually abused when they have not. These accounts are emotional and impassioned, but

have not. These accounts are emotional and impassioned, but do not contain the kind of balanced data required to study this phenomenon in an intellectually rigorous, impartial and scientific way. The result is promulgation of pseudo-scientific misinformation in the popular media that will decrease the likelihood of a meaningful study of the important issues relating to dissociation, trauma, and the complex problem of assessing autobiographical memory in a therapy session. (Lowenstein, p. 4)

Some professionals argue that the FMS hypothesis is part of the current "backlash" against recent efforts to accurately acknowledge the prevalence and harm caused by sexual abuse. According to Dr. A. Matsakis:

Experts in the field of early childhood sexual abuse interpret the rise of the false memory accusation as a form of societal resistance against acknowledging that child sexual abuse exists and is so extensive.[308]

To quote Jennifer Freyd, Ph.D., the daughter of FMSF founding member and Executive Director, Pamela Freyd, "Therapists get blamed for memories of incest, in a way that reminds me of a tendency to shoot the messenger" (Freyd, 1993). Dr. Jennifer Freyd, a Professor of Psychology at the University of Oregon, accused her father, Peter Freyd, of having sexually abused her in childhood. This accusation is denied by Peter Freyd and his denial is supported by his wife (who is also his stepsister), Pamela Freyd. Thus was the FMSF created.

Peter Freyd was a self-acknowledged alcoholic whose alcoholism was so severe that it required hospitalization. Although it is well-known that alcoholics sometimes have blackouts and engage in behaviors that they do not remember later, Pamela Freyd has been steadfast in proclaiming her husband's innocence. Instead Pamela Freyd blames Jennifer Freyd's therapist for Jennifer Freyd's identification of her father as her childhood abuser because the abuse memory in question was a recovered memory, which is to say that the memory occurred shortly after Jennifer began psychotherapy with the particular therapist in question.[309]

Dr. Jennifer Freyd denies that her therapist implanted any inappropriate thoughts and cites numerous instances of sexually inappropriate behavior by her father that appear to have fallen just short of incest and which were ongoing, not recovered memories. In relating her experiences, Dr. Freyd implicates several members of the FMSF professionals were apparently involved in the psychological treatment of this troubled family. These same professionals subsequently accepted positions on this board in violation of the generally accepted ethical proscription against therapists taking on dual roles with their clients (Freyd, 1993). Jennifer Freyd is an expert in the area of psychology that deals with thought processes including memory and the author of *Betrayal Trauma* (1996). A letter by her uncle William Freyd,[310] strongly supports her position in her dispute with her parents.

One of the most important benefactors and founding members of the FMSF is Ralph Underwager, Ph.D., an ordained minister and psychologist who made a name for himself as a professional expert witness. Underwager is known for his testimony in support of accused, and sometimes convicted, child abusers. Dr. Underwager was a member of the FMSF advisory board until a scandal arose after he made statements that appeared supportive of paedophilia in a periodical devoted to that subject called *Paidika* published in the Netherlands. In *Paidika,* Dr. Underwager is quoted as saying, "Paedophiles need to become more positive and make the claim that paedophilia is an acceptable expression of God's will for love and unity among human beings." (Geraci, 1993, p. 12).

Underwager is the author of a number of publications on the subject of the sexual abuse of children that are frequently cited in legal cases. One of his major forensic works was found to have numerous distortions and errors in a study supported by a grant by the New England Commissioners of Child Welfare Agencies.[311] Before taking a leadership role in the FMSF, Underwager was prominently involved with a similar group called VOCAL, Victims of Child Abuse Laws. Author Michael Newton cited Underwager as follows: " 'It is more desirable that a thousand children in abuse situations are not discovered,' he told the press, 'than for one innocent person to be convicted' " (1993, p. 355). Marjorie Orr, a survivor advocate and journalist in Great Britain reported:

> a troubling case in which Underwager's declarations played a
> key role in getting the children's testimony disallowed,
> thereby helping to free the alleged child molester. Since then
> I've read a Canadian court judgment (*R. v. Sean G. R.,* 1993)
> disqualifying his expert witness and rebuking him for
> misleading the court. I've also read the judge's ruling that
> dismissed Underwager's defamation suit against Anna Salter
> and Paddy Toth (*Underwager and Wakefield v. Salter et al.,*
> 1994). In dismissing the case, the appeal court judge pointed
> out that Underwager's books (co-authored with Wakefield)

had failed to carry the medical and scientific communities. Because of this failure, and because other courts had rejected Underwager's testimony for this very reason, the court held that trial judges could appropriately exclude Underwager's testimony. (Orr, 1995, p.22)

Another of the better known and vocal of the FMSF Advisory Board is Dr. Richard Ofshe, the primary author of the book, *Making Monsters*. In this book, Richard Ofshe and journalist, Ethan Watters argue the FMSF position that there is "a new class of sexual predator" found among what they call "recovered memory therapists." The term recovered memory therapy is also a term invented by FMSF advocates which has no meaning in the professional community. However, this term allows FMSF proponents to build a straw man that they can then attack. Unfortunately their straw man typically has very little to do with reality.

In the "Preface" to *Making Monsters* Dr. Ofshe thanks the "Thurston County Prosecutor's Office for retaining him to analyze the allegations against Paul Ingram and thereby giving him the opportunity to study the effects of recovered memory techniques in a unique fashion." (p. x). However, psychiatrist Robert Rockwell, M.D. states that "the appeals judge found Richard Ofshe not a credible witness." Dr. Rockwell goes on to write about the case citing court records and a statement by Captain Tom Lynch:

(From the Report of Proceedings volume VII of a hearing held on Feb 1, 1990, before the Judge of the Superior Court, Robert H. Peterson. p 910-913.) The Judge says: My problems with Dr. Ofshe's testimony are just these. No. 1 he is not a clinical psychologist. He is a professor of sociology at—in Berkeley. He's not able to treat—he's not able to treat this defendant for the conditions that Dr. Lennon found that he had.
2. he's not an expert in sex abuse or with matters with regard to victims of sex abuse.
3. his experiment that he engaged in here was odd in my judgment. The first day he came to Thurston County was February 2nd. And on that very first day he went to the defendant and gave the defendant, when he was allegedly working for the state, a false set of facts, but a set of facts that came pretty close to what one of the victims had accused the defendant of. But he said this person said this, and this person said this. Now, what do you say about it. And then told him to go back to the cell, and come back with a scenario as to what happened. And he came back with a scenario.

In that he had a police officer making false statements to a defendant, I think the state would come under very heavy criticism for that. And Dr. Hatcher said that it is not an appropriate technique that he would have used. And if one were going to use a technique like that, one would wait until you had exhausted all other avenues, then come back and say nothing fits here, I'm going to try and experiment, rather than doing it on the very first day. So there would be—there would be no tainting. If you're going to be doing things like that would you pick something that is totally foreign from anything that could probably be true?

I think I would say, why don't you pick a scenario of a female and male that live in Shelton, or Tacoma, or someplace else, and see if you could get them to come back with details regarding that. He didn't do that. And I find that it's an odd experiment, and the time is odd.

The next problem I've got with Dr. Ofshe is he finds the defendant to be in a hypnotic state, or trance, on November 29th from reading a dry record. I find that to be strange. I wonder if that can be done. I have great cause for concern with that. I find that really, he is considerably less qualified than Hatcher, Peterson, and Lennon to give opinions in this area. He does say in his report, "I have no opinion if the daughters were raped here."

And the last thing that concerns me is that the defendant appeared in court on May 1st 1989, pled guilty. Then on May 16th about two and a half weeks later, Dr. Ofshe calls the defendant and there is a long conversation that they hold over the telephone. Hour and a half telephone call. And in that conversation, it's a odd scenario, because usually the defendant is going to say "I'm innocent and the doctor, or interrogator is going to say, "No you're guilty."

In this case the doctor says, "You're innocent, " and the defendant says, "No I'm guilty." And the defendant says, twice, "Well, one of us is right (and you're wrong)." (Rockwell, 1995, pp. 318–319)

This scenario seems odd in light of Dr. Ofshe's vociferous criticism of therapists that he alleges use unconventional techniques or persuasion. Yet in this case, he appears to be doing both. So who is really creating false memories? In how many cases of sexual abuse does the FMSF encourage guilty perpetrators to deny their guilt because the FMSF has publicized its propaganda that the recollections of victims often cannot be trusted. Dr. Mark F. Schwartz writes:

> In St. Louis there are 1,000 reports of sexual abuse of children each year. Multiply that number by each state for over 30 years and it equals a lot of "non-false memory." In our perpetrators' program, many individuals who had previously acknowledged their perpetrations have begun carrying around "false memory" articles to fuel their denial, resulting in more perpetrations. (Schwartz, 1993, p. 3)

Michelle Landsberg, journalist for the Toronto Star, reported an interesting case of "false innocence belief syndrome". She described the case of physician Leo Pilo whose license to practice medicine was revoked by the Canadian medical board after he admitted having sexual contact with four of his female patients when they were children. When Pilo was later sued in civil court by one of his victims, Dr. Harold Merskey, an eminent Canadian psychiatrist and board member of the FMSF argued as an expert for the defense that the plaintiff had "false memory syndrome." This false memory argument was offered even though Dr. Pilo previously had admitted his guilt to the Canadian medical board. The plaintiff prevailed when the court ordered Pilo to pay her $95,000.

The FMSF has a brief, but checkered history. Unfortunately, in spite of the dubious source from which it originates, the FMSF harms both clients who are in recovery and therapists sincerely attempting to provide a professional and ethical service. Further, the FMS hypothesis muddies the waters rather than adding clarity to an already problematic concern for all those involved with mental health. This confusion makes it more difficult for therapists and clients to recognize that indeed some memories are false—there simply is no such thing as "false memory syndrome."

It is healthy for people both with and without abuse memories to scrutinize their memories for accuracy and to accept that the truth of many memories may be uncertain. There is simply no evidence that the memories people have in therapy or "recovered memories" are any more or less accurate than any other memories (Dalenberg, 1996).

Dr. Loftus "mall study" is often cited by FMSF apologists as evidence that false memories can indeed be implanted. However, there is considerable controversy surrounding the methodology, science, and ethics regarding Dr. Loftus' "study" (Brown, Scheflin, & Hammond,

1998; Crook and Dean, 1999a, 1999b; Whitfield, 1995). According to Dr. Loftus:

> The trick was to design a study powerful enough to prove that it is possible to implant a false memory while also winning the approval of the university's Human Subjects Committee, which reviews proposed research projects to ensure that they will not be harmful to participants. (Loftus & Ketcham, 1994, p. 91)

The design that was ultimately accepted by the Human Subjects Committee involved 24 subjects, 3 males and 21 females, recruited by Dr. Loftus' among undergraduate students at the University of Washington. The research subjects were told that they were engaged in the study of memory and specifically why some events were remembered and others, not. The participants were provided a booklet that contained three true incidents with details provided by a relative. A fourth event was also described about a fabricated incident in which the subject was lost as a child in a shopping mall or department store. Each participant was asked to review his or her own booklet and to write what was remembered about each of the four events. Six of the participants (25%) expressed the belief that the false event actually happened. One to two weeks later, the participants were told that the study was actually designed to find out if people could be made to believe that false memories were true. They were asked to review the four events in their booklets and identify the false belief.

> Of the 24 total, 19 subjects correctly chose the getting-lost memory as the false one, while the remaining five [20.8%] incorrectly thought that one of the true events was the false one (Loftus & Pickrell, 1995, p. 723).

It is not clear how one should interpret the discrepancies regarding the research subjects' endorsement of true versus false memories. Is it possible that the researchers made some errors in what they assumed were true memories? Is it possible that some of the individuals had in fact been lost in a mall and in a sense their acknowledgment of that particular memory was not actually an error? While these findings are certainly not definitive and even though they do not address the issue of traumatic memory, they have been used by proponents of the false memory theory to support specific claims against therapists, e.g., in civil suits.

The FMS Foundation presents the argument that unscrupulous therapists implant "false memories" as a vehicle for producing symptoms that require long-term psychotherapy. In fact, the precursors of these recollections such as flashbacks and other psychiatric symptoms frequently antedate therapy and are often the reason that such individuals seek therapy in the first place. Furthermore, a disproportionate number of adults who make allegations of childhood abuse often have histories of chronically disabling psychological disorders. Given their marginal level of coping, many of them are unemployable and without any insurance benefits. Many, if they are lucky, are on disability. Any therapist who works with this patient population is likely doing a considerable amount of work at a discounted fee or even pro bono. Conversely, a number of therapists, notably George Ganaway, a member of the FMSF advisory board, are contracted by insurance companies to scrutinize claims for psychotherapy related to allegations of memories of childhood abuse.[312]

If there is indeed a question of "false memories," how can we be sure that the false ones are not those of the accused perpetrators, rather than those of the alleged victims?[313] The appearance of normalcy is not an assurance that criminal behavior cannot be present. Certainly Ted Bundy, John Wayne Gacy and John Hinkley led many to perceive them as "normal," giving no outward sign of their chaotic inner world and the secrets of their heinous criminal acts.

To date, there have been successful civil and criminal prosecutions against individuals who perpetrated criminal acts that were undetected at the time they occurred and were only brought to public awareness days, weeks, months or years later, when the victims or witnesses were capable of providing testimony. Doubtless, there have been some occurrences of false accusations of criminal behavior lodged against individuals. However, it is imperative that all allegations of wrongdoing be given a fair hearing. Victims deserve to have the crimes against them be fully investigated and explored. A false accusation can result in some significant discomfort to the accused, perhaps even imprisonment. An incorrect accusation of "false memory" can cost the credibility, safety, and even the lives of the victims in question.

This of course is not merely a recent problem exploited by the False Memory Syndrome Foundation, but as anyone familiar with the literature of child abuse knows, there is a long history of public denial and resistance to the idea that children are being harmed, especially when it is alleged that abuse is ongoing in their own families. Masson's (1992) book, *The Assault on Truth*, cites examples of brutality toward children during Freud's time in which children were given little or no protection by the legal or medical professions. Breiner (1990) also writes a well-researched history of child abuse practices throughout a variety of cultures illustrating the widespread nature of this phenomenon.

There appear to be at least two major obstacles that stand in the way of our solving the problems of child abuse in our culture. First, there is a lack of understanding regarding the various factors that increase the likelihood of child abuse occurring. Many people simply do not understand it, and others do not particularly want to. This leads us to a second factor — denial. Through denial, the victim is able to temporarily survive the assault, the perpetrator is able to discard his or her feelings of guilt and shame, and the rest of us do not need to get involved because it "didn't happen." Unfortunately, denial only works for so long, and then thoughts, sensations, memories, and feelings that were previously safely locked away often come crashing into the survivor's conscious awareness, frequently in the form of nightmares and flashbacks.

Alice Miller (1990) writes about the denial of child abuse in a more institutionalized form — within the profession and practice of psychoanalysis. In her book, *Thou Shalt Not Be Aware: Society's Betrayal of the Child,* she speaks as a trained psychoanalyst disillusioned with her profession's abandonment of the legitimate concerns of child abuse. In direct contrast to the mistaken notion promoted by the FMSF that therapists are obsessed with finding evidence of child abuse in their patients she correctly notes the tendency of psychoanalysts to go to the other extreme, ignoring such reports and reinforcing denial in their patients:

> Sometimes I have to ask myself how many children's corpses psychoanalysts require as proof before they will stop ignoring their patient's childhood suffering or trying to talk them out of it. . . . It is unlikely that analysts will be able to alter the incidence of child abuse, but as long as they go on espousing theories that can be used to deny and cover up flagrant mistreatment, they will prevent their patients as well as the general public from becoming conscious of the truth. They will be lending support to the collective repression of a phenomenon whose consequences directly affect each one of us. (1990, p. 212)

But is child abuse really such a frequent occurrence? In a national survey focusing on a variety of questions pertinent to modern Americans, James Patterson and Peter Kim (1992) found that one in seven of their respondents acknowledged a history of sexual abuse in childhood. However, the investigators also found that these individuals were also very secretive about their abuse histories. Almost half stated that prior to the survey they had never told anyone about their abuse. Given this level of reluctance to talk about sexual abuse, one has to wonder if these researchers may have also missed detecting some actual survivors of sexual abuse. Even if their data do not under report the frequency of childhood sexual abuse, it does point to the enormity of this problem in our culture.

The arguments used to deny the existence of child abuse have, with some variation, also been used in an attempt to deny that ritual abuse exists. In his book, *Raising Hell: An Encyclopedia of Devil Worship and Satanic Crime*, Michael Newton (1993) observes that "cult apologists" utilize seven basic arguments that he examines individually, finding each to be without merit. As Newton demonstrates, citing the cult of the Hindu goddess Kali, the Ku Klux Klan, the Mafia, and the Yakuza, there are many examples of clandestine organizations that are both acknowledged and denied, even by the highest government sources.

History demonstrates that heinous acts can and do occur within the midst of great civilizations. There is no shame attached to our ability to recognize that human beings are capable of committing atrocities. It is, however, shameful that we often ignore the outcries of the victims, many of whom not only describe past abuses but also an awareness of present threats and dangers. Although it is reasonable to assume that not all outcries are accurate, we will never know if we do not properly investigate them.

NOTES

[301] Nevertheless, this is consistent with the results of other studies (e.g., Bottoms, Shaver, & Goodman, 1991; Perry, 1992) discussed in Chapter 6 of this book.

[302] However, if we restate the argument to say that allegations have been made that some destructive cults operate at a national or international level then, at least, we have stated a problem that is easier to put to scrutiny.

[303] California came later. See Ad Veritatem IX°, (1990, pp. 95–97).

[304] Ironically the book in which this misinformed chapter appears is highly recommended by Ken Lanning (1992).

[305] See Christopher Simpson's (1993) *The Splendid Blond Beast*. He cites the Office of the United States Chief Counsel for the Prosecution of Axis Criminality (1946, p. 753).

[306] In Parkin's (1987) book *Memory and Amnesia*, he states that amnesia for crime "has been widely documented" (p. 162) although citing a study by Taylor and Kopelman (1984): "Amnesia was not observed in any person charged with a non-violent crime" (Parkin, 1987, p. 162).

[307] See *False Prophets of the False Memory Syndrome* [videotape].

[308] In A. Matsakis. (1994). *Post-traumatic stress disorder*. Oakland, CA: New Harbinger Publications, p. 310. The author also cites three other publications in support of her quoted statement: J. Herman (1992). *Trauma and recovery*. New York: Basic Books; C. Courtois (1988). Healing the incest wound. New York: W.W. Norton; and J.

Briere and   J. Conte (1993).   Self reported amnesia for abuse in adults molested as children. *Journal of Traumatic Stress, 6*, 21-31.

[309] It should be noted however that Dr. Jennifer Freyd states that the memory came to her while she was at her home not while she was in her therapist's office.

[310] This letter is quoted in Chapter 15 of this book.

[311] See the unpublished monograph, *Accuracy of Expert Testimony in Child Sexual Abuse Cases* by Anna C. Salter, Ph.D. and available from the author.

[312] By Ganaway's own report featured on *ABC Primetime*, he is engaged by a number of insurance companies to review claims for services rendered by mental health professionals to individuals who allege histories of child abuse.

[313] Even Michael Yapko acknowledges in his book, *Suggestions of Abuse,* (1994, p. 91) that "Therapists and researchers have no reliable means to distinguish authentic from false memories." It is not surprising that this book is an indictment against therapists who respect their patient's reports of child abuse memories. He acknowledges the support and assistance of many of the members of the FMSF advisory board and thoughtfully provides the address and telephone number of the FMSF headquarters (p. 213) in a chapter subheading entitled, "Some Therapy Guidelines for the Falsely Accused."

Appendix: A Proposed Diagnosis in DSM Format

309.82 Cult and Ritual Trauma Disorder

Diagnostic Features

The essential feature of Cult and Ritual Trauma Disorder is clinically significant distress or functional impairment with either: (1) disturbing or intrusive recollections of abuse, or (2) the presence of involuntary dissociated mental states, either or both of which are the result of ritual (circumscribed or ceremonial) abuse. Dissociated mental states may take the form of unwanted or intrusive dissociated alter identities, trance states, automatisms, catalepsy, stupor, or coma or coma-like states. These dissociated mental states may appear in a spontaneous manner or they may be triggered by particular stimuli or cues or by the individual's experience of distress.

Ritual abuse consists of traumatizing procedures that are conducted in a circumscribed or ceremonial manner. Such abuse may include the actual or simulated killing or mutilation of an animal, the actual or simulated killing or mutilation of a person, forced ingestion of real or simulated human body fluids, excrement or flesh, forced sexual activity, as well as acts involving severe physical pain or humiliation. Frequently, these abusive experiences employ real or staged features of deviant occult or religious practices, but this is not always the case. Some reports of this phenomenon indicate that the abuse may occur outdoors, in a residence, day care, laboratory or hospital setting as well as other locations. Ritual abuse may occur in a group setting, but occasionally it is perpetrated by an individual.

Associated Features and Disorders

Associated descriptive features and mental disorders.   Evidence of psychological trauma is usually present and many individuals with Cult and Ritual Trauma Disorder also exhibit some symptoms of Post-traumatic Stress Disorder, if not actually meeting the criteria for this diagnosis as well. Intrusive and often fragmentary memories of abuse, alternating terror and emotional numbing, nightmares, amnesia, anxiety, panic, flashbacks, phobic avoidance, and signs of increased arousal are often present. These individuals typically report chronic depression, often with cyclical characteristics.

Dissociation of identity is a feature of Cult and Ritual Trauma Disorder, and Dissociative Identity Disorder or Dissociative Disorder Not otherwise specified, are frequently concurrently diagnosed.

Features of Borderline Personality Disorder are also often exhibited and occasionally individuals with Cult and Ritual Trauma Disorder will also experience brief psychotic episodes, sometimes with auditory or visual hallucinations. More commonly these individuals experience or act out strong self-destructive urges including attempted or actual suicide and self-mutilation. Frequently there is a strong desire to injure the self in a manner that produces blood (e.g., "I have to see blood"). Sometimes the individual will report a desire to taste, touch, or smell their own blood. Chronic and unmodulated anger and sometimes rage alternate with other mood states to create the impression that the individual is unpredictable in mood and unable to manage anger.   Strong feelings of dependency alternate with social aloofness. Narcissism and self-hatred are frequently experienced separately and together.

In children (in addition to the above) motoric hyperactivity, impulsivity and problems in attention and concentration are seen at a rate which exceeds the baseline for children without psychiatric disorders.

Associated laboratory findings. Individuals with Cult and Ritual Trauma Disorder typically show evidence of psychological trauma and dissociation on psychological testing.

Associated physical examination findings and general medical conditions. There may be scars from self-inflicted injuries or physical abuse. Somatic symptoms with or without objective medical findings typically include headaches, gastrointestinal, and genito-urinary complaints, but other reports of physical pain may be present. In some cases, physical pain will not reflect a current injury but will be a psychological component of implicit memories (e.g., "body memories") associated with previous abuse. These individuals also frequently show evidence of mild neuropsychological impairment that in some cases may result from a history of head trauma. Others have argued that psychological trauma in childhood may cause mild neuropsychological deficits in some individuals (e.g., van der Kolk, 1987) but further research is needed to clarify this question.

Prevalence

The prevalence of Cult and Ritual Trauma Disorder is unknown due to a lack of reliable information. The alleged secrecy associated with ritual abuse may make the accurate tabulation of such statistics difficult or impossible.

Course

The clinical course of these individuals is typically chronic with periodic exacerbations and sometimes partial remission of symptoms. Some of these individuals report that they continue to participate in ritual abuse either as a victim, a perpetrator or both, typically while in a dissociated state.

Familial Pattern

A history of sexual or ritual abuse is frequently reported among family members. In particular, transgenerational victimization is a commonly indicated pattern, consistent with the familial trends associated with non-ritual sexual abuse of children. However, the extent to which ritual abuse is a transgenerational phenomenon is presently unknown. Features of dissociation are also frequently seen in family members.

Differential Diagnosis

Cult and Ritual Trauma Disorder must be distinguished from **Delusional Disorder** and other **psychotic disorders** where delusional beliefs are better able to account for the reports of abuse particularly when it can be demonstrated that the allegations of abuse are false. However, there are also cases where these diagnoses can exist concurrently with Cult and Ritual Trauma Disorder, particularly when corroborating evidence of such abuse exists in an individual who is also exhibiting delusional or other psychotic symptoms. Cult and Ritual Trauma Disorder must be distinguished from **Malingering** in situations where there may be forensic or financial gain and from **Factitious Disorder** where there may be a maladaptive pattern of help-seeking behavior. The possibility of suggestibility should also be evaluated and ruled out as a possible alternative explanation for the individual's reports of ritual abuse.

Diagnostic criteria for 309.82 Cult and Ritual Trauma
Disorder

A.   The presence of clinically significant distress or
     functional impairment with either (1) or (2):

     (1) disturbing or intrusive recollections of abuse.
     (2) involuntary dissociated mental states consisting
          of at least one of the following:

          (a) dissociated alter identities
          (b) involuntary trance states
          (c) automatisms
          (d) catalepsy
          (e) stupor, coma or coma-like states.

B.   The disturbance described in A is the result of ritual
     (circumscribed or ceremonial) abuse.

C.   The disturbance described in A cannot be better accounted
     for by Delusional Disorder or another psychotic disorder in
     which delusions are present, Malingering or Factitious Disorder
     or as a consequence of the patient's suggestibility.

References

Abse, D.W. (1983). Multiple personality. In S. Akhtar (Ed.), *New psychiatric syndromes: DSM III and beyond* (pp. 339–361). New York: Jason Aronson.

Adler, M. (1986). *Drawing down the moon.* Boston, MA: Beacon Press.

Ad Veritatem IX° (1990). An introduction to the history of the O.T.O. In Hymenaeus Beta X° (Ed.), The *Equinox*, vol. 3, no. 10 (pp. 87–99). York Beach, ME: Samuel Weiser.

Ahmed, R. (1968). *The black art.* New York: Paperback Library.

Alexander, D. (1990, March). Giving the devil more than his due. *The Humanist*, pp. 5–14.

Allen, T.B. (1993). *Possessed: The true story of an exorcism.* New York: Doubleday.

American Psychiatric Association. (1980). *Diagnostic and statistical manual of mental disorders* (3rd ed.). Washington, DC: Author.

American Psychiatric Association. (1987). *Diagnostic and statistical manual of mental disorders* (3rd ed., revised). Washington, DC: Author.

American Psychiatric Association. (1993). *DSM-IV Draft Criteria.* Washington, DC: Author.

American Psychiatric Association. (1994). *Diagnostic and statistical manual of mental disorders* (4th ed.). Washington, DC: Author.

Andrews, B., Morton, J., Bekerian, D.A., Brewin, C.R., Davies, G.M., & Mollon, P. (1995, May). The recovery of memories in clinical practice: Experiences and beliefs of British Psychological Society practitioners. *The Psychologist*, pp. 209–214.

Armstrong, J.G., & Loewenstein, R.J. (1990). Characteristics of patients with multiple personality and dissociative disorders on psychological testing. *Journal of Nervous & Mental Disorders, 178,* 448–454.

Ashe, G. (1974). *Do what you will: A history of anti-morality.* London: W. H. Allen.

Asimov, I. (1968). *Asimov's guide to the Bible.* New York: Avon.

Assagioli, R. (1975). *Psychosynthesis: A manual of principles and techniques.* London: Turnstone Press.

Atkinson, J.M. (1992). Shamanisms today. *Annual Review of Anthropology, 21,* 307–330.

Axelrod, G. (Producer), & Frankenheimer, J. (Producer/Director). (1962). *The Manchurian candidate* [Videotape]. Culver City, CA: MGM/UA.

Baigent, M., Leigh, R., & Lincoln, H. (1983). *Holy blood, holy grail.* New York: Dell.

Baigent, M., Leigh, R., & Lincoln, H. (1986). *The messianic legacy.* New York: Dell.

Bailey, B., & Darden, B. (1993). *Mad man in Waco.* Waco, TX: WRS Publishing.

Bainbridge, W.S. (1978). *Satan's power: A deviant psychotherapy cult.* Berkeley, CA: University of California Press.

Bainbridge, W.S. (1991). Social construction from within: Satan's process. In J.T. Richardson, J. Best, & D.G. Bromley (Eds.), *The Satanism scare* (pp. 297–310). New York: Aldine de Gruyter.

Bakan, D. (1965). *Sigmund Freud and the Jewish mystical tradition.* New York: Schocken.

Baker, R.A. (1992). *Hidden Memories: Voices and visions from within.* Buffalo, NY: Prometheus Books.

Barber, M. (1980). *The trial of the Templars.* Cambridge, UK: Cambridge University Press.

Barnett, H.G. (1972). *Indian Shakers: A messianic cult of the Pacific Northwest.* Carbondale: Southern Illinois University Press.

Barton, B. (1990). *The secret life of a Satanist: The authorized biography of Anton LaVey.* Los Angeles: Feral House.

Baskin, W. (1974). *The sorcerer's handbook.* New York: Philosophical Library.

Bauer, S.F., & Hornick, E.J. (1968). Lunar effect on mental illness: The relationship of moon phase to psychiatric emergencies. *American Journal of Psychiatry, 125,* 696–697.

Beck, J.C. (1979). *To windward of the land:* The *occult world of Alexander Charles.* Bloomington: Indiana University Press.

Beck, M. (1993a, October 11). The book of Koresh. *Time,* pp. 26, 27, 30.

Beck, M. (1993b, March 15). Thy kingdom come. *Newsweek,* pp. 52–55.

Believe the Children. (1987, June). Multi-victim multi-perpetrator ritualized abuse survey. Unpublished manuscript. P.O. Box 797, Cary, IL 60013.

Bellafante, G. (1995, May 22). Chronicle of a witch hunt. *Time,* pp. 69–70.

Belsky, J. (1993). Etiology of child maltreatment: A developmental-ecological analysis. *Psychological Bulletin, 114,* 413–434.

Benner, D.G., & Joscelyne, B. (1984). Multiple personality as a borderline disorder. *Psychiatric Clinics of North America, 7,* 89–99.

Bennetts, L. (1993, June). Nightmares on main street. *Vanity Fair,* pp. 42, 45, 46, 48, 50, 52, 58, 60, 62.

Blackman, S., & Catalina, D. (1973). The moon and the emergency room. *Perceptual & Motor Skills, 37,* 624–626.

Blavatsky, H.P. (1877/1988). *Isis unveiled,* vol. 1–2. Pasadena, CA: Theosophical University Press.

Blavatsky, H.P. (1888/1988). *The secret doctrine,* vol. 1–2. Pasadena, CA: Theosophical University Press.

Bliss, E.L. (1980). Multiple personalities: A report of 14 cases with implications for schizophrenia and hysteria. *Archives of General Psychiatry, 37,* 1388–1397.

Bliss, E.L. (1984a). Spontaneous self-hypnosis in multiple personality disorder. *Psychiatric Clinics of North America, 7,* 135–148.

Bliss, E.L., (1984b). A symptom profile of patients with multiple personalities, including MMPI results. *Journal of Nervous & Mental Disease, 172,* 197–202.

Bliss, E.L., & Jeppsen, E.A. (1985). Prevalence of multiple personality among inpatients and outpatients. *American Journal of Psychiatry, 142,* 250–251.

Blood, L. (1994). *The new Satanists.* New York: Warner Books.

Boddy, J. (1988). Spirits and selves in Northern Sudan: The cultural therapeutics of possession and trance. *American Ethnologist, 15,* 4–27.

Bok, B.J. (1975). A critical look at astrology. *Humanist, 35*(5), 6–9.

Bottoms, B.L., & Davis, S.L. (1997). The creation of satanic ritual abuse. *Journal of Social and Clinical Psychology, 16*, 112–132.

Bottoms, B.L., Diviak, K.R., & Davis, S.L. (1997). Jurors' reactions to satanic ritual abuse allegations. *Child Abuse and Neglect, 21*, 845–859.

Bottoms, B.L., Shaver, P.R., & Goodman, G.S. (1996). An analysis of ritualistic and religion related child abuse allegations. *Law and Human Behavior, 20*, 1–34.

Bottoms, B.L., Shaver, P.R., & Goodman, G.S. (1991, August). *Profile of ritualistic and religion-related abuse allegations reported to clinical psychologists in the United States.* Paper presented at the ninety-ninth annual convention of the American Psychological Association, San Francisco, CA.

Bourguinon, E. (1973). Introduction: A framework for the comparative study of altered states of consciousness. In E. Bourguinon (Ed.), *Religion, altered states of consciousness, and social change* (pp. 3–35). Columbus: Ohio State University Press.

Bourguinon, E. (1974). Cross-cultural perspectives on the religious uses of altered states of consciousness. In I.I. Zaretsky & M.P. Leone (eds.), *Religious movements in contemporary America* (pp. 228–243). Princeton, NJ: Princeton University Press.

Bowart, W. (1994). *Operation mind control, researcher's edition.* [available from W. H. Bowart, P.O. Box 35072, Tuscon, AZ 85740-5072].

Bowman, E.S. (1993). Clinical and spiritual effects of exorcism in fifteen patients with multiple personality disorder. *Dissociation, 6*, 222–238.

Boyce, M. (1979). *Zoroastrians: Their religious beliefs and practices.* London: Routledge & Kegan Paul.

Bramly, S. (1977). *Macumba: The teachings of Maria-José.* New York: St. Martin's Press.

Braude, S.E. (1991). *First person plural: Multiple personality and the philosophy of mind.* London: Routledge.

Braun, B.G. (1984). Hypnosis creates multiple personality: Myth or reality? *International Journal of Clinical & Experimental Hypnosis, 32*, 191–197.

Braun, B.G. (1988a). The BASK (behavior, affect, sensation, knowledge) model of dissociation. *Dissociation, 1*(1), 4–23.

Braun, B.G. (1988b). The BASK model of dissociation: Clinical applications. *Dissociation, 1*(2), 16–23.

Breiner, S.J. (1990). *Slaughter of the innocents: Child abuse through the ages and today.* New York: Plenum Press.

Breault, M., & King, M. (1993). *Inside the cult.* New York: Signet.

Bromley, D.G., & Shupe, A.D. (1981). *Strange gods: The great American cult scare.* Boston, MA: Beacon Press.

Brown, D., Schleflin, A.W., & Hammond, D. C. (1998). *Memory, trauma treatment, and the law.* New York: W.W. Norton.

Buck, O.D. (1983). Multiple personality as a borderline state. *Journal of Nervous and Mental Disease, 171*, 62–65.

Burkert, W. (1983). *Homo Necans: The anthropology of ancient Greek sacrificial ritual and myth.* Berkeley: University of California Press.

Burkert, W. (1987). *Ancient mystery cults.* Cambridge, MA: Harvard University Press.

Burrows, W.E. (1986). *Deep black.* New York: Berkeley Books.

Burton, R. (1927). *The anatomy of melancholy.* New York: Tudor.

Bybee, D. & Mowbray, C. (1993). An analysis of allegations of sexual abuse in a multi-victim day-care case. *Child Abuse and Neglect, 17*, 767-783.

Campbell, R.J. (1989). *Psychiatric dictionary* (6th ed.). New York: Oxford University Press.

Cannon, W.B. (1942). Voodoo death. *American Anthropologist, 44,* 169–181.

Cantwell, A. (1988). *AIDS and the doctors of death.* Los Angeles, CA: Aries Rising Press.

Carus, P. (1974). *The history of the devil and the idea of evil.* La Salle, IL: Open Court Publishing.

Cavendish, R. (1967). *The black arts.* New York: Perigee Books.

Cervantes, F. (1994). *The devil in the New World: The impact of diabolism on New Spain.* New Haven: Yale University Press.

Chancellor, E.B. (1925). *The Hell Fire Club.* Vol. 4, *The lives of rakes.* London: Phillip Allan.

Chavez, F.A. (1974). *My penitente land: Reflections on Spanish New Mexico.* Albuquerque: University of New Mexico Press.

Children at risk: Ritual abuse in America [Videotape]. (1992). Ukiah, CA: Cavalcade Productions.

Clary, W.F., Burstin, K.J., & Carpenter, J.S. (1984). Multiple personality and borderline personality disorder. *Psychiatric Clinics of North America, 7,* 89–100.

Clymer, R.S. (1920). *The fraternitas rosae crusis.* Quakertown, PA: Philosophical Publishing.

Cohen, B.M., & Cox, C.T. (1995). Telling *Without talking: Art as a Window into the World of Multiple Personality.* New York: W.W. Norton & Co.

Cohen, S.B. (1984). Tests of susceptibility/hypnotizability. In W.C. Wester & A.H. Smith (Eds.), *Clinical hypnosis: A multidisciplinary approach* (pp. 73–81). Philadelphia: J.B. Lippincott.

Cohn, N. (1975). *Europe's inner demons.* New York: Basic Books.

Colquhoun, I. (1975). *The sword of wisdom.* Channel Islands: Neville Spearman.

Comstock, C. (1991, February). Critical issues task report. *ISSMP&D News,* p. 7.

Comstock, C., & Vickery, D. (1992). The therapist as victim: A preliminary discussion. *Dissociation, 5,* 155–158.

Condon, R. (1959). *The Manchurian candidate.* New York: Jove Books.

Confer, W.N., & Ables, B.S. (1983). *Multiple personality: Etiology, diagnosis, and treatment.* New York: Human Sciences Press.

Coons, P.M. (1985). Children of parents with Multiple Personality Disorder. In R. P. Kluft (Ed.), *Childhood antecedents of multiple personality* (pp. 152–165). Washington, DC: American Psychiatric Press.

Coons, P.M. (1994). Reports of satanic ritual abuse: Further implications about pseudomemories. *Perceptual & Motor Skills, 78,* 1376–1378.

Coons, P.M. (1997). Satanic ritual abuse: First research and therapeutic implications. In George A. Fraser, (Ed.), *The dilemma of ritual abuse: Cautions and guidelines for therapists* (pp. 105–117). Washington, DC: American Psychiatric Press.

Coons, P.M., & Grier, F. (1990). Factitious disorder (Munchausen type) involving allegations of satanic ritual abuse: A case report. *Dissociation, 3,* 177–178.

Coons, P.M., & Stern, A.L. (1986). Initial and follow-up psychological testing on a group of patients with multiple personality disorder. *Psychological Reports, 58,* 43–49.

Core, D. (1991). *Chasing Satan: An investigation into Satanic crimes against children.* London: Gunter Books.

Couliano, I.P. (1990). *The tree of gnosis: Gnostic mythology from early Christianity to modern nihilism.* San Francisco, CA: HarperSanFrancisco.

Couliano, I.P. (1991). *Out of this world: Otherworldly journeys from Gilgamesh to Albert Einstein.* Boston, MA: Shambhala.

Cowan, J.G. (1992). *The elements of the Aborigine tradition.* Rockport, ME: Element.

Crapanzo, V. (1977). Introduction. In V. Crapanzo & V. Garrison (Eds.), *Case studies in spirit possession* (pp. 1–40). New York: John Wiley & Sons.

Crook, L.S., & Dean, M. (1999a). Logical falacies and ethical breeches. *Ethics & Behavior, 9*, 61-68.

Crook, L.S., & Dean, M. (1999b). Lost in a shopping mall — a breech of professional ethics. *Ethics & Behavior, 9*, 39-50.

Crouch, B., & Damphouse, K. (1991). Law enforcement and the satanic crime connection: A survey of "cult cops." In J.T. Richardson, J. Best, & D.G. Bromley (Eds.), *The Satanism scare* (pp. 191–204). New York: Aldine de Gruyter.

Crowley, A. (1988). *Gems from the Equinox: Instructions by Aleister Crowley for his own magical order.* Las Vegas, NV: Falcon Press.

Crowley, A. (1989). *Magick without tears.* Las Vegas, NV: Falcon Press.

Crowley, A. (1990). The O.T.O. Gnostic Mass. In Hymenaeus Beta X° (Ed.), The *Equinox*, vol. 3, no. 10 (pp. 123–140). York Beach, ME: Samuel Weiser.

Crowley, A. (1991). *Magick in theory and practice.* Secaucus, NJ: Castle Books.

Crowley, A. (1992). *Liber aleph vel CXI: The book of wisdom or Folly.* York Beach, ME: Samuel Weiser.

Crowley, V. (1989). *Wicca: The old religion in the new age.* London: Aquarian Press.

Culling, L.T. (1992). *Sex magick.* St. Paul, MN: Llewellyn Publications.

Cumont, F. (1956). *The mysteries of Mithra.* New York: Dover.

Da Costa, H.J. (1964). *The Dionysian artificers.* Los Angeles: Philosophical Research Society.

Dalenburg, C.J. (1996). Accuracy, timing and circumstances of disclosure in therapy of recovered and continuous memories of abuse. *Journal of Psychiatry and Law, 24*, 229–275.

Dallam, S.J. (May/June, 1997). Is there a false memory epidemic? *Treating Abuse Today*, pp. 29–38.

Dallam, S.J. (November, 16, 1998). *Analysis of empirical evidence of a false memory epidemic.* Paper presented at the 15th International Fall Conference of the International Society for the Study of Dissociation, Seattle, WA.

Danforth, L. M. (1989). *Firewalking and religious healing: The Anastenaria of Greece and the American firewalking movement.* Princeton, NJ: Princeton University Press.

Daraul, A. (1990). A history of secret societies. New York: Carol Publishing.

Darley, A.M. (1968). *The passionists of the Southwest, or the Holy Brotherhood.* Glorieta, NM: Rio Grande Press.

Darwin, C. (1958). *The origin of species.* New York: Mentor Books.

Davies, N. (1981). *Human sacrifice in history and today.* New York: William Morrow.

Davis, W. (1985). *The serpent and the rainbow.* New York: Simon & Schuster.

Davis, W. (1988). *Passage of darkness: The ethnobiology of the Haitian zombie.* Chapel Hill: The University of North Carolina Press.

De Camp, J.W. (1992). *The Franklin cover-up: Child abuse, Satanism and murder in Nebraska.* Lincoln, NE: AWT.

De Martino, E. (1972). *Primitive magic: The psychic powers of shamans and sorcerers.* Dorset, England: Prism Press.

Deren, M. (1991). *Divine horsemen: The living gods of Haiti.* Kingston, NY: McPherson.

Devil worship. (1965). In E. Podolsky (Ed.), *Encyclopedia of aberrations* (pp. 186–187). New York: Citadel Press.

Devine, M.J. (1992). *Magic from Mexico: Folk magic, prayers spells & recipes as taught by the wise women of Guadalupe.* St. Paul, MN: Llewellyn Publications.

Dickstein, L.J., Hinz, L.D., & Eth, S. (1991). Treatment of sexually abused children and adolescents. *American Psychiatric Press Review of Psychiatry, 10,* 346–366.

Dingwall, E.J. (1963). *Some human oddities: Studies in the queer, the uncanny and the fanatical.* New Hyde Park, NY: University Books.

Dodds, E.R. (1951). *The Greeks and the irrational.* Berkeley, CA: University of California Press.

Dodds, E.R. (1971, March). Supernormal phenomena in classical antiquity. *Society for Psychical Research, Proceedings.*

Driscoll, L.N., & Wright, C. (1991). Survivors of childhood ritual abuse: Multigenerational Satanic cult involvement. *Treating Abuse Today, 1,* 5–13.

Drury, N. (1987). *The Shaman and the magician: Journeys between the worlds.* London: Arkana.

Drury, N. (1989). *The occult experience: Magic in the New Age.* Garden City Park, NY: Avery.

Dumont, L.E., & Altesman, R.I. (1989). *A parent's guide to teens and cults.* Washington, DC: PIA Press.

Dunn, G.E., Paolo, A.M., Ryan, J.J., & Van Fleet, J.N. (1994). Belief in the existence of multiple personality disorder among psychologists and psychiatrists. *Journal of Clinical Psychology,* 50, 454–457.

DuQuette, L.M., Hyatt, C.S., & Wilson, D.P. (1992). *Aleister Crowley's illustrated goetia.* Scottsdale, AZ: New Falcon Publications.

Durant, W. (1950). *The story of civilization.* Vol. 4: *The age of faith.* New York: Simon & Schuster.

Eberle, P. & Eberle, S. (1993). *The abuse of innocence: The McMartin Preschool trial.* Buffalo, NY: Prometheus Books.

Eliade, M. (1964). *Shamanism: Archaic techniques of ecstasy.* New York: Pantheon.

Encyclopedia of witchcraft & demonology. (1974). London: Octopus Books.

Evans-Pritchard, E.E. (1931). Sorcery and native opinion. *Africa, 4,* 23–28.

Evans-Pritchard, E.E. (1980). *Witchcraft oracles and magic among the Azande.* Oxford: Clarendon Press.

Faller, K. C. (1994, Spring). Ritual abuse: A review of research. *APSAC Advisor,* pp. 1, 19–27.

Feldman, G.C. (1993). *Lessons in evil, lessons from the light: A true story of Satanic abuse and spiritual healing.* New York: Crown Publishers.

Fielding, C. (1989). *The practical Qabalah.* York Beach, ME: Samuel Weiser.

Filoramo, G. (1990). *A history of gnosticism.* Cambridge, MA: Blackwell.

Finkelhor, D., Williams, L.M., Burns, N., & Kalinowski, M. (1988, March). *Sexual abuse in day care: A national study, final report.* Family Research Laboratory, University of New Hampshire, Durham, NH.

Finkelhor, D., Williams, L., & Burns, N. (1988). *Nursery crimes: Sexual abuse in day care.* Newbury Park, CA: Sage Publications.

Fletcher, C. (1990). *What cops know.* New York: Pocket Books.

Flint, I. (1991). *The rise of magic in early medieval Europe.* Princeton, NJ: Princeton University Press.

Flowers, S.E. (1990). *Fire & ice: Magical teachings of Germany's greatest secret occult order.* St. Paul, MN: Llewellyn Publications.

Flynn, K., & Gerhardt, G. (1989). *The silent brotherhood.* New York: Signet.

Fortune, D. (1984). *The mystical Qabalah.* York Beach, ME: Samuel Weiser.

Fraser, G.A. (1993). Exorcism rituals: Effects on multiple personality disorder patients. *Dissociation, 6,* 239–244.

Frater U∴.D∴. (1991). *Secrets of the German sex magicians: A practical handbook for men & women.* St. Paul, MN: Llewellyn Publications.

Frazer, J.G. (1963). *The golden bough: A study in magic and religion* (abridged edition). New York: Macmillan.

Freud, A. (1946). *The ego and mechanisms of defense.* New York: International Universities Press.

Freud, S. (1962). The neuro-psychoses of defence. In J. Strachey, A. Freud, A. Strachey & A. Tyson (Eds.), *The standard edition of the complete psychological works of Sigmund Freud,* vol. 3 (pp. 45–61). London: Hogarth Press.

Freud, S. (1966a). Letter 56. In J. Strachey, A. Freud, A. Strachey & A. Tyson (Eds.), *The standard edition of the complete psychological works of Sigmund Freud,* vol. 1 (p. 242). London: Hogarth Press.

Freud, S. (1966b). Letter 57. In J. Strachey, A. Freud, A. Strachey & A. Tyson (Eds.), *The standard edition of the complete psychological works of Sigmund Freud,* vol. 1 (pp. 242–244). London: Hogarth Press.

Freyd, J. (1993, August). *Theoretical and personal perspectives on the delayed memory debate.* A presentation for the Center for Mental Health at Foote Hospital's Continuing Education Conference: Controversies around recovered memories of incest and ritualistic abuse. Ann Arbor, MI.

Freyd, W. (1995, May/June). Raised voices: No doubt. *Treating Abuse Today,* p. 38.

Friesen, J.G. (1989). Treatment for multiple personality disorder: Integrating alter personalities and casting out evil spirits. *Journal of Christian Healing, 11*(3), 4–16.

Friesen, J. G. (1991). *Uncovering the mystery of MPD: Its shocking origins, its surprising cure.* San Bernardino, CA: Here's Life Publishers.

Friesen, J.G. (1992). *More than survivors: Conversations with multiple-personality clients.* San Bernardino, CA: Here's Life Publishers.

Galanter, M. (1989). *Cults: Faith, healing, and coercion.* New York: Oxford University Press.

Ganaway, G. (1989). Historical truth versus narrative truth: Clarifying the role of exogenous trauma in the etiology of multiple personality and its variants. *Dissociation, 2,* 205–220.

Ganaway, G. (1990, November). A psychodynamic look at alternative explanations for Satanic ritual abuse in MPD patients. Paper presented at Seventh International Conference on Multiple Personality/Dissociative States, Chicago.

Gardner, R.A. (1991). *Sex abuse hysteria: Salem witch trials revisited.* Cresskill, NJ: Creative Therapeutics.

Garrett, C. (1987). *Spirit possession and popular religion: From the Camisards to the Shakers.* Baltimore, MD: Johns Hopkins University Press.

Garrison, V. (1977). The "Puerto Rican Syndrome" in psychiatry and *Espiritismo.* In V. Crapanzo & V. Garrison (Eds.), *Case studies in spirit possession* (pp. 383–449). New York: John Wiley & Sons.

George, L. (1995). *The encyclopedia of heresies and heretics.* London: Robson Books.

Geraci, J. (1993, Winter). Interview: Hollida Wakefield and Ralph Underwager. *Paidika,* pp. 2–12.

Gersi, D. (1991). *Faces in the smoke: An eyewitness experience of Voodoo, shamanism, psychic healing and other amazing human powers.* Los Angeles, CA: Jeremy P. Tarcher.

Gibbs, N. (1993, December 27). Angels among us. *Time,* pp. 56–65.

Girard, R. (1972). *Violence and the sacred.* Baltimore, MD: Johns Hopkins University Press.

Goldstein, E. (1992). *Confabulations: Creating false memories, destroying families.* Boca Raton, FL: SIRS Books.

Golston, J.C. (1992). Ritual abuse: Raising hell in psychotherapy. *Treating Abuse Today, 2*(6), 5–16.

Gonzalez-Wippler, M. (1984). *Rituals and spells of Santeria.* New York: Original Publications.

Gonzalez-Wippler, M. (1987). *Santeria: African magic in Latin America.* New York: Original Publications.

Gonzalez-Wippler, M. (1992). *The Santeria experience: A journey into the miraculous.* St. Paul, MN: Llewellyn Publications.

Goodman, F. (1989). *Magic symbols.* London: Brian Trodd Publishing House.

Goodman, F.D. (1973). Apostolics of Yucatán: A case study of a religious movement. In E. Bourguinon (Ed.), *Religion, altered states of consciousness, and social change* (pp. 178–218). Columbus: Ohio State University Press.

Goodman, F.D. (1988). *How about demons?* Bloomington: Indiana University Press.

Goodman. G.S., Qin, J., Bottoms, B.L., and Shaver, P.R. (1994). *Characteristics and sources of allegations of ritualistic child abuse: Final report to the National Center on Child Abuse and Neglect.* [unpublished manuscript].

Gottlieb, A., & Graham, P. (1993). *Parallel worlds: An anthropologist and a writer encounter Africa.* New York: Crown Publishers.

Gould, C. (1992). Diagnosis and treatment of ritually abused children. In D.K. Sakheim & S.E. Devine (Eds.), *Out of darkness: Exploring Satanism and ritual abuse* (pp. 207–248). New York: Lexington Books.

Gould, C. (1993a, September). *Coercive control: Young minds held captive.* Presented at the National Conference on Crimes Against Children, Washington, DC.

Gould, C. (1993b, September). *Treating dissociation in children.* Presented at the National Conference on Crimes against Children, Washington, DC.

Gould, C., & Cozolino, L. (1992). Ritual abuse, multiplicity, and mind control. *Journal of Psychology and Theology, 20,* 194–196.

Grant, K. (1989). Aleister Crowley. In R. Cavendish (Ed.), *Encyclopedia of the unexplained: Magic, occultism and parapsychology* (pp. 70–72). London: Arkana.

Graves, R. (1955). *The Greek myths,* vols. 1–2. New York: Penguin Books.

Greaves, G.B. (1989). Precursors of integration in the treatment of Multiple Personality Disorder: Clinical reflections, *Dissociation, 2,* 224–230.

Greaves, G.B. (1992). Alternative hypotheses regarding claims of Satanic cult activity: A critical analysis. In D.K. Sakheim & S.E. Devine (Eds.), *Out of darkness: Exploring Satanism and ritual abuse* (pp. 45–72). New York: Lexington Books.

Green, T.A. (1991). Accusations of Satanism and racial tensions in the Matamoros cult murders. In J.T. Richardson, J. Best, & D.G. Bromley (Eds.), *The Satanism scare* (pp. 237—248). New York: Aldine de Gruyter.

Gregory, A.K. (1966). Introduction. In T.K. Oesterreich. *Possession: Demoniacal and other among primitive races, in antiquity, the Middle Ages and modern times* (pp. v–xvi). New Hyde Park, NY: University Books.

Guest, J.S. (1987). *The Yezidis: A study in survival.* London: KPI.

Guiley, R.E. (1989). *The encyclopedia of witches and witchcraft.* New York: Facts on File.

Guirdham, A. (1977). The great heresy. Saffron Walden, England: C.W. Daniel.

Haining, P. (1975). *An illustrated history of witchcraft.* New York: Pyramid Books.

Hales, R.E., Yudofsky, S.C., & Talbott, J.A. (1994). *The American Psychiatric Press Textbook of Psychiatry,* 2nd ed., Washington, DC: American Psychiatric Press.

Harner, M. (1990). *The way of the shaman.* New York: HarperCollins.

Harrison, B.G. (1993, December). Desperately seeking Satan. *Mirabella*, pp. 38, 40, 43.

Haskins, J. (1978). *Voodoo and hoodoo*. Chelsea, MI: Scarborough House.

Hassan, S. (1988). *Combating cult mind control*. Rochester VT: Park Street Press.

Hawkins, T.R. (1993). *A pastoral approach to multiple personality disorder and demonization*. Unpublished manuscript.

Hayes, J.A., & Mitchell, J.C. (1994). Mental health professionals' skepticism about multiple personality disorder. *Professional Psychology: Research & Practice, 25,* 410–15.

Hector, H. (1991). *Satanic ritual abuse and multiple personality disorder*. Rochester, MN: National Counseling Resource Center.

Hendrickson, K.M., McCarty, T., & Goodwin, J.M. (1990). Animal alters: Case reports. *Dissociation, 3,* 218–221.

Henney, J.H. (1973). The Shakers of St. Vincent: A stable religion. In E. Bourguinon (Ed.), *Religion altered states of consciousness, and social change* (pp. 219–263). Columbus: Ohio State University Press.

Herman, J.L., Perry, J.C., & van der Kolk, B.A. (1989). Childhood trauma in borderline personality disorder. *American Journal of Psychiatry, 146,* 490–495.

Hess, D.J. (1990). Ghosts and domestic politics in Brazil: Some parallels between spirit possession and spirit infestation. *Ethos, 18,* 407–438.

Hicks, R. (1990a). Police pursuit of Satanic crime: I. *Skeptical Inquirer, 14*(2), 276–286.

Hicks, R. (1990b). Police pursuit of Satanic crime: II. *Skeptical Inquirer, 14*(2), 378–389.

Hicks, R.D. (1991). *In pursuit of Satan: The police and the occult*. New York: Prometheus Books.

Higgins, K.M. (1987). *Nietzsche's Zarathustra*. Philadelphia, PA: Temple University Press.

Hilberg, R. (1992). *Perpetrators, victims, bystanders: The Jewish catastrophe*. New York: HarperCollins.

Hill, S., & Goodwin, J. (1989). Satanism: Similarities between patient accounts and pre-Inquisitional historical sources. *Dissociation, 2,* 39–43.

Holmberg, D. (1983). Shamanic soundings: Femaleness in the Tamang ritual structure. *Signs: Journal of Women's Cultural Sociology, 9* (1), 40–58.

Horevitz, R. (1994). Dissociation and multiple personality: Conflicts and controversies. In S.J. Lynn & J.W. Rhue (Eds.), *Dissociation: Clinical and theoretical perspectives* (pp. 434–461). New York: Guilford.

Horevitz, R.P., & Braun, B.G. (1984). Are multiple personalities borderline? *Psychiatric Clinics of North America, 7,* 69–88.

"The Horos Case" (1902, Jan. 18). *Lancet, 2*, pp. 174–175.

Howard, M. (1989). *The occult conspiracy: Secret societies – their influence and power in world history*. Rochester, VT: Destiny Books.

Howe, E. (1989). German occult groups. In R. Cavendish (Ed.), *Encyclopedia of the unexplained: Magic, occultism and parapsychology* (pp. 89–92). London: Arkana.

Hoyt, C.A. (1989). *Witchcraft* (2nd ed.). Carbondale: Southern Illinois University Press.

Hudson, P. (1991). *Ritual child abuse: Discovery, diagnosis and treatment*. Sarasota, CA: R & E Publishers.

Huxley, A. (1952). *The devils of Loudun*. New York: Harper & Row.

Huxley, F. (1989). *The way of the sacred*. London: Bloomsbury Books.

Huysmans, J.K. (1986). *Là Bas (Lower depths)*. London: Daedalus.

Hyatt, C.S., Duqette, L.M., & Ford, G. (1991). *Taboo: The ecstasy of evil.* Scottsdale, AZ: New Falcon Publications.

Hyatte, R. (Trans.). (1984). *Laughter for the devil: The trials of Gilles de Rais, companion-in-arms of Joan of Arc (1440).* Cranbury, NJ: Associated University Presses.

Idel, M. (1988). *Kabbalah: New perspectives.* New Haven, CT: Yale University Press.

Inglis, B. (1989). *Trance: A natural history of altered states of mind.* London: Paladin.

Jackson, B. (1993, September). *The role of ritual abuse and the sexual exploitation of children.* Presented at the National Conference on Crimes Against Children, Washington, DC.

Jacobs, L. (Ed.). (1990). *The Jewish mystics.* London: Kyle Cathie.

Jameson, R.D. (1984). Cannibalism. In M. Leach & J. Fried (Eds.), *Funk & Wagnalls standard dictionary of folklore, mythology, and legend* (pp. 186–189). San Francisco: Harper & Row.

Jenkins, P., & Maier-Katkin, D. (1991). Occult survivors: The making of a myth. In J.T. Richardson, J. Best, & D.G. Bromley (Eds.), *The Satanism scare* (pp. 127–144). New York: Aldine de Gruyter.

John, A. (1989). *Unholy trinity: The Adrian Lim ritual child killings.* Singapore: Times Books.

Johns, J. (1969). *King of the witches: The world of Alex Saunders.* New York: Coward-McCann.

Johnston, J. (1989). *The edge of evil: The rise of Satanism in North America.* Dallas, TX: Word Publishing.

Jonker, F., & Jonker-Bakker, P. (1991). Experiences with ritualistic child sexual abuse: A case study from the Netherlands. *Journal of Child Abuse and Neglect, 15,* 191–196.

Jonker, F., & Jonker-Bakker, I. (1997). Effects of ritual abuse: The results of three surveys in the Netherlands, *Journal of Child Abuse & Neglect, 21,* 541–556.

Kaczynski, R. (1993, June 21). Of heresy and secrecy: Evidence of Golden Dawn teachings on mystic sexuality. *Eidolon,* pp. 4–7.

Kahaner, L. (1988). *Cults that kill: Probing the underworld of occult crime.* New York: Warner Books.

Kantrowitz, B. (1993, March 15). The messiah of Waco. *Newsweek,* pp. 56, 57, 58.

Kaplan, H.I., & Sadock, B.J. (Eds.) (1995). Comprehensive *Textbook of Psychiatry/VI.* Baltimore: Williams & Wilkins.

Katchen, M.H. (1992). The history of satanic religions. In D.K. Sakheim & S.E. Devine (Eds.), *Out of darkness: Exploring Satanism and ritual abuse* (pp. 1–19). New York: Lexington Books.

Kelly, S.J. (1992, Jan.) *Ritualistic abuse: Recognition, impact and current controversy.* Paper presented at the Conference on Responding to Child Maltreatment, San Diego, CA.

Kelly, S. (1993). Ritualistic abuse of children in day care centers. In M. Langone (Ed.), *Recovery from cults* (pp. 340-351). New York: Norton.

Kertzer, M.N. (1993). *What is a Jew?* New York: Macmillan.

Kilduff, M., & Javers, R. (1978). *The suicide cult: The inside story of the Peoples Temple sect and the massacre in Guyana.* New York: Bantam Books.

Kilroy, J. (1990). *Sacrifice: The drug cult murder of Mark Kilroy at Matamoros.* Dallas: Word Publishing.

King, F. (1970). *The rites of modern occult magic.* New York: Macmillan.

King, F. (1971). *Sexuality, magic and perversion.* London: Spearman.

King, F. (1989a). *Modern ritual magic: The rise of Western occultism.* New York: Avery.

King, F. (1989b). Satanism. In R. Cavendish (Ed.), *Encyclopedia of the unexplained: Magic, occultism and parapsychology* (pp. 219–221). London: Arkana.

King, F. (1991). *Witchcraft and demonology.* New York: Crescent Books.

Kligman, G. (1981). *Calus: Symbolic transformation in Romanian ritual.* Chicago: University of Chicago Press.

Kluckhohn, C. (1962). *Navaho witchcraft.* Boston, MA: Beacon Press.

Kluft, R.P. (1984). Treatment of multiple personality disorder: A study of 33 cases. *Psychiatric Clinics of North America, 7,* 9–29.

Kluft, R.P. (1985) (Ed.) *Childhood antecedents of multiple personality.* Washington, DC: American Psychiatric Press.

Knapp, B. (1977). The golem and ecstatic mysticism. *Journal of Altered States of Consciousness, 3,* 355–369.

Knight, S. (1986). *The brotherhood: The secret world of the freemasons.* London: Dorset Press.

Koch, K., & Lechler, A. (1970). *Occult bondage and deliverance.* Grand Rapids, MI: Kernel Publications.

Koehler, K., Ebel, H., & Vartzopoulos, D. (1990). Lycanthropy and demonmania: Some psychopathological issues. *Psychological Medicine, 20,* 629–633.

Kroger, W.S., & Fezler, W.D. (1976). *Hypnosis and behavior modification: Imagery conditioning.* Philadelphia, PA: J.B. Lippincott.

Kroll, J. (1988). *The challenge of the borderline patient: Competency in diagnosis and treatment.* New York: W.W. Norton.

Kurath, G.P. (1984). Sun dance. In M. Leach & J. Fried (Eds.), *Funk & Wagnalls standard dictionary of folklore, mythology, and legend* (pp. 1088–1089). San Francisco: Harper & Row.

La Barre, W. (1962). *They shall take up serpents: Psychology of the southern snake-handling cult.* Minneapolis: University of Minnesota Press.

La Barre, W. (1975). Anthropological perspectives on hallucination and hallucinogens. In R.K. Siegel & L.J. West (Eds.), *Hallucinations: Behavior, experience, and theory* (pp. 9–52). New York: John Wiley & Sons.

Lacarriere, J. (1991). *The Gnostics.* San Francisco: City Light Books.

Lacayo, R. (1993, March 15). Cult of death. *Time,* pp. 36–39.

La Fontaine, J.S. (1994). *The extent and nature of organized and ritual abuse: Research findings.* London: HMSO.

La Fontaine, J.S. (1998). *Speak of the devil: Tales of satanic abuse in contemporary England.* Cambridge: Cambridge University Press.

Lame Deer, J. (1972). *Lame Deer seeker of visions: The life of a Sioux medicine man.* New York: Simon & Schuster.

Lanning, K.V. (1989, October). Satanic, occult, ritualistic crime: A law enforcement perspective. *Police Chief,* pp. 88–107.

Lanning, K.V. (1992). *Investigator's guide to allegations of "ritual" child abuse.* Quantico, VA: National Center for the Analysis of Violent Crime.

Larner, C. (1974). Is all witchcraft really *witchcraft? New Society, 30,* 81–83.

Larson, B. (1989a). *Larson's new book of cults.* Wheaton, IL: Tyndale House.

Larson, B. (1989b). *Satanism: The seduction of America's youth.* Nashville, TN: Thomas Nelson Publishers.

Larson, B. (1989c). *Straight answers on the new age.* Nashville, TN: Thomas Nelson.

Lasalandra, M., & Merenda, M. (1990). *Satan's harvest.* New York: Dell.

Laughlin, H.P. (1970). *The ego and its defenses.* New York: Appleton-Century-Crofts.

Laurence, L., & Weinhouse, B. (1994). *Outrageous practices: The alarming truth about how medicine mistreats women*. New York: Fawcett Columbine.

LaVey, A.S. (1966). *The Satanic bible*. New York: Avon Books.

LaVey, A.S. (1972). *The Satanic rituals*. Secaucus, NJ: University Books.

LaVey, A.S. (1989). *The Satanic witch*. Los Angeles, CA: Feral House.

L. Bathurst IX° (1990). Liber LII [Book 52]: Manifesto of the O.T.O. In Hymenaeus Beta X° (Ed.), The *Equinox*, vol. 3, no. 10 (pp. 87–99). York Beach, ME: Samuel Weiser.

Leacock, S., & Leacock, R. (1975). *Spirits of the deep: A study of an Afro-Brazilian cult*. Garden City, NY: Anchor Books.

Leavitt, F. (1994). Clinical correlates of alleged satanic abuse and less controversial sexual molestation. *Child Abuse & Neglect,* 18, 387–392.

Leavitt, F. (1997). False attribution of suggestibility to explain recovered memory of childhood sexual abuse following extended amnesia. Journal of *Child Abuse & Neglect,* 21, 265–272.

Leavitt, F. (1998). Measuring the impact of media exposure and hospital treatment on patients alleging satanic ritual abuse. *Treating Abuse Today,* 8 (4), pp. 28–29.

Leavitt, F. & Labott, S. (1998). Revision of the Word Association Test for assessing association of patients reporting satanic ritual abuse in childhood. *Journal of Clinical Psychology, 54,* 933—943.

Lemonick, M. D. (1993, August). Secrets of the Maya. *Time,* pp. 44–50.

Lester, D., Brokopp, G.W., & Prieb, K. (1969). Association between full moon and completed suicide. *Psychological Reports, 25,* 598.

Lewis, I.M. (1971). *Ecstatic religion: An anthropological study of spirit possession and shamanism*. Baltimore, MD: Penguin Books.

Lieban, R.W. (1967). *Cebuano sorcery: Malign magic in the Philippines*. Berkeley, CA: University of California Press.

Lieber, A.L., & Sherin, C.R. (1972). Homicides and the lunar cycle: Toward a theory of lunar influence on human emotional disturbance. *American Journal of Psychiatry,* 29, 69–74.

Linedecker, C.L. (1993). *Massacre at Waco, Texas*. New York: St. Martin's Paperbacks.

Linehan, M. M. (1993). *Cognitive behavioral treatment for borderline personality disorder*. New York: Guilford Press.

Lipstadt, D. (1986). *Beyond belief*. New York: Free Press.

Lipstadt, D. (1993). *Denying the Holocaust: The growing assault on truth and memory*. New York: Free Press.

Lissner, I. (1961). *Man, God and magic*. New York: G.P. Putnam's Sons.

Livy, T. (1976). *Rome and the Mediterranean: Books XXI-XLV of the history of Rome from its foundation*. London: Penguin Books.

Lockwood, C. (1993). *Other altars: Roots and realities of cultic and Satanic ritual abuse and multiple personality disorder*. Minneapolis, MN: CompCare.

Loftus, E. (1999). Lost in the mall: Misrepresentations and misunderstandings. *Ethics & Behavior, 9,* 51-60.

Loftus, E. F., & Ketcham, K. (1994). *The myth of repressed memory*. New York: St. Martin's Press.

Loftus, E. F., & Pickrell, J. E. (1995). The formation of false memories. *Psychiatric Annals, 25,* 720-725.

Lowe, T. (1913). *Adoptive masonry illustrated*. Chicago, IL: Ezra Cook.

Lowenstein, R.J. (1992, December). President's message. *ISSMP&D News,* pp. 1, 2, 4.

Luhrmann, T.M. (1989). *Persuasions of the witch's craft.* Cambridge, MA: Harvard University Press.

Lund, D.S. (1991, April). Psychiatrists debate the extent of ritual abuse. *The Psychiatric Times,* pp. 54, 57.

Lynn, S.J., & Rhue, J.W. (Eds.) (1994). *Dissociation.* New York: Guilford Press.

Lyons, A. (1988). *Satan wants you: The cult of devil worship in America.* New York: Mysterious Press.

Macfarlane, A. (1970). *Witchcraft in Tudor and Stuart England.* London: Routledge & Kegan Paul.

MacGregor, G. (1979). *Gnosis: A renaissance in Christian thought.* Wheaton, IL: Theosophical Publishing House.

Macoy, R. (1989). *A dictionary of freemasonry.* New York: Bell Publishing.

Mai, F. (1995). Psychiatrists' attitudes to multiple personality disorder: A questionnaire study. *Canadian Journal of Psychiatry, 40,* 154–57.

Mair, L. (1971). *Witchcraft.* New York: McGraw-Hill.

Maloney, H.N., & Lovekin, A.A. (1985). *Glossolalia: Behavioral science perspectives on speaking in tongues.* New York: Oxford University Press.

Mandelsberg, R.G. (Ed.). (1991). *Cult killers.* New York: Pinnacle Books.

Mannix, D.P. (1959). *The Hell Fire Club.* New York: Ballantine Books.

Marchetti, V., & Marks, J.D. (1974). *The CIA and the cult of intelligence.* New York: Dell.

Markman, R.H., & Markman, P.T. (1992). *The flayed god: The Mesoamerican mythological tradition: Sacred texts and images from pre-Columbian Mexico and Central America.* New York: HarperCollins.

Marks, J. (1979). *The search for the "Manchurian candidate": The CIA and mind control.* New York: W.W. Norton.

Marrs, T. (1990). *New age cults and religions.* Austin, TX: Living Truth Publishers.

Martin, M. (1976). *Hostage to the devil.* New York: Harper & Row.

Martin, W. (1980). *The new cults.* Santa Ana, CA: Vision House.

Marwick, M. (1982). Introduction. In M. Marwick (Ed.), *Witchcraft and sorcery* (pp. 11–19). Harmondsworth, UK: Penguin Books.

Masson, J.M. (1992). *The assault on truth: Freud's suppression of the seduction theory.* New York: HarperCollins.

Mather, G.A., & Nichols, L.A. (1993). *Dictionary of cults, sects, religions and the occult.* Grand Rapids, MI: Zondervan.

Mathers, S.L.M. (Trans. and Ed.). (1974). *The key of Solomon the king.* York Beach, ME: Samuel Weiser.

McCormick, D. (1958). *The Hell-Fire Club: The story of the amorous knights of Wycombe.* London: Jarrolds Publishers.

McDougal, D. (1995, May 20). The people versus McMartin. *TV Guide,* pp. 28–29.

McDowell, J., & Stewart, D. (1992). *The deceivers.* San Bernardino, CA: Here's Life.

McMinn, M.R., & Wade, N.G. (1995). Beliefs about the prevalence of dissociative identity disorder, sexual abuse, and ritual abuse among religious and nonreligious therapists. *Professional Psychology: Research and Practice. 26,* 257–261.

McShane, C. (1993). Satanic sexual abuse: A paradigm. *Affilia, 8,* 200–212.

Menninger, K. (1930). *The human mind.* New York: Alfred A. Knopf.

Mercer, J. (1991). *Behind the mask of adolescent Satanism.* Minneapolis, MN: Deaconess Press.

Metraux, A. (1959). *Voodoo in Haiti.* New York: Oxford University Press.

Michelet, J. (1992). *Satanism and witchcraft.* New York: Citadel Press.

Miller, A. (1990). *Thou shalt not be aware: Society's betrayal of the child.* New York: Meridian.

Miller, S.D. (1989). Optical differences in cases of multiple personality disorder. *Journal of Nervous & Mental Disorders, 177,* 480–486.

Mischel, W., & Mischel, F. (1958). Psychological aspects of spirit possession. *American Anthropologist, 60,* 249-260.

Montgomery, J.W. (Ed.) (1976). *Demon possession.* Minneapolis, MN: Bethany House.

Moody, E.J. (1974). Magical therapy: An anthropological investigation of contemporary Satanism. In I.I. Zaretsky & M.P. Leone (Eds.), *Religious movements in contemporary America* (pp. 355–382). Princeton, NJ: Princeton University Press.

Moore, R.I. (1975). *Documents of medieval history,* vol. 1: *The birth of popular heresy.* New York: St. Martin's Press.

Moriarity, A. (1992). *The psychology of adolescent Satanism: A guide for parents, counselors, clergy, and teachers.* Westport, CT: Praeger.

Moriarity, A.R., & Story, D.W. (1990). Psychological dynamics of adolescent Satanism. *Journal of Mental Health Counseling, 12,* 186–198.

Morton, A. (1977). Dawit: Competition and integration in an Ethiopian wuqabi cult group. In V. Crapanzo & V. Garrison (Eds.), *Case studies in spirit possession* (pp. 193–233). New York: John Wiley & Sons.

Mossiker, F. (1969). *The affair of the poisons.* New York: Alfred A. Knopf.

Mulhern, S. (1991a). Embodied alternative identities: Bearing witness to a world that might have been. *Psychiatric Clinics of North America, 14,* 769–786.

Mulhern, S. (1991b). Satanism and psychotherapy: A rumor in search of an inquisition. In J.T. Richardson, J. Best, & D.G. Bromley (Eds.), *The Satanism scare* (pp. 145–172). New York: Aldine de Gruyter.

Mulhern, S. (1994). Satanism, ritual abuse, and multiple personality disorder: A sociohistorical perspective. *The International Journal of Clinical and Experimental Hypnosis, 42,* 265–288.

Murphy, J. (1988). *Santeria: An African religion in America.* Boston, MA: Beacon.

Murray, M.A. (1921). *The witch-cult in Western Europe.* Oxford: Oxford University Press.

Murray, M.A. (1933). *The god of the witches.* London: Sampson Low, Marston & Co.

Musopole, A.C. (1993). Witchcraft terminology, the Bible and African Christian theology: An exercise in hermeneutics. *Journal of Religion in Africa, 23,* 347–354.

Myers, J.E. (1994). *The backlash: Child protection under fire.* Newbury Park, CA: Sage Publications.

Nagel, S.B. (1989). Addictive behaviors: Problems in treatment with borderline patients. In J.F. Masterson, & R. Klein (Eds.), *Psychotherapy of the disorders of the self* (pp. 395–410). New York: Brunner Mazel.

Nethercot, A.H. (1961). *The first five lives of Annie Besant.* London: Hart-Davis.

Nethercot, A.H. (1963). *The last four lives of Annie Besant.* London: Hart-Davis.

Neusner, J., Frerichs, E.S., Flesher, P.V. (Eds.). (1989). *Religion, science, and magic: In concert and conflict.* New York: Oxford University Press.

Nevius, J. (1968). *Demon possession.* Grand Rapids, MI: Kregel Publications.

Newton, M. (1993). *Raising hell: An encyclopedia of devil worship and satanic crime.* New York: Avon Books.

Newton, M. (1997, April). *Guilty as charged.* Presentation at Dreamweavers Conference, Sponsored by Believe the Children, International Council on Cultism and Ritual Trauma, Survivors and Victims Empowered, and Mothers Against Sexual Abuse, Chicago.

Nitzsche, J.C. (1975). *The genius figure in antiquity and the Middle Ages.* New York: Columbia University Press.

Noblitt, J. R. (1979). Celestial concomitants of human behavior (doctoral dissertation, North Texas State University, 1978). *Dissertation Abstracts International, 39,* 5572B.

Noblitt, J. R. (1993a). *Cult and ritual trauma disorder* [videotape]. Dallas, TX: Center for Counseling & Psychological Services.

Noblitt, J.R. (1993b, Spring). A proposal that the DSM add the diagnosis, Cult and Ritual Trauma Disorder, to a future revision. *The Society for the Investigation, Treatment & Prevention of Ritual and Cult Abuse News,* p. 2.

Noblitt, J.R. (1995). Psychometric measures of trauma among psychiatric patients reporting ritual abuse, Psychological Reports, 77, 743-747.

Noblitt, J.R. (1998a). *Accessing dissociated mental states.* [Self-published monograph available through the Center for Counseling and Psychological Services, P.C., 9601 White Rock Trail, Suite 103, Dallas, TX 75238].

Noblitt, J.R. (1998b, March) *Techniques for induction of trance phenomenon without suggestion.* Paper presented at the 40th Annual Meeting of the American Society of Clinical Hypnosis, Fort Worth, TX.

Noll, R. (1989). Multiple personality, dissociation, and C. G. Jung's complex theory. *Journal of Analytical Psychology, 34,* 353–370.

Noll, R. (1990). *Bizarre diseases of the mind.* New York: Berkeley.

Noll, R. (1992). Possession syndrome. In R. Noll (Ed.), *The encyclopedia of schizophrenia and the psychotic disorders* (pp. 245–246). New York: Facts on File.

North, C.S., Ryall, J.M., Ricci, D.A., & Wetzell, R.D. (1993). *Multiple personalities, multiple disorders.* New York: Oxford University Press.

Novello, P., & Primavera, A. (1992). An ethnological approach to self-injurious behavior [Letter to the editor]. *American Journal of Psychiatry, 149,* 1763.

Oesterreich, T.K. (1966). *Possession: Demoniacal and other among primitive races, in antiquity, the Middle Ages and modern times.* New Hyde Park, NY: University Books.

Ofshe, R.J. (1992). Inadvertent hypnosis during interrogation: False confession due to dissociative state; misidentified multiple personality and the satanic cult hypothesis. *International Journal of Clinical and Experimental Hypnosis, 3,* 125–156.

Ofshe, R., & Waters, E. (1994). *Making monsters: False memories, psychotherapy and sexual hysteria.* New York: Charles Scribner's Sons.

Ogloff, J.R.P., & Pfeifer, J. (1992). Cults and the law: A discussion of the legality of alleged cult activities. *Behavioral Sciences & the Law, 10,* 117–140.

Oke, I. (1989). *Blood secrets: The true story of demon worship and ceremonial murder.* New York: Prometheus Books.

Oksana, C. (1994). *Safe passage to healing: A guide for survivors of ritual abuse.* New York: HarperCollins.

Olson, K. (1992). *Exorcism: Fact or fiction.* Nashville, TN: Thomas Nelson Publishers.

Orne, M.T., & Bates, B.L. (1992). Reflections on Multiple Personality Disorder: A view from the looking glass of the past. In A. Kales, C. M. Pierce, & M. Greenblatt (Eds.), *The mosaic of contemporary psychiatry in perspective* (pp. 247–260). New York: Springer-Verlag.

Osborn, R.D. (1968). The moon and the mental hospital: An investigation of one area of folk-lore. *Journal of Psychiatric Nursing and Mental Health Services, 6,* 88–93.

Overton, M. (1994, November 16). Copies of Wilson file missing in burglary. *Gilmer Mirror,* pp. 1, 7A.

Pagels, E. (1981). *The gnostic gospels*. New York: Vintage Books.

Pagels, E. (1988). *Adam, Eve, and the serpent*. New York: Random House.

Parkin, A.J. (1987). *Memory and amnesia: An introduction*. Cambridge, MA: Basil Blackwell.

Parrinder, G. (1970). *Witchcraft: European and African*. London: Faber & Faber.

Partner, P. (1990). *The Knights Templar & their myth*. Rochester, VT: Destiny Books.

Passantino, G., Passantino, B., & Trott, J. (1989). The true Lauren Stratford story. *Cornerstone, 18*, (90), pp. 23–28.

Patterson, J., & Kim, P. (1992). *The day America told the truth*. New York: Penguin Books.

Pattison, E.M. (1974). Ideological support for the marginal middle class: Faith healing and glossolalia. In I.I. Zaretsky & M.P. Leone (Eds.), *Religious movements in contemporary America* (pp. 418–455). Princeton, NJ: Princeton University Press.

Peck, M. S. (1983). *People of the lie: The hope for healing human evil*. New York: Simon & Schuster.

Perry, N.E. (1992). *Therapist's experiences of the effects of working with dissociative patients*. Paper presented at the 9th Annual Meeting of the International Society for the Study of Multiple Personality and Dissociation, Chicago.

Piggott, S. (1987). *The Druids*. New York: Thames & Hudson.

Pike, A. (1871/1966). *Morals and dogma of the ancient and accepted rite of freemasonry*. Washington, DC: L.H. Jenkins.

Pistone, J. (1992). *The ceremony: The Mafia initiation tapes*. New York: Dell.

Pokorny, A.D. (1964). Moon phases, suicide, and homicide. *American Journal of Psychiatry, 121*, 66–67.

Pokorny, A.D. (1968). Moon phases and hospital admissions. *Journal of Psychiatric Nursing and Mental Health Services, 6*, 325–327.

Pokorny, A.D., & Jachimczyk, J. (1974). The questionable relationship between homicide and the lunar cycle. *American Journal of Psychiatry, 131*, 827–829.

Potter, C.F. (1984). Infanticide. In M. Leach & J. Fried (Eds.), *Funk & Wagnalls standard dictionary of folklore, mythology, and legend* (pp. 522–524). San Francisco: Harper & Row.

Powers, W. K. (1977). *Oglala religion*. Lincoln: University of Nebraska Press.

Pressel, E. (1973). Umbanda in São Paulo: Religious innovation in a developing society. In E. Bourguinon (Ed.), *Religion, altered states of consciousness, and social change* (pp. 264–318). Columbus: Ohio State University Press.

Pressel, E. (1977). Negative Spirit possession in experienced Brazilian Umbanda spirit mediums. In V. Crapanzo & V. Garrison (Eds.), *Case studies in spirit possession* (pp. 333-364). New York: John Wiley & Sons.

Putnam, F.W. (1989). *Diagnosis and treatment of multiple personality disorder*. New York: Guilford Press.

Putnam, F.W. (1991). Commentary: The satanic ritual abuse controversy. *Child Abuse & Neglect, 15*, 175–179.

Putnam, F.W., Guroff, J.J., Silberman, E.K., Barban, L., & Post, R.M. (1986). The clinical phenomenology of multiple personality disorder: A review of 100 recent cases. *Journal of Clinical Psychiatry, 47*, 285– 293.

Raschke, C.A. (1990). *Painted black*. New York: HarperCollins.

Ravenscroft, K. (1965). Voodoo possession: A natural experiment in hypnosis. *International Journal of Clinical and Experimental Hypnosis, 13*, 157–182.

Razran, G. (1971). *Mind in evolution: An East-West synthesis of learned behavior and cognition*. New York: Houghton Mifflin.

Regardie, I. (1987). *What you should know about the Golden Dawn.* Phoenix, AZ: Falcon Press.

Regardie, I. (1989). *The Golden Dawn* (6th ed.). St. Paul, MN: Llewellyn.

Regardie, I. (1993). *The eye in the triangle: An interpretation of Aleister Crowley.* Phoenix, AZ: New Falcon Publications.

Ribi, A. (1990). *Demons of the inner world: Understanding our hidden complexes.* Boston, MA: Shambhala.

Rigaud, M. (1985). *Secrets of Voodoo.* San Francisco: City Lights Books.

Ritual Abuse Task Force, Los Angeles County Commission for Women. (1989). *Ritual abuse: Definitions, glossary, the use of mind control.* Los Angeles: Author.

Robbins, R.H. (1981). *The encyclopedia of witchcraft and demonology.* New York: Bonanza Books.

Robertson, P. (1991). *The new world order.* Dallas, TX: Word Publishing.

Robinson, J.J. (1989). *Born in blood: The lost secrets of freemasonry.* New York: M. Evans.

Robinson, J.J. (1991). *Dungeon, fire and sword: The Knights Templar in the crusades.* New York: M. Evans & Co.

Robinson, J.M. (Ed.). (1988). *The Nag Hammadi Library in English.* San Francisco: Harper & Row.

Robinson, P. (1991). *The new world order.* Dallas, TX: Word Publishing.

Rockwell, R.B. (1995). Incidious deception. *Journal of Psychohistory, 22,* 312-328.

Rogers, A. (1994). *For survival's sake workbook.* Lewiston, NY: Rogers.

Rose, E.S. (1993, January). Surviving the unbelievable: Cult ritual abuse. *Ms.,* pp. 40–45.

Ross, C.A. (1989). *Multiple personality disorder: Diagnosis, clinical features and treatment.* New York: John Wiley & Sons.

Ross, C.A. (1995). *Satanic ritual abuse: Principles of treatment.* Toronto: University of Toronto Press.

Ross, C.A. (1997). *Dissociative identity disorder: Diagnosis, clinical features and treatment of multiple personality.* New York: John Wiley & Sons.

Rowan, J. (1990). *Subpersonalities: The people inside us.* London: Routledge.

Rudolph, K. (1987). *Gnosis: The nature & history of Gnosticism.* San Francisco, CA: HarperSanFrancisco.

Russell, J.B. (1972). *Witchcraft in the middle ages.* Secaucus, NJ: Citadel Press.

Russell, J.B. (1984). *Lucifer: The devil in the middle ages.* Ithaca, NY: Cornell University Press.

Russell, J.B. (1988). *The prince of darkness: Radical evil and the power of good in history.* Ithaca, NY: Cornell University Press.

Russell, J.B. (1991). The historical Satan. In J.T. Richardson, J. Best, & D.G. Bromley (Eds.), *The Satanism scare* (pp. 41–48.). New York: Aldine de Gruyter.

Russell, N. (1993, September). *Ritualized crimes against children.* Presented at the National Conference on Crimes Against Children, Washington, DC.

Ryder, D. (1992). *Breaking the circle of Satanic ritual abuse.* Minneapolis, MN: CompCare Publishers.

Ryder, D. (1994). *Cover-up of the century: Satanic ritual crime and world conspiracy.* Carmel, CA: Ryder Publishing.

S., Joe (1991). *Out of hell again.* Rocky River, OH: State of the Art Publishing.

St. Clair, D. (1987). *Say you love Satan.* New York: Dell.

Saitoti, T. O. (1986). *The worlds of a Maasai warrior: An autobiography.* New York: Dorset.

Saks, E.R., & Behnke, S.H. (1997). *Jekyll on trial: Multiple personality disorder and criminal law*. New York: New York University Press.

Salter, A. (1991). *Accuracy of expert testimony in child sexual abuse cases: A case study of Ralph Underwager and Hollida Wakefield*. Unpublished manuscript.

Sargant, W. (1974). *The mind possessed: A physiology of possession, mysticism and faith healing*. Philadelphia, PA: J.B. Lippincott.

Schele, L., & Miller, M.E. (1986). *The blood of kings: Dynasty and ritual in Maya art*. Fort Worth, TX: Kimball Art Museum.

Schetky, D.H. (1991). The sexual abuse of infants and toddlers. *American Psychiatric Press Review of Psychiatry, 10,* 308-319.

Schlesinger, A.M. (1978). *Robert Kennedy and his times*. Boston, MA: Houghton Mifflin.

Schumaker, J.F. (1995). *The corruption of reality: A unified theory of religionhypnosis, and psychopathology*. Amherst, NY: Prometheus Books.

Schutte, J.W. (1994). Repressed memory lawsuits: Potential verdict predictors. *Behavioral Sciences and the Law, 12,* 409–416.

Schwartz, M.F. (1993, Summer). False memory blues. *Masters and Johnson Report,* p. 3.

Schwartz, R.C. (1987, March). Our multiple selves: Applying systems thinking to the inner family, *Networker,* 80–83.

Scot, R. (1972). *The discoverie of witchcraft*. New York: Dover.

Sebald, H. (1995). *Witch-children: From Salem witch-hunts to modern courtrooms*. Amherst, NY: Prometheus Books.

Segal, R.A. (Ed.). (1992). *The Gnostic Jung*. Princeton, NJ: Princeton University Press.

Sex abuse, lies and videotape. (1995, Spring). *Believe the Children Newsletter,* pp. 1, 4.

Shapiro, J.O., Streiner, D.L., Gray, A.L., Williams, N.L., & Soble, C. (1970). The moon and mental illness: A failure to confirm the Transylvania effect. *Perceptual & Motor Skills, 30,* 827–830.

Shaw, J.D., & McKenney, T.C. (1988). *The deadly deception*. Lafayette, LA: Huntington House.

Short, M. (1989). *Inside the brotherhood: Further secrets of the freemasons*. New York: Dorset Press.

Shupe, A.D., & Bromley, D.G. (1985). *A documentary history of the anti-cult movement*. Arlington, TX: University of Texas at Arlington Center for Social Research.

Sifakis, C. (1987). *The Mafia encyclopedia*. New York: Facts on File.

Silverstein, E., & Howard, S. (1985). *A man called horse* [Videotape]. Farmington Hills, MI: CBS/Fox Video.

Simmons, M. (1974). *Witchcraft in the Southwest*. Lincoln: University of Nebraska Press.

Simpson, C. (1993). *The splendid blond beast: Money, law and genocide in the twentieth century*. New York: Grove Press.

Sliker, G. (1992). *Multiple mind: Healing the split in psyche and world*. Boston, MA: Shambhala.

Smith, M. (1993). *Ritual abuse: What it is, why it happens, how to help*. San Francisco: HarperSanFrancisco.

Smith, M., & Pazder, L. (1980). *Michelle Remembers*. New York: Congdon & Lattes.

Snow, B. & Sorenson, T. (1990). *Ritualistic child abuse in a neighborhood setting*. Journal of Interpersonal Violence, 5, 474–487.

Solomon, R. (1983). The use of the MMPI with multiple personality patients. *Psychological Reports, 53,* 1004–1006.

Somé, M.P. (1993). *Ritual: Power, healing and community.* Portland, OR: Swan, Raven.

Somé, M.P. (1994). *Of water and the spirit: Ritual, magic, and initiation in the life of an African shaman.* New York: G.P. Putnam's Sons.

Spanos, N.P. (1996). *Multiple identities and false memories: A sociocognitive perspective.* Washington, DC: American Psychological Association.

Spanos, N.P., Weeks, J.R., Menary, E., & Betrand, L.D. (1986). Hypnotic interview and age regression procedures in elicitation of multiple personality symptoms: A simulation study. *Psychiatry, 49,* 298–311.

Spence, L. (1993). *An encyclopedia of occultism.* New York: Carol Publishing.

Spiegel, H. (1974). The grade 5 syndrome: The highly hypnotizable person. *International Journal of Clinical & Experimental hypnosis 22,* 303–319.

Spiegel, H., & Spiegel, D. (1978). *Trance and treatment: Clinical uses of hypnosis.* New York: Basic Books.

Stanton, B. (1992). *Klanwatch: Bringing the Ku Klux Klan to justice.* New York: Mentor.

Steffon, J.J. (1992). *Satanism: Is it real?* Ann Arbor, MI: Servant Productions.

Steiger, B. (1971). *Kahuna magic.* West Chester, PA: Whitford Press.

Stern, C.R. (1984). The etiology of multiple personalities. *Psychiatric Clinics of North America, 7,* 149–160.

Stevens, P. (1991). The demonology of Satanism: An anthropological view. In J.T. Richardson, J. Best, & D.G. Bromley (Eds.), *The Satanism scare* (pp. 21–39). New York: Aldine de Gruyter.

Still, W. (1990). *New world order: The ancient plan of secret societies.* Lafayette, LA: Huntington House.

Stratford, L. (1988). *Satan's underground.* Eugene, OR: Harvest House.

Summers, A. (1993). *Official and confidential: The secret life of J. Edgar Hoover.* New York: G.P. Putnam's Sons.

Summers, M. (1992). *The history of witchcraft and demonology.* Secaucus, NJ: Castle Books.

Suster, G. (1987). Modern scholarship and the origins of the Golden Dawn. In Israel Regardie, *What you should know about the Golden Dawn* (pp. 159–178). Phoenix, AZ: Falcon Press.

Symonds, J. (1958). *Madame Blavatsky, medium and magician.* London: Oldhams.

Symonds, J. (1979). Introduction. In, J. Symonds & K. Grant (Eds.), The *confessions of Aleister Crowley* (pp. 13–25). London: Arkana.

Symonds, J., & Grant, K. (Eds.). (1979). The *confessions of Aleister Crowley.* London: Arkana.

Tallant, R. (1990). *Voodoo in New Orleans.* Gretna, LA: Pelican Publishing.

Tannahill, R. (1975). *Flesh and blood: A history of the cannibal complex.* New York: Dorset Press.

Tasman, A., Kay, J., & Lieberman, J.A. (1997). *Psychiatry.* Philadelphia: W.B. Saunders.

Tasso, J., & Miller, E. (1976). The effects of the full moon on human behavior. *Journal of Psychology, 93,* 81–83.

Taussig, M. (1989). The nervous system: homesickness and Dada. *Stanford Humanities Review, 1*(1), 44-81.

Taylor, P.J., & Kopelman, M.D. (1984). Amnesia for criminal offenses. *Psychological Medicine, 14,* 581–588.

Telushkin, J. (1991). *Jewish Literacy: The most important things to know about the Jewish religion, its people, and its history.* New York: William Morrow.

Terry, M. (1987). *The ultimate evil.* Garden City, NY: Doubleday.

Thomas, G. (1989). *Journey into madness: The true story of secret CIA mind control and medical abuse.* New York: Bantam Books.

Thomas, K. (1971). *Religion and the decline of magic.* New York: Charles Scribner's Sons.

Tice, P. (1994, Spring). The Bogomils: Gnostics of old Bulgaria. *Gnosis*, pp. 55–60.

Tierney, P. (1989). *The highest altar: Unveiling the mystery of human sacrifice.* London: Penguin Books.

Tompkins, P. (1990). *This tree grows out of hell: Mesoamerican and the search for the magical body.* San Francisco, CA: HarperSanFrancisco.

Torrey, E.F. (1972). *The mind game: Witch doctors and psychiatrists.* New York: Emerson Hall.

Towers, E.D. (1986). *The man & the myth.* Wellingborough, England: Crucible.

Trevor-Roper, H.R. (1968). *The European witch-craze of the sixteenth and seventeenth centuries and other essays.* New York: Harper & Row.

Trott, J., & Hertenstein, M. (1992). Selling Satan: The tragic history of Mike Warnke. *Cornerstone, 21* (98). (Reprint available from publisher of *Cornerstone* magazine).

Tucker, R. (1989). *Strange gospels.* London: Marshall Pickering.

Turell, S.C., & Armsworth, M.W. (2000). Differentiating incest survivors who self-mutilate. *Child Abuse and Neglect, 24*, 237–249.

Ulansey, D. (1989). *The origins of the Mithraic mysteries: Cosmology & salvation in he ancient world.* New York: Oxford University Press.

Underwager, R., &Wakefield, H. (1994). Misinterpretation of a primary prevention effect. *Issues in Child Abuse Accusations, 6*, 96–107.

Unger, M.F. (1971). *Demons in the world today: A study of occultism in the light of God's word.* Wheaton, IL: Tyndale House.

U.S., Office of the United States Chief Counsel for the Prosecution of Axis Criminality (1946). *Nazi conspiracy and aggression*, vol. 3. Washington, DC: USGPO.

Valliere, P., Bybee, D., & Mobray, C. (1988, Apr.). *Using the Child Behavior Checklist in child sexual abuse research: Longitudinal and comparative analysis.* Paper presented at the National Symposium on Child Victimization, Anaheim, CA.

Valeri, V. (1985). *Kingship and sacrifice: Ritual and society in ancient Hawaii.* Chicago: University of Chicago Press.

van Biema, D. (1995, April 3). Prophet of poison. *Time*, pp. 26–33.

Vankin, J. (1992). *Conspiracies, cover-ups and crimes.* New York: Dell.

Vetter, G.B. (1973). *Magic and religion: Their psychological nature, origin and function.* New York: Philosophical Library.

Victor, J.S. (1993). *Satanic panic: The creation of a contemporary legend.* Chicago, IL: Open Court.

Waite, A.E. (1970). *A new encyclopedia of freemasonry.* New York: Weathervane Books.

Waldinger, R.J., & Gunderson, J.G. (1987). *Effective psychotherapy with borderline patients: Case studies.* New York: Macmillan.

Walker, B. (1989a). Mystery religions. In R. Cavendish (Ed.), *Encyclopedia of the unexplained: Magic, occultism and parapsychology* (pp. 153–155). London: Arkana.

Walker, B. (1989b). Tantrism. In R. Cavendish (Ed.), *Encyclopedia of the unexplained: Magic, occultism and parapsychology* (pp. 242-244). London: Arkana.

Walker, B.G. (1983). *The woman's encyclopedia of myths and secrets.* San Francisco, CA: HarperSanFrancisco.

Walsh, B.W., & Rosen, P.M. (1988). *Self-mutilation: Theory, research, & treatment.* New York: Guilford Press.

Warmington, E.H., & Rouse, P.G. (Eds.). (1956). *Great dialogues of Plato.* New York: Mentor Books.

Warnke, M.A. (1972). *The Satan seller.* Plainfield, NJ: Logos International.

Warnke, M.A. (1991). *Schemes of Satan.* Tulsa, OK: Victory House.

Waterman, J., Kelly, R.J., Olivieri, M.K., McCord, J. (1993). *Beyond the playground walls: Sexual abuse in preschools.* New York: Guilford Press.

Webb, J. (1974). *The occult underground.* La Salle, IL: Open Court Publishing Co.

Webb, J. (1989). Gnosticism. In R. Cavendish (Ed.), *Encyclopedia of the unexplained: Magic, occultism and parapsychology* (pp. 94–99). London: Arkana.

Weigle, M. (1976). *Brothers of light, brothers of blood: The Penitentes of the Southwest.* Albuquerque: University of New Mexico Press.

Weinstein, H.M. (1990). *Psychiatry and the CIA: Victims of mind control.* Washington, DC: American Psychiatric Press.

Weinstein, M. (1980). *Earth magic: A Dianic book of shadows.* Custer, WA: Phoenix Publishing.

Weiskott, G.N. (1974). Moon phases and telephone counseling calls *Psychological Reports, 35,* 752–754.

Weiskott, G.N., & Tipton, G.B. (1975). Moon phases and state hospital admissions. *Psychological Reports, 37,* 486.

Weissman, J. (1993). *Of two minds: Poets who hear voices.* Hanover, NH: University Press of New England.

Weitzenhoffer, A. M. (1989). *The practice of hypnotism: Volume 1: Traditional and semi-traditional techniques and phenomenology.* New York: John Wiley & Sons.

White, V. (1992). Some notes on Gnosticism. In R.A. Segal (Ed.), The *Gnostic Jung* (pp. 197–218). Princeton, NJ: Princeton University Press.

Whitfield, C.L. (1995). *Memory and abuse: Remembering and healing the effects of trauma.* Deerfield Beach, FL: Health Communications.

Wilson, C. (1971). *The occult: A history.* New York: Random House.

Wilson, C. (1984). *A criminal history of mankind.* New York: Carroll & Graf Publishers.

Wilson, C. (1988). *Beyond the occult.* New York: Carroll & Graf Publishers.

Wilson, I. (1988). *Jesus: The evidence.* San Francisco, CA: Harper & Row.

Winchell, R.M., & Stanley, M. (1992). Dr. Winchell and Dr. Stanley reply [Letter to the editor]. *American Journal of Psychiatry, 149,* 1763–1764.

Witkin, G., Cary, P., & Martinez, A. (Dec. 27, 1993/Jan. 3, 1994). Through a glass very darkly: Cops, spies and a very odd investigation. *U.S. News and World Report,* p.30.

World Health Organization. (1992). *The ICD-10 classification of mental and behavioural disorders: Clinical descriptions and diagnostic guidelines.* Geneva, Switzerland: author.

Wright, H.B. (1957). *Witness to witchcraft.* New York: Funk & Wagnalls.

Wright, L. (1993a, May 17). Remembering Satan — part I. *New Yorker,* pp. 60–81.

Wright, L. (1993b, May 24). Remembering Satan — part II. *New Yorker,* pp. 54–76.

Wright, L. (1994). *Remembering Satan.* New York: Knopf.

Yank, J.R. (1991). Handwriting variations in individuals with multiple personality disorder. *Dissociation, 4,* 2–12.

Yap, P.M. (1960). The possession syndrome: A comparison of Hong Kong and French findings. *Journal of Mental Science, 106,* 114–137.

Index

About the Authors

JAMES RANDALL NOBLITT is a clinical psychologist in Dallas, Texas, where he is Director of the Center for Counseling and Psychological Services.

PAMELA SUE PERSKIN is Executive Director of the International Council on Cultism and Ritual Trauma and a lecturer on child abuse.

The Center for Counseling and Psychological Services, PC, is located at 9601 White Rock Trail, Suite 103, Dallas, Texas 75238.

ISBN 0-275-96664-X

90000>

EAN

9 780275 966645

HARDCOVER BAR CODE